COBOL

COBOL
BY GEORGE JACKSON

TAB BOOKS Inc.
BLUE RIDGE SUMMIT, PA. 17214

FIRST EDITION

FIFTH PRINTING

Printed in the United States of America

Reproduction or publication of the content in any manner, without express permission of the publisher, is prohibited. No liability is assumed with respect to the use of the information herein.

Copyright © 1982 by TAB BOOKS Inc.

Library of Congress Cataloging in Publication Data

COBOL.

Includes index.
1. COBOL (Computer program language) I. Title.
QA76.73.C25T7   001.64′24   81.18220
ISBN 0-8306-0051-5   AACR2
ISBN 0-8306-1398-6 (pbk.)

Contents

Introduction vii

1 Introduction to COBOL 1
History and Background—Benefits Derived from Using COBOL — COBOL and the Computer — The COBOL System—COBOL Modules and Levels—COBOL Interpreters

2 Program Organization 11
Describing the Data—Items and Groups—Records—Files—Summary—Stating the Procedures for Problem Solution—Identifying the Program—Describing the Equipment—A Sample Application—Definition of Application—Description of Data — Procedural Steps — Physical Environment Description—Program Identification—The Coding Form—Symbols, Rules and Notations Used in a COBOL Program

3 Data Description 23
The COBOL Character Set—Data Types and Classes—The Data Division—The Working-Storage Section—Sample Problem

4 The Procedure Division 50
Expressions—Conditions—Statements and Sentences—Procedure Formation—Sample Problem

5 The Environment Division 85
Configuration Section—Source Computer—Object Computer—Special Names—Input-Output Section—Sample Problem

6 The Identification Division 92
Program ID—Author—Installation—Date Written—Date Compiled—Security—Remarks—Sample Problem

7	**COBOL Reference Format**	**95**
	Purpose of Reference Format—Standard Procedure—Using the Reference Format	
8	**Segmentation**	**100**
	Organization—Segmentation Control—Segment Limit	
9	**The COBOL Library**	**103**
	Use in the Environment Division—Use in the Data Division—Use in the Procedure Division	
10	**Table Handling**	**107**
	Defining Table—Reference of Table Items—Summary of General Rules for Subscripting and Indexing—Subscripting and Indexing: A Comparative Sample Problem—COBOL Table Handling Features—Comparisons Involving Index Names and/or Index Data Items	
11	**Sorting**	**123**
	Sort Operation—Input and Output Procedures—Types of Sort Programs—Programming Considerations—Examples of a Sort Program	
12	**Mass Storage**	**134**
	File Handling	
	Glossary—COBOL	**138**
	Glossary—Data Processing	**154**
	Appendix A—Operation of Computers	**267**
	Appendix B—Assignment Codes	**283**
	Index	**287**

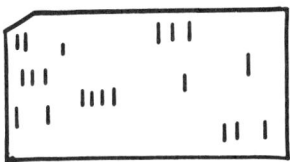

Introduction

Common Business Oriented Language (COBOL) was developed and defined in the 1960s by a cooperative, volunteer effort of the Federal Government, users in industry, and computer hardware and software manufacturers under the supervision of the Conference of Data Systems Languages (CODASYL). The standardization of COBOL was completed in August, 1968 by the work of the United States of America Standards Institute (USASI).

In general, COBOL is a specific language by which data processing procedures may be precisely described in a standard form. The language is intended not only as a means for presenting business programs to computers but also as a means of communicating such procedures among individuals.

This book is designed to acquaint the reader with the fundamental knowledge of data processing using the COBOL language and will cover sequential access, segmentation, library, table handling, sorting, mass storage, random access and report writing. A comprehensive glossary is included.

In preparing this book for publication, a deep bow, and thanks, is due many individuals, manufacturers, organizations and agencies. Special thanks to the UNIVAC Division of Sperry Rand Corp., the United States of America Standards Institute and the Superintendent of Documents, and the U.S. Government Printing Office.

Chapter 1

Introduction to COBOL

The need for improved communication has long existed between all elements concerned with the proper functioning of business, educational, and technical organizations since seldom did these various organizations speak the same language. Management had difficulty understanding the technician, the analyst had difficulty understanding the accountant, and so on. Then, with the introduction of the computer, all had difficulty applying computer techniques to their own individual needs and producing results that could be understood by persons other than those with computer training.

Unlike conventional digital computers that accept and produce only digital results, COBOL enables problems and solutions to be formed in the English language, acceptable to all persons involved in a particular data processing application, and readily understood by the casual observer. As in the English language, COBOL contains many types of words with which meaningful thoughts are formed.

Meaningful is the key descriptor in this or any language. In human discourse, a word is meaningful because, at some point in time, this word has been defined and associated with a particular concept or object. In COBOL, a word is meaningful either because the programmer has given it meaning by relating it to a specific quantity, or because it is an inherent, built-in part of the language.

The COBOL language program employs many types of words. It uses nouns that are established by the programmer to name the various data elements upon which the program operates. It uses verbs which are supplied by the COBOL system to direct the manner in which the data is treated. It also uses certain selected words to improve the readability of the language or to complete the meaning of a sentence. For example, the following sentence illustrates these various words:

SUBTRACT DEDUCTIONS
FROM GROSS-PAY GIVING NET-PAY.

Here, DEDUCTIONS, GROSS-PAY, and NET-PAY are nouns assigned by the programmer to name specific quantities. SUBTRACT is a verb supplied by the COBOL language to direct that particular arithmetic operation. FROM and GIVING are words included in the COBOL language to complete the meaning of the sentence. Often, such words as IS, ARE, and ON are included in statements to improve readability and may be omitted.

In summary then, the COBOL language is one part of a system which provides a method of stating computer problems and solutions in English. It comprises a fundamental set of English words and symbols used to define and create a program. It further permits the definition and naming of data according to the individual dictates of the user rather than the peculiarities of the computer. It forms a functional language that is largely independent of computer make or model.

HISTORY AND BACKGROUND

On May 28 and 29, 1959, a meeting was called in the Pentagon for the purpose of considering both the desirability and feasibility of establishing a common language for the programming of electronic computers in business data processing. Representatives from users, government installations, computer manufacturers, and other interested parties were present. There was almost unanimous agreement that the project was both desirable and feasible at that time. The concept of three committees or task forces was agreed upon. They were called the Short Range, Intermediate Range, and Long Range committees, with appropriate time scales.

The Short Range group was composed of six manufacturers and three government representatives. This committee held its first meeting on June 23, 1959. At that time it was decided that the tasks of the committee fell into four general areas. Working groups were established as follows:

- Data Description
- Procedural Statements
- Application Survey
- Usage and Experience

The first two of these groups held frequent meetings and prepared proposals for consideration by the full short range committee which met for the purpose of preparing a report to the Executive Committee. Materials developed by the third and fourth groups were used later, in the course of the development of COBOL. The report to the Executive Committee stated that the Short Range Committee felt it had prepared a framework upon which an effective common business language could be built. It was recognized that the report contained rough spots and needed additions. It further requested that the Short Range Committee be authorized to complete and publish the system by December 1959. It also requested that the Short

Range Committee continue beyond December in order to monitor the implementation. Both of these requests were approved.

The Committee held meetings between September and November, 1959, and proceeding steadily in its task of resolving problems and completing the language. The name "COBOL", a COmmon Business Oriented Language, was adopted.

The COBOL System was reviewed and approved by the Short Range Committee during the week of November 16-20, 1959. Final editing and initial distribution of the report to the Executive Committee was completed December 17, 1959.

After acceptance by the Executive Committee of CODASYL, the report was published April 1960 by the Government Printing Office under the title:

"COBOL—A report to the Conference on Data Systems Languages, Including Initial Specifications for a Common Business Oriented Language (COBOL) for Programming Electronic Digital Computers."

A Maintenance Committee was created by the Executive Committee of the CODASYL group to be responsible for initiating and reviewing changes to keep COBOL up-to-date. This Maintenance Committee was comprised of user and manufacturer groups. The Maintenance Committee considered and agreed on a number of revisions to COBOL.

In order to devote concentrated attention to publishing a revised and updated "COBOL-1960", the Executive Committee created a Special Task Group. The product of this task group was the COBOL-1961 manual published in mid-1961. In mid-1963, the Maintenance Committee released COBOL-1961 Extended.

The organizations participating in the Maintenance Committee or the Special Task Group were:

Air Materiel Command, United States Air Force
Allstate Insurance Company
Bendix Corporation, Computer Division
The Boeing Company
Burroughs Corporation
Chase Manhattan Bank
Control Data Corporation
David Taylor Model Basin, Bureau of Ships, U.S. Navy
DuPont Company
General Electric Company
General Motors Corporation
International Business Machines Corporation
Lockheed Aircraft Corporation
Minneapolis-Honeywell Regulator Company
National Cash Register Company
Owens-Illinois Incorporated
Philco Corporation

Radio Corporation of America
Royal McBee Corporation
Space Technology Laboratories, Incorporated
Southern Railway Company
Standard Oil Company (N.J.)
Sylvania Electric Products, Inc.
Univac Division of Sperry Rand Incorporated
United States Steel Corporation
Westinghouse Electric Corporation

In January 1964, the COBOL Maintenance Committee was reorganized to provide a true industry group and to broaden its scope of activities. As the result of this reorganization, the COBOL committee was formed and three subcommittees were established: the Language Subcommittee, the Evaluation Subcommittee, and the Publication Subcommittee. The Language Subcommittee took over the functions of the old Maintenance Committee. The Publication Subcommittee was charged with the production of official COBOL publications and with liaison with the United States of America Standards Institute (USASI) as to the content of the COBOL Information Bulletin (a collection of material relating to COBOL which is distributed to the COBOL community). The Evaluation Subcommittee's task was the analysis and evaluation of compiler implementations and user surveys. This subcommittee provides information to the COBOL Committee regarding the use of COBOL. In November 1965, the COBOL Committee released COBOL-Edition 1965.

In 1961, a portion of the Intermediate Range Committee was combined with the Long Range Committee to form the Development Committee. This committee was comprised of a Systems Group and a Language Structure Group. Although there were occasional joint meetings of these two groups, it was concluded that it would be more fruitful to operate these groups as two separate committees. Accordingly, the CODASYL Executive Committee in April 1965, approved the reorganization of these two groups and designated them as follows:

"(a) The CODASYL Systems Committee (CSC) with the objective of developing a data systems language which uses general, easily understood language as the medium expression; is independent of machines; and can be used as a common language for and between all digital computer systems as well as a medium for human communication.

(b) The CODASYL Language Structures Committee (CLSC) with the objective of developing a unifying structure for the specification of data processing systems which places emphasis on the nature of the data processin results to be accomplished rather than on the sequence of steps required; results in a language that is convenient to use by people concerned with a variety of data processing problems rather than with computer programming; and is readily implementable on data processing machines.

In July 1965, CLSC was dissolved at its own request.

The American Standards Association (ASA) Sectional Committee X3 for Computers and Information Processing was established in 1960 under the sponsorship of the Business Equipment Manufacturers' Association (BEMA). ASA X3 in turn, established the X3.4 Sectional Subcommittee to work in the area of common programming language standards. Subsequently, Working Group X3.4.4 for Processor Specifications and COBOL Standards was formed with the primary goal of the group being the production of an American COBOL standard.

On December 17, 1961, invitations to an organizational meeting of the X3.4.4 Working Group were sent to manufacturer and user groups who might be interested in participating in the development of an American COBOL standard. The first meeting of the X3.4.4 Working Group was held in New York City on January 15 and 16, 1963. In August 1966, the ASA became the United States of America Standards Institute.

Since that first meeting back in January 1963, many meetings have been held and on August 30, 1966, the X3.4.4 Working Group approved the content and format for a proposed USASI standard COBOL. The resultant proposed standard is based upon the elements contained in CODASYL COBOL-Edition 1965 and, as such, represents a proper subset of the total COBOL language as defined in that publication.

BENEFITS DERIVED FROM USING COBOL

The following are some of the many advantages in using COBOL:

Demonstrated Compatibility

The capability of using a program written on one computer and, with minor modification, running it on another computer of a different make or model, is a proven fact. This reduces the reprogramming time considerably from the time required to recode applications written in an equipment-oriented language.

Increased Communication

Since COBOL uses English-like statements, the program is intelligible to all who understand the application. This makes available to the programming effort, the knowledge and efforts of many experts formerly excluded.

Faster Programming

Since the programmer is freed from the constraints of the equipment-oriented languages, the time required to program new or altered applications is reduced. Emphasis is shifted from the programming effort involved in detailed coding to problem definition and analysis.

Increased Program Accuracy

COBOL uses built-in standard conventions, based on extensive user and systems experience, to develop efficient coding techniques. Because these techniques are automatically introduced into the program, greater coding efficiency is achieved. The debugged coding segments at the user's command minimize the chance of program error and simplify design.

Reduced Training Time

New programming personnel can be trained to write productive programs in substantially less time than it takes to train them in equipment-oriented languages. With COBOL, it is not necessary to have a large staff of trained programmers. The more complicated, time-consuming techniques of computer coding need be taught only to those few people selected to become highly-skilled, career programmers.

Reduced Programming Costs

The ability to program a problem faster, and for the most part more accurately, reduces the cost of programming. Reprogramming costs are also reduced, since programs produced for one system may be modified to run on other systems without being entirely recoded.

These are just some of the benefits to be derived from the use of COBOL. As the user becomes more familiar with COBOL, many other advantages of the system become evident.

COBOL AND THE COMPUTER

Digital computers will only accept and act upon a fixed set of instructions, expressed in a specific manner. However, though the number and sophistication of instructions may vary from computer to computer, certain general concepts remain the same. Each computer will have instructions to implement at least the following functions:

- Data Movement
- Arithmetic Operations
- Decision Making
- Input/Output Operations

Each of these functions may comprise many instructions and the format for their specification varies with the myriad makes and models of computers presently available on the market. Unlike the various equipment-oriented languages (oriented to a single computer or to a single family of computers) which cater to the peculiarities of the individual computer instruction repertoire, COBOL operates at a functional level. That is, it provides in English, facilities for treating the above-stated functions in terms of the problem to be solved rather than in terms of the computer to be programmed.

Certainly, the COBOL language is not free-form English. It is stylized and, to that extent, restricted. Unlike the human brain, the computer cannot accept nuances of expression; it cannot discern vocal inflection; it cannot recognize physical gestures meant for emphasis. Therefore, with built-in restrictions, governed by what the computer can and cannot accept, the

COBOL language operates within certain well-defined boundaries established by very definite rules of procedure. However, any language, whether it is designed for computers or human beings, contains many rules for construction and use. These rules enhance the usefulness of the language as a vehicle for discourse and communication. The programmer must familiarize himself with the fundamental rules and procedures of the COBOL language to gain proficiency in problem definition, analysis, and solution.

THE COBOL SYSTEM

The COBOL system actually comprises two main elements: the program and the program processor (compiler).

When we refer to the program, we are actually referring to two programs as follows:

The Source Program

That set of written entries and statements prepared by the programmer and designed to perform the following functions:
1. Describe the data.
2. Instruct the computer by a set of procedural steps on how to treat the data to effect a logical solution to the problem.
3. Identify the program.
4. Describe the equipment being used.

The Object Program

That set of coded instructions and data acceptable to the computer which carries through the logic expressed in the source program, together with the storage assignments for the data to be processed.

To translate a problem-oriented COBOL source program into a machine or equipment—oriented object program written in a code form acceptable to the specific computer, a COBOL program processor (compiler) is provided. The compiler is a program which analyzes the words and characters of a COBOL-language program and produces a new program in a code acceptable to the particular computer. From a single COBOL statement, the compiler may produce many computer instructions. The compiler is entered into the computer together with the source program. In a sense, the compiler is a program whose input data is the source program and whose output is the object program. The object program is the one the computer actually runs when it is time to use the program.

When translating the source program to object program, the program processor may perform the following functions:

Decoding

The intended meaning of individual characters or groups of characters written in the source language are ascertained and converted into computer-acceptable instructions and data.

Conversion

Numerical information is converted from one number base to another (i.e., decimal to binary) and from fixed to floating point notation or vice versa, if required.

Selection

A required routine may be selected from a library of routines.

Generation

Required subroutines are generated from various parameters and skeletal coding specified in the source program.

Allocation

Actual storage locations are assigned in memory to the various program elements.

Assembly

Subroutines (supplied, selected, or generated) are integrated into the program.

Recording

Detailed information concerning the object program is recorded and may be printed.

COBOL MODULES AND LEVELS

In order to more effectively implement the uses for which COBOL was designed, the COBOL language has been revised to include eight functional processing modules. The new organization is oriented toward the functional processing concept while still retaining the original divisional structure (Identification, Environment, Data, and Procedure) within each module. These modules are as follows:

- Nucleus
- Table Handling
- Sequential Access
- Random Access
- Sort
- Report Writer
- Segmentation
- Library

Each functional processing module is divided into two or more levels. These levels provide a hierarchy within each module and in all cases, a lower level constitutes a proper subset of the next higher level. This hierarchal modular structural, illustrated in Fig. 1-1, enables the user to

	FUNCTIONAL PROCESSING MODULES							
NUCLEUS	TABLE HANDLING	SEQUENTIAL ACCESS	RANDOM ACCESS	SORT	REPORT WRITER	SEGMENTATION	LIBRARY
LEVEL 2	LEVEL 3	LEVEL 2	LEVEL 2	LEVEL 2	LEVEL 2	LEVEL 2	LEVEL 2
	LEVEL 2		LEVEL 1	LEVEL 1	LEVEL 1	LEVEL 1	LEVEL 1
LEVEL 1	LEVEL 1	LEVEL 1	NULL	NULL	NULL	NULL	NULL

Fig. 1-1. The minimum COBOL system that can be implemented is Level 1 Nucleus, Level 1 Table handling, and Level 1 sequential file handling.

tailor his COBOL complier such that he obtains only as much computing power as he needs for his particular application.

COBOL INTERPRETERS

There are a few COBOL interpreters available for the microcomputers. An interpreter differs from a compiler in that when the source code is interpreted it is not stored as an object program. Instead, each instruction is executed immediately. Since the interpretation takes time, an interpreter is much, much slower than a compiled program, and has the added disadvantage of requiring more memory because the interpreter and source code must both reside in memory at run time. The advantage is that an interpreter is usually more interactive with the user, and is a less expensive piece of software to buy than a compiler.

Since the source code is identical, it is sometimes advantageous to develop a program on an interpreter system and, when it is completely debugged, compile it on a system that has a program processor.

Chapter 2

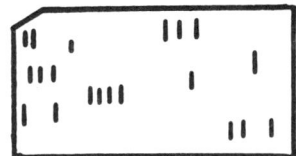

Program Organization

A program written in language designed for the easy expression of a class of problems or procedures is called a *source program*. This program must contain four basic elements to solve a given problem:
1. A description of the data to be processed.
2. A set of procedures or operations establishing how the data is to be treated.
3. A description of the equipment to be used.
4. Information that will label and identify a particular application.

A generator, assembler, translator, or compiler routine is used to perform the mechanics of translating the source program into an object program in machine language. This chapter discusses the components of the source program and illustrates the organization of a COBOL program by providing a narrative English discussion of a sample application.

DESCRIBING THE DATA

The first element listed above that must receive attention requires that the programmer describe each element of data upon which the object program is expected to operate. In doing so, at least the following information must be included:

A. The name by which the program is to identify a particular datum.
B. The class of data (i.e., is it alphabetic, numeric, or alphanumeric?).
C. The length of the datum in terms of characters.
D. The location of special symbols such as the currency sign, comma, decimal point, etc.
E. The relative position of this datum within a record with respect to the other data to be operated on.

When the programmer provides this information, he is stating that, at object time, he will have an element of data to be processed and that the

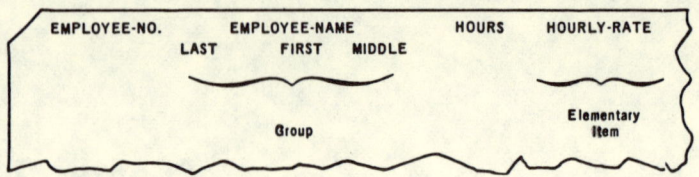

Fig. 2-1. Elementary items and groups.

compiler should provide storage space based upon the requisites he has expressed. For example, suppose a programmer wishes to process data such as an employee's salary. First, he would assign a name to the datum, such as SALARY. Then he would state that the field is numeric (or alphanumeric if it contains characters other than digits), state the maximum size of the field, and show the position of both currency sign and decimal point. He would then show its relationship to the other data in the employee's record. The compiler, based on this information, would reserve a storage area for the data and, as the salary for each employee was fed in at run time, it would be placed in this location preparatory to being processed by the instructions in the program.

The COBOL language provides specific rules and procedures for supplying this information. Chapter 3 of this book discusses them in detail.

ITEMS AND GROUPS

The smallest unit of data is the elementary item. This is a datum which is not further subdivided into smaller units when referenced in the program. The HOURLY-RATE field on an employee's weekly time card (Fig. 2-1) is an example of an elementary item; it is not broken into smaller units.

On the same weekly time card, there is a field called EMPLOYEE-NAME. This datum, however, is subdivided into smaller units called LAST, FIRST, MIDDLE. In this case, we are no longer dealing with a single unit of data, but with a group, the individual components of which are elementary items relating to the entire group named EMPLOYEE-NAME.

When organizing data, it is also possible to have groups of groups. This is illustrated by the following example: Assume that the ACME FIREARMS COMPANY maintains an inventory stock for the various parts necessary for the production of rifles and shotguns. The data pertaining to these parts might be organized as shown in Fig. 2-2.

GRADE and TYPE are elementary items and each designates a single quantity of particular item. For example, under SHOTGUN BARRELS, GRADE 1 could be 12 gauge, GRADE 2 may be 16 gauge and GRADE 3 could represent 20-gauge. The same gauges could apply to the receivers. The types of stocks could represent different grades of wood; field, fancy, etc. BARREL, RECEIVER STOCK, and SIGHTS are groups comprising several related items. SHOTGUN and RIFLES are also groups however, instead of being groups of items, they are groups of groups.

To reiterate, elementary items are the smallest data units and are not further subdivided. Groups are larger data units comprising several elementary items or several groups.

RECORDS

Related elementary items and groups are combined to form records. In the time card example, for instance, the card for each employee might constitute a single or logical record. Though the format would remain the same, the values of the various items would obviously change from employee to employee. The same holds true for the example of the ACME FIREARMS COMPANY. In that example, the entire series of items and groups might be combined into one logical record called INVENTORY-ON-HAND.

Information for processing is read into the computer in complete records. It is not possible to read in only a part of a record. Similarly, only complete records may be written; that is, made available for output on some form of external medium such as magnetic tape or punched cards.

FILES

A file is a set of records. Not all the records in a particular file need have the same format. When a record is read in for processing, it replaces the previous record of that file. If it is necessary to have more than one record of a particular file available to the program at a specific time, the first record must be moved to an intermediate work area before the second record may be read in. The exact method of doing this is discussed in subsequent Chapters.

The word "file" is used in COBOL because of the similarity to the file cabinet used in any office. For example, each drawer might be equated to a record in which is contained various types of related data. The file cabinet would also be labeled in some manner to indicate the contents. Similarly, a data processing file often has a label record to provide identification. Usually there is one label at the beginning of the file and another at the end. These label records serve as checking devices to ensure that the proper data is being read and that the file has been completed.

There is no direct relationship between the length of a tape file and a reel of tape. A tape file may be contained on many reels of tape or a single

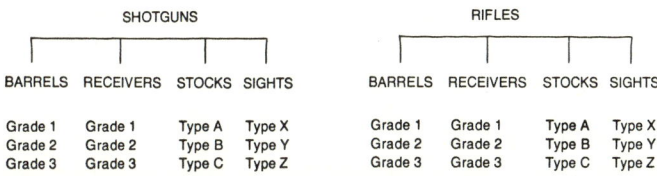

Fig. 2-2. Groups of groups.

tape may contain many files. Other files, such as printer files and card files, have their own unique characteristics.

SUMMARY

The diagram in Fig. 2-3 illustrates the rank structure used in COBOL to describe data. Each file consists of a set of records. There may be one type of record or several types of records. Each type of record is usually described as a set of elementary items; however, a record itself may be treated as an elementary item if it is not further subdivided. It is often convenient to group two or more elementary items. These groups may then be further grouped into groups of groups, and so forth.

STATING THE PROCEDURES FOR PROBLEM SOLUTION

Once the data has been described and organized, the programmer may concentrate on the various operations or procedures necessary to solve his problem using the four major functions available to him.

1. Data Movement
2. Arithmetic
3. Decision-Making
4. Input/Output

In addition, the programmer has at his command Control functions which enable him to alter the sequence of program operation or cause repetitive cyclings of certain program steps.

When establishing the various procedures for problem execution, the programmer need not be aware of the internal details of the computer being used. He may concentrate fully on problem logic.

The various functions operate as follows:

1. Input/output functions permit communication with the external media, such as magnetic tapes or punched card equipment, to obtain the specific records that are to be processed or to deliver final records to output.
2. Decision-making capabilities permit comparisons of data to determine which of several possible operations are to be performed.
3. Arithmetic functions permit the necessary calculations to be made on the data.
4. Control functions permit selected operations to be performed or repeated a specific number of times.
5. Data-movement instructions permit the movement or assembling of the data into groupings. They are covered in Chapter 4 of this book.

IDENTIFYING THE PROGRAM

Having described the data and established the procedures for problem execution, the programmer will identify the program. He might wish to include such things as the date the program was written, the programmer's name, the name of the particular installation, and so forth. The mechanics by which this information is entered into the COBOL program are covered in detail in Chapter 6.

DESCRIBING THE EQUIPMENT

A description of the equipment is necessary to the proper operation of a COBOL program. The descriptions of the computers to be used for both compilation and object running of the program must be provided. This could include memory size and descriptions of the relationship between the logical records and their physical format on the input/output media. Names may be assigned to specific peripherals to facilitate referencing in the program. This section, because it deals with specifications of the equipment being

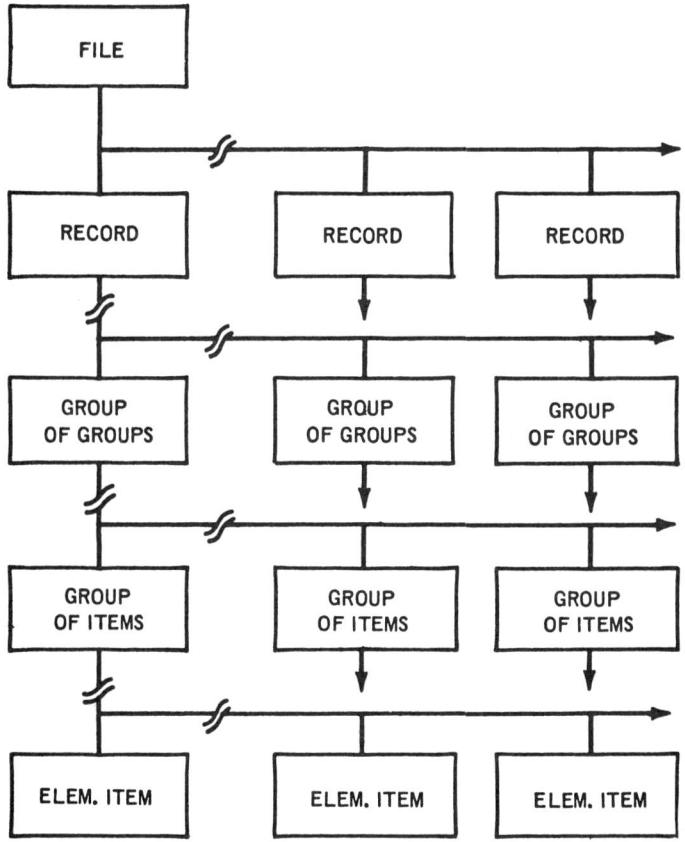

Fig. 2-3. File hierarchy.

used, is largely computer-dependent. Details for providing this information are given in Chapter 5.

A SAMPLE APPLICATION

A typical data processing problem is presented here using common English sentences to provide the following information:

1. A general definition of the problem or application.
2. A general description of the data.
3. A general description of the actions which will be performed on the data.
4. A description of the manner in which the computing equipment is described.

Using this information as a guide, a COBOL solution is developed throughout the book as the individual elements comprising the COBOL language are discussed. The final solution is shown in full at the end of the manual.

There are many ways of approaching any data processing problem, and the following is not intended to represent an optimum solution. The purpose of this problem is to illustrate the use of as many fundamental COBOL features as is practical, while providing a comparison of the COBOL compiler language to the English language.

DEFINITION OF APPLICATION

A sporting goods retailing chain updates its central warehouse inventory file on a daily basis to assure an adequate supply of goods for its many local dealers.

Each change of stock is recorded on a punched card, called a detail transaction. All detail transactions are then collected and sorted or arranged into order by stock item number and transaction code. This detail transaction file is run against the existing master inventory file to build an updated master inventory file.

As the updated master inventory file is created, a list is made of all stock items that have fallen below their minimum stock levels, and of new stock items which have been entered into the file on that particular update run. This list is called the stock replenishment or stock reorder list.

DESCRIPTION OF DATA

Two input files and two output files are used; the input master inventory file, the input detail transaction file, the output (updated) master inventory file, and the output stock reorder list file. In addition to the input and output files, certain other data items must be defined for intermediate arithmetic or logical results and for constant information, such as page headings. Detailed descriptions and examples of this information will be presented in the continuation of the sample problem discussion in Chapter 3.

PROCEDURAL STEPS

The data having been described, the actions to be taken at run time are specified. The program begins by opening the files (i.e., initializing each file to prepare it for releasing or accepting data). Then data is read in stock number sequence, and the various manipulative, logical, and arithmetic operations performed. This done, the files are closed and the run terminated. A detailed description of the procedural steps, including a flow chart, is given at the continuation of the sample problem discussed in Chapter 4.

PHYSICAL ENVIRONMENT DESCRIPTION

This section of the program describes those aspects of the total problem which depend upon the characteristics of the computing equipment. The following information must be considered:

- (a) The computer on which the compilation will be performed.
- (b) The computer on which the compiled object program will be executed.
- (c) Special mnemonic names which will be defined as equivalent to standard hardware names.
- (d) Hardware assignments for the several filers.
- (e) Data transfer, including buffering, between the computer memory and the hardware media.

This information is discussed in detail in the sample problem discussion in Chapter 5.

PROGRAM IDENTIFICATION

This section of the program identifies or labels the program. It may also contain any other information desired as to authorship, date of writing or compiling, security, and any other comments regarding the functional or peripheral aspects of the problem. Detailed information on program identification will be given with the sample problem in Chapter 6.

THE CODING FORM

Figure 2-4 shows the layout of a typical COBOL programming form and an explanation of the columns are given in Table 2-1. On this form the programmer enters all information needed by the COBOL compiler, observing certain rules of format and content as defined in this book. Each line of written information represents the information to be entered into one 80-column punched card. Table 2-1 explains the several divisions of the form.

SYMBOLS, RULES, AND NOTATIONS USED IN A COBOL PROGRAM

The various language elements that comprise a COBOL program must be written in formats that adhere to fixed and precise rules of presentation. Before discussing these individual formats, it is necessary to understand the various symbols, rules, and notations used in describing them. Each format statement will indicate the following information:

1. The order of presentation.
2. Those words that are requisite to the proper functioning of the statement.
3. Those words that are optional and included at the discretion of the user.
4. That information that must be supplied by the user.
5. Those elements in the statement that involve a choice by the user.
6. Those functions of the particular statement that are optional.

In free form, the MULTIPLY statement might appear in the following manner:

Multiply a data name or a literal by another data name with the result rounded; on size error execute an imperative statement.

This, of course, tells us something about the order of presentation, but very little else about the format. Let us then establish the first rule of format presentation.

(a) All words inherent or built into the COBOL language are specified as uppercase.

MULTIPLY a data name or a literal BY another data name with the result ROUNDED; ON SIZE ERROR execute an imperative statement.

(b) All uppercase words which are underlined are required or key words. Those uppercase words not underlined are optional and may be included at the user's discretion to improve readability.

MULTIPLY a data name or a literal BY another data name with the result ROUNDED; ON SIZE ERROR execute an imperative statement.

All uppercase words, whether underlined or not, are a part of the COBOL language and must be spelled exactly as indicated.

(c) All lower case words *in italics* represent variable terms which must be supplied by the user. In the sample statement, there are four such elements to be supplied by the user; two data names (which shall be designated data-name-1 and data-name-2 in order of their appearance), a literal, and an imperative-statement.

(d) Elements of a statement involving a choice are surrounded by braces [ ].

MULTIPLY { data-name-1 / literal } BY data-name-2 with the result

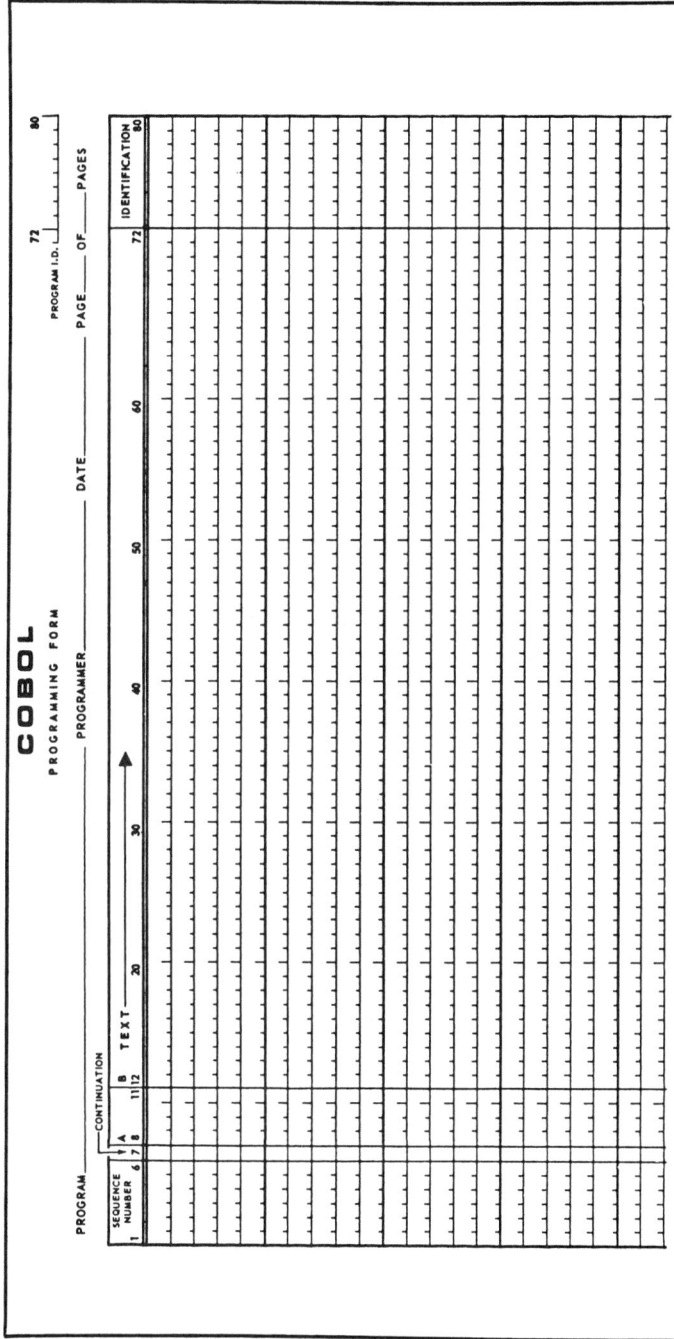

Fig. 2-4. A programming sheet.

ROUNDED; ON SIZE ERROR imperative-statement.

In some instances, the choice can be made by default. For example:

$$\left[;\text{BLOCK CONTAINS [integer-1 TO] integer-2} \left\{ \begin{array}{c} \underline{\text{RECORDS}} \\ \text{CHARACTERS} \end{array} \right\} \right]$$

The programmer must choose either RECORDS or CHARACTERS. If RECORDS is chosen, the word RECORDS must be written because it is a key word (indicated by the underline). However, if CHARACTERS is the choice, CHARACTERS is not a key word and the programmer may or may not write it at his discretion. When the programmer writes a BLOCK CONTAINS entry and neither RECORDS nor CHARACTERS is written, the COBOL compiler assumes that CHARACTERS was chosen and generates machine code based on this assumption.

(e) Optional functions which may be included or omitted at the user's discretion are surrounded by brackets.

$$\text{MULTIPLY} \left\{ \begin{array}{c} \text{data-name-1} \\ \underline{\text{literal}} \end{array} \right\} \underline{\text{BY}} \text{ data-name-2 [ROUNDED]}$$

[; ON SIZE ERROR imperative statement.]

(f) In some statements, certain portions may be used as many times as needed by the programmer. This repeatability is indicated by the ellipsis (. . .). Brackets or braces are used as delimiters to indicate the portion of the statement which is repeatable. From the foregoing, the following rule can be formed:

Given an ellipsis in a statement, scan the statement from right to left beginning at the bracket or brace immediately to the left of the ellipsis until the logically matched bracket or brace is found; the ellipsis applies to the words within the logically matched brackets or braces.

The following two examples illustrate the application of this rule.
Example 1:

<u>ALTER</u> procedure-name-1 <u>TO</u> [<u>PROCEED TO</u>] procedure-name-2
[procedure-name-3 <u>TO</u> [<u>PROCEED TO</u>] procedure-name-4] . . .

Scanning this example from right to left, starting at the bracket immediately to the left of the ellipsis, it can be seen that the logically matching bracket is the bracket preceding <u>procedure-name-3</u>. Thus,

Table 2-1. Punch Card Column Use.

COLUMNS	DESIGNATION	CONTENTS
1-6	SEQUENCE NUMBER	A numeric entry; used only by the programmer (not the COBOL processor) to establish a sequence among the various lines of coding (optional).
7	CONTINUATION	A hyphen (-); used when an entry extended past one line has a break occurring in the middle of a word. The hyphen is written in column 7 of the next contiguous line on which the word is completed. A word may be interrupted in any column, the rest of the line space filled, and completed on the next line. Parentheses are considered punctuation and do not require a hyphen in column 7 when they are split from the word they surround.
8-72	TEXT	All COBOL- formatted information, in the form of names, statements, information, instructions, etc., that is to be compiled into the object program. Note that two left-margin limits designated "A" and "B" are shown. These are needed for program alignment. Major definitive names are begun at margin A (column 8). Margin B (column 12) is used for subordinate items and for continuations of entries from the last preceding line.
73-80	IDENTIFICATION	Card deck information (optional).

the entire second line of the statement can be written as many times as the programmer chooses. The brackets surrounding PROCEED TO in both lines of the statement perform their normal function, i.e., they indicate which portion of the statement is optional.

Example 2:

$$\underline{\text{MOVE}} \left\{ \begin{array}{c} \text{identifier-1} \\ \underline{\text{literal}} \end{array} \right\} \quad \underline{\text{TO}} \quad \left\{ \text{identifier-2} \right\} \ldots$$

Once again, scanning from right to left, starting at the brace immediately to the left of the ellipsis, the logically matching brace is the brace immediately preceding identifier-2. The programmer may write as many different identifiers following the word TO as he chooses. The first set of braces in the statement perform their normal function; the programmer must choose either identifier-1 or literal.

The preceding illustrates the various elements of a COBOL statement. Certain language elements used in the examples (data-name, literal, identifier, imperative-statement) are discussed in later Chapters.

Chapter 3

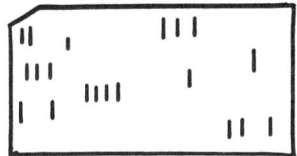

Data Description

It will be necessary for you to describe the data you are going to use in your program to the compiler. This is done in a section called the DATA DIVISION. However, before you can do this, you yourself must be familiar with the form the data will take. The first part of this chapter addresses itself to this need, and the second part deals with the DATA DIVISION itself, and the third part is a sample problem.

THE COBOL CHARACTER SET

Before learning a new language, it is necessary to learn the allowable characters that make up that language. The complete COBOL character is made up of a total of 51 characters. Notice the absence of a few symbols often found on the standard typewriter, and that there are no lower case letters. The following list shows the character set:

The ten digits (0, 1, . . . ,9)
The 26 capital letters (A, B, . . . ,Z)
Space (or blank)
Plus sign (+)
Minus sign or hyphen (−)
Asterisk (*)
Stroke (/)
Equal sign (=)
Currency sign ($)
Comma (,)
Period (.)
Semicolon (;)
Apostrophe (')
Left parenthesis (
Right parenthesis)
Greater than symbol (>)
Less than symbol (<)

23

DATA TYPES AND CLASSES

When working with a computer, we can divide all of the data into three groups. Data that comes into or is sent out of the program while it is running, and is generally arranged into files, is said to be variable data. Data that is developed in the computer during the run, and must be stored somewhere temporarily is called temporary data. Data that the programmer supplied before the program was run, that stays in memory for the entire run and never changes its constant data.

When programming in COBOL specifically, the descriptions of these groups fall into two neat catagories. There is data with a user supplied name, and data assigned to a reserved word name. The following is a description of these two types of data, including their use, capabilities, restrictions, and method of describing them to the COBOL compiler.

User-Supplied Names

An element of data may be named by a variable or it may literally occur within the body of the program with its value interpreted as being that of the digits or letters comprising it. For example, if the following were written, ADD 125 to A, the compiler would treat the 125 literally as the integer 125, but A, a variable, would have to be described more fully. The following tells the rules for forming and using named data and literal data.

Data Names. Programmer invented names can be used to represent any data. They may contain only letters, digits, and embedded hyphens. They may not contain embedded spaces or any special characters. They are ended by either a space, a period followed by a space, a comma followed by a space, or a semi-colon followed by a space. They must not be a COBOL word, or longer than 30 characters, though that number varies from compiler to compiler. At least one character must be a letter.

Condition Names. A data name may represent not only a variable or constant, but it also may represent an initially specified *set* of values. This data form is referred to as a conditional variable. Each specific value associated with the conditional variable may also be a constant to facilitate referencing.

For example, suppose that an automobile supply dealer uses punched cards to maintain his spare parts inventory. Suppose further that each part is coded in the following way:

PART	CODE NO.
Mufflers	00764
Carburetors	92486
Batteries	39635
Tail Pipes	42666
Sparkplugs	84980

On each inventory card there might be a field called PART-TYPE. This field has a specific code number appearing on it. Names are assigned to each code number to speed up referencing. For example:

CODE NO.	CONSTANT
00764	MUFF
92486	CARB
39635	BATT
42666	TAIL
84980	SPARK

PART-TYPE can be defined as a conditional variable with a set of condition names associated with it. These assignments are made in the data description section of the program, and thereafter the programmer refers to the condition names instead of the code numbers. Thus, when a card is read, the specific value of the PART-TYPE field is determined as follows:

IF MUFF GO TO . . .

This statement would generate a test of the content of the PART-TYPE field against the value 00764 and produce the same results as if the following were written:

IF PART-TYPE EQUALS 00764 GO TO . . .

The exact method of specifying condition names, and assigning values to them, will be discussed later in this chapter. Condition names may only be specified in a statement expressing an alternative course of action (a decision).

Literal Data. There are two types of literal data; numeric and non-numeric. A literal is an item of data that has a constant value. The value it has is identical to the digits or letters comprising the item. This is different from a data name because the value of a data name can change at any moment and its value has nothing whatever to do with the characters which make up its data name.

The numeric literals are what you've been calling numbers all your life. Examples:

150789
−125.3
+25.675
3.0

Numeric literals may not contain more than 18 digits and may contain only digits and a plus sign or minus sign, and/or a decimal point. If no sign is used, it is assumed to be positive, and if a sign *is* present, it must appear as the left-most character. If a decimal point is not used, the numeric literal is treated as an integer. Integral value literals (counters) must be written in this fashion. Finally, if a decimal point *is* used, it must not be the rightmost character.

Nonnumeric literals are frequently used to establish what will be printed as page titles, column headings, and the like. They have other uses but are most often used to dress up the printed page. Examples:

'COMPANY PAYROLL'
'CLASS OF 1977 ROSTER'
'F.I.C.A. DEDUCTIONS'
'$ EQUIVALENT'

Nonnumeric literals may not exceed 120 characters (again, this varies with compilers), and must be bounded by quotes. Any word, including a COBOL reserved word, may be used.

Reserved Names

Certain data names are inherent in the structure of the COBOL language and need no description. When employed, they must conform precisely to the rules established for their use. When these names are encountered in a program, the compiler can interpret them in only one way. Therefore, the programmer should make certain that he does not specify in his program a problem oriented name that is also a reserved name. The only exception to this rule is the case of nonnumeric literals.

There are two types of reserved data names; figurative constants and the special register TALLY.

Figurative Constants. These are COBOL reserved words which are understood by the computer to have predefined constant values. There are six, and they are described below:

FIGURATIVE CONSTANT	REPRESENTS
ZERO, ZEROS, ZEROES	Represents the value 0, or a sequence of one or more 0's depending on the context of the statement.
SPACE, SPACES	Represents a sequence of one or more blank characters or spaces depending on the context of the statement.
HIGH-VALUE, HIGH-VALUES	Represents one or more of the characters that has the highest value in the computer's collating sequence.
LOW-VALUE, LOW-VALUES	Represents one or more of the characters that has the lowest value in the computer's collating sequence.
QUOTE, QUOTES	Represents a sequence of quotation marks.
ALL (any literal)	Calls for a sequence of the specified literal. The length of the sequence is limited by the receiving field.

Special Register. TALLY is the name of a variable whose length is equivalent to a five decimal—digit integer. Its primary use is to hold data produced by the EXAMINE verb. TALLY is provided for in each compilation and need not be described by the programmer.

THE DATA DIVISION

This important division describes the organization of the data that will be used by the program. It is made up of two sections: the FILE SECTION and the WORKING-STORAGE SECTION. These section names are reserved names. For your purposes, consider the FILE SECTION to be mandatory and the WORKING-STORAGE SECTION to be optional.

File Section

The File Section contains two types of descriptive entries. They are:
1. File description entries pertaining to each file handled by the program.
2. Record description entries for each record in a given file

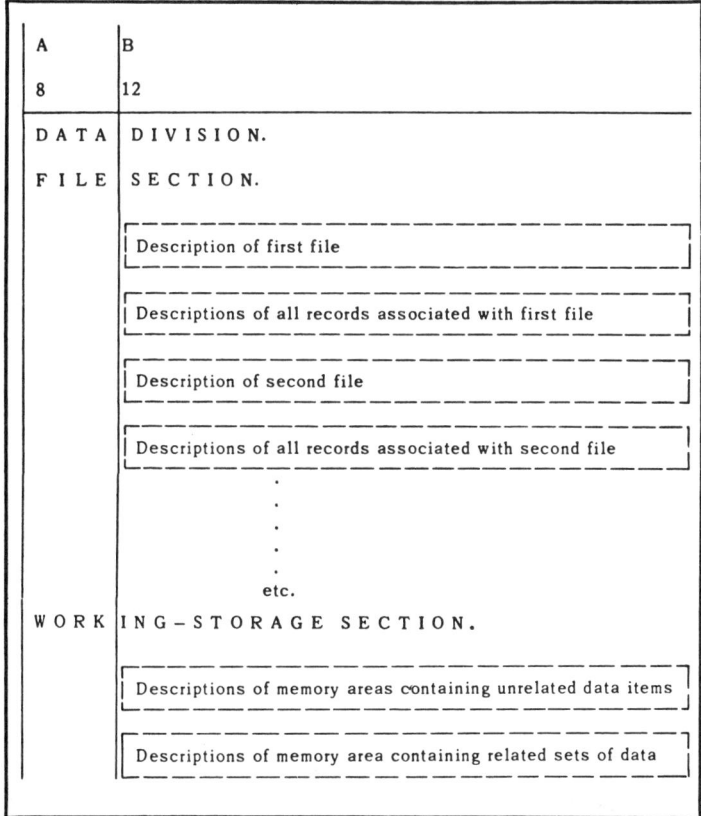

Fig. 3-1. The data division.

```
003000 DATA DIVISION.
003100 FILE SECTION.
003200 FD  OLD-MASTER-INVENTORY
003210     LABEL RECORD IS STANDARD
003250     VALUE OF ID IS 'MSTINVP'
003300     BLOCK CONTAINS 50 RECORDS
003400     DATA RECORD IS MASTER-RECORD.
                      .
                      .
                      .
                      .
                      .
006100 FD  NEW-MASTER-INVENTORY
006110     LABEL RECORD IS STANDARD
006120     BLOCK CONTAINS 50 RECORDS
006130     VALUE OF ID IS 'MSTINVP'
006140     DATA RECORD IS MASTER-RECORD.
```

Fig. 3-2. Notice that order is not important and not all of the clauses are required. The RECORD CONTAINS clause is only for documentation on modern systems and may be omitted.

File Description. Every file that is used by a COBOL program is described in its FILE SECTION by a File Description (FD) entry. An FD entry begins with the letters FD coded at Margin A. (8th column). The remainder of the entry consists of four clauses which are coded at Margin B (12th column). This is the form of the FD entry:

FD file-name;
RECORD CONTAINS integer CHARACTERS;

LABEL RECORDS ARE $\left\{\begin{array}{c} \text{OMITTED} \\ \text{or} \\ \text{STANDARD} \end{array}\right\}$;

DATA $\left\{\begin{array}{c} \text{RECORD IS} \\ \text{or} \\ \text{RECORDS ARE} \end{array}\right\}$ $\underline{\text{record-name-1,}}$ $\underline{\text{record-name-2,}}$ etc.

Listed below are each of the clauses included in the File Description Complete Entry Format.

1. RECORD CONTAINS-In this clause you specify how many characters there are in each record in the file. If it were a file of data cards, you'd use a value of 80 for the integer (since a data card is 80 character positions long), and the clause would say:

RECORD CONTAINS 80 CHARACTERS

When integer-1 and integer-2 are both used, integer-1 refers to the number of characters in the smallest size data records, and integer-2 refers to the number of characters in the largest size data records contained in the file. When only integer-2 is used, it represents the exact number of characters in the data record. Both integer-1 and integer-2 must be positive numeric literals. The format of this clause is as follows:

[;RECORD CONTAINS [integer-1 TO] integer-2 CHARACTERS]

2. LABEL-Label records may be specified at both the beginning and end of a file. This clause permits the identification of these label records. The LABEL clause must appear for each file description. The format is:

$$;\underline{\text{LABEL}} \left\{ \begin{array}{l} \underline{\text{RECORDS}} \text{ ARE} \\ \underline{\text{RECORD}} \text{ IS} \end{array} \right\} \left\{ \begin{array}{l} \underline{\text{STANDARD}} \\ \underline{\text{OMITTED}} \\ \text{data-name-1,} \\ \text{[data-name-2]}\ldots \end{array} \right\}$$

If the user has a standard form for label records, then the STANDARD option may be used. the OMITTED option specifies that no explicit labels exist for the file or for the device to which the file is assigned. Data-name-1 is the name of a label record which must be the subject of a record description entry associated with the file. The name must not appear in the DATA RECORDS clause of the File Description.

3. DATA RECORDS-This clause gives the name by which you intend to refer to the records in this file. In most cases all the records in a file will have their items of data in exactly the same arrangement, and when that is so, the clause is used in this form:

DATA RECORD IS GRADE-CARD.

In this example we have announced that all records in the file are of one type, and that we will call each of them by the same record name, GRADE-CARD.

This clause is optional and serves only to document the various records in each file. These records may have different sizes and formats, and can be listed in any order, however any record name used here *must* be described in the record description area. The general format of this clause is:

$$\left[;\underline{\text{DATA}} \left\{ \begin{array}{l} \underline{\text{RECORDS}} \text{ ARE} \\ \underline{\text{RECORD}} \text{ IS} \end{array} \right\} \text{data-name-1} \quad [, \text{data-name-2}] \ldots \right]$$

4. BLOCK CONTAINS-This clause specifies the size of the physical record or block on tape. The physical grouping in no way affects the logic of the program; however, it may affect the amount of magnetic tape needed to store data in a tape file. With this in mind, the programmer should attempt to establish the most efficient correlation between the physical and logical record. There must be at least one record per block. Blocks may not contain partial records (i.e., records may not overlap blocks).

The format for this clause is as follows:

$$\left[\text{;}\underline{\text{BLOCK}}\text{ CONTAINS [integer-1 }\underline{\text{TO}}\text{] integer-2}\begin{Bmatrix}\text{RECORDS}\\\text{CHARACTERS}\end{Bmatrix}\right]$$

This clause is not necessary in three instances. The first of these is when the hardware device assigned to the file has only one physical record size. The second is when a physical record contains only one complete logical record, e.g., one card. The last condition is when a standard physical record size is established by the user regardless of optional sizes permitted by the equipment. If logical records of various sizes are grouped into a physical record, the end of each record must be clearly defined in the individual record description entry.

If the clause is used, integer-1 and integer-2 must be unsigned (positive) numeric literals. Also, if only integer-2 is used, it represents the exact size of physical record. If both integer-1 and integer-2 are used, they indicate the minimum (integer-1) and maximum (integer-2) size of the physical record. When the CHARACTERS option is selected, the physical record size is specified as the number of characters contained within the physical record regardless of the types of characters used to represent the items within the physical record. Whenever logical records of varying size are grouped into one physical record, the end of the logical record must be explicitly defined in the record description entry except when the user's standard technique is used.

Record Organization. In order to indicate to the compiler the manner in which the data is organized, COBOL provides a system of level numbers of level indicators. Each data entry begins with a level number to indicate its position relative to other data being processed. For example, all records are assigned a level number of 01. Each subordinate entry (group items, elementary items, etc.) then takes a higher level number. Therefore, a record might be organized in the following manner:

```
01 (name and description of first record)
   02 (name and description of first group)
      03 (name and description of first item in first group)
      03 (name and description of second item in first group)
                         .
                         .
                         .
      03 (name and description of nth item in first group)
   02 (name and description of second group)
                         -
                         .
01 (name and description of second record)
                         .
```

Record Description. When you describe a record, what you actually do is describe the arrangement of data items on the record. A system of level-numbers is used in COBOL to indicate the hierarchy of the items of data. Like the file description, the record description comprises a number of independent clauses. These clauses may be used to describe data, or they may describe intermediate work areas.

1. The lower the rank of a data name in the hierarchy, the higher is the level number assigned to it.
2. The lower the rank of a data name, the farther to the right are it and its level number coded.
3. Data names of equal rank are given the same level number and are coded starting in the same column.
4. Level number 01 is always coded at Margin A.
5. Level numbers 02 through 49 are coded at or to the right of Margin B.
6. Two spaces are left between a level number and its corresponding data name.
7. Each level number is coded four columns to the right of the next lower level number.

DATA ITEM	MNEMONIC NAME	DESCRIPTION (Size and Type)	PURPOSE
Stock item number	SEQ-STOCK-NUMBER	6 alphanumeric	Unique number for each stock item to determine position in file.
Vendor number	NUMBER-MANUFACTURER	3 numeric	Code number associated with vendor.
Vendor catalogue number	MFR-CATALOG-NUMBER	10 alphanumeric	Order key specified to vendor.
Item unit description	DESCRIPTION	30 alphanumeric	Description of one order unit of the stock item.
Units on hand	ON-HAND-UNITS	4 numeric	Number of units in current stock.
Price per unit	COST-PER-UNIT	6 numeric	Wholesale price of one unit in dollars and cents.
Total wholesale value	TOTAL-WHOLESALE-VALUE	10 numeric	Product of price per unit times units on hand.
Minimum unit quantity	MIN-STOCK-UNIT-QUANTITY	4 numeric	Reorder level.

```
003500 01  MASTER-RECORD.
003600     03 SEQ-STOCK-NUMBER PICTURE IS X(6).
003700     03 NUMBER-MANUFACTURER PICTURE IS 9(3).
003900     03 MFR-CATALOG-NUMBER PICTURE IS X(10).
004000     03 DESCRIPTION PICTURE IS X(30).
004100     03 ON-HAND-UNITS PICTURE IS 9(4) USAGE IS COMPUTATIONAL.
004300     03 COST-PER-UNIT PICTURE IS 9(4)V99.
004400     03 TOTAL-WHOLESALE-VALUE PICTURE IS 9(8)V99.
004500     03 MIN-STOCK-UNIT-QUANTITY PICTURE IS 9(4).
```

Fig. 3-3. MASTER-RECORD, which was used in the DATA RECORD IS clause of the file descriptions in Fig. 3-2 is defined according to the specifications on the table. PICTURE tells the compiler how the data will look.

There must be a level number for each elementary item, group, or record described. Level numbers begin at 01, which is reserved for use on the line containing the record name. Numbers 02 through 49 can be used as level numbers for your data names.

Data Description Clauses

Value. The VALUE OF clause specifies the value of an item in a label record. One possible use of this clause is to permit the user to enter the name of the file about to be processed in the label record. Thus, a test as to whether or not the proper file is about to be processed can be made before entering the processing stage. The format is:

$$\left[\text{;VALUE OF} \quad \underline{\text{data-name-1}} \text{ IS} \left\{ \frac{\underline{\text{data-name-2}}}{\text{literal-1}} \right\} \left[, \underline{\text{data-name-3}} \text{ IS} \left\{ \frac{\underline{\text{data-name-4}}}{\text{literal-2}} \right\} \right] \cdots \right]$$

In the general format, data names 1, 3, etc., should be qualified where necessary (see Qualification of Data) but can't be subscripted or indexed. Figurative constants may be used in place of the literals specified in the format. If label records are standard, then the supplied data names must be fixed names established by the individual implementor; data names 2, 4, etc., must be defined in the WORKING-STORAGE SECTION.

Filler. FILLER may be used in place of data name to indicate a portion of a record that is to contain no addressable data; e.g., a spacer between two data items that are to be printed. This specification cannot appear at a 01 level. The only other clause that may be specified with FILLER in the File Section is PICTURE. In effect, FILLER may be considered a special name for data to which no data name has been assigned, and no direct reference to FILLER may be made in the program. However, it may be referenced through the group or record of which it is a subset.

The format is as follows:

$$\text{level-number} \left\{ \begin{array}{c} \underline{\text{data-name}} \\ \underline{\text{FILLER}} \end{array} \right\}$$

Usage. The clause indicates to the compiler the most frequent use of the data being described and thereby dictates the format of internal representation. Data may be used in two ways:
1. As an element in a computational procedure.
2. As an element in an operation in which the data is formated for display.

DATA-ITEM	MNEMONIC NAME	DESCRIPTION	PURPOSE
Stock item number	STK-NUMBER-PRINT	6 alphanumeric	Printed stock item number.
Vendor number	NO-MFR	3 numeric	Printed code number associated with vendor.
New stock flag	FLAG-NEW-STOCK	1 alphabetic	Printed "N" if a new stock item; otherwise blank.
Vendor catalog number	MFR-ORDER-NUMBER	10 alphanumeric	Printed order key specified to vendor.
Item unit description	ITEM-DESCRIPTION	30 alphanumeric	Printed description of one order unit of the stock item.
Units on hand	UNITS-ON-HAND	4 numeric	Printed number of units in current stock.
Emergency reorder flag	EMERGENCY-REORDER-FLAG	3 alphabetic	Printed EEE when an emergency stock shortage; otherwise blank.
Minimum unit quantity	MIN-UNITS	4 numeric	Printed reorder level.
Price per unit	UNIT-COST	8 alphanumeric	Wholesale price of one unit of stock item in edited format.

Fig. 3-4. The file description and record description will be developed from the specifications on this table.

The format is:

In order to improve the efficiency of the object program, it is desirable to indicate to the COBOL compiler just how data is going to be used. The USAGE clause can be written at any level. When written at a group level it applies to each item in the group, however, the group itself is not COMPUTATIONAL and cannot be used in computations. The USAGE clause of an item may not contradict the usage of a group to which the item belongs. Thus, an item cannot be described as COMPUTATIONAL when it is part of a group item specified as DISPLAY.

If the USAGE clause is not specified for an item, or for any group to which the item belongs, it is assumed to be DISPLAY. The usage specified in this clause does not restrict in any way the operation of any verb on the data, except that COMPUTATIONAL implies numeric class. However, it does affect the way in which the data is represented inside the computer, and this will affect the efficiency of the object program. Example:

    03 ON-HAND-UNITS PICTURE IS
    9(4) USAGE IS COMPUTATIONAL.

The above example is an instance of correct use of the USAGE clause. However, if PICTURE IS X(4) or A(4), the USAGE IS COMPUTATIONAL clause would be illegal. The abbreviation COMP could have been used in place of COMPUTATIONAL; they are logically equivalent. Specifying one USAGE does not preclude an item from being used according to the other. For example, COMPUTATIONAL usage might be specified for most numeric items; this does not prevent their being displayed. The opposite is also true.

A COMPUTATIONAL item may only be *compared* with a numeric item. You cannot use the verb EXAMINE. There are no other restrictions on the use of a COMPUTATIONAL item as an operand in any statement. That is, you may DISPLAY, MOVE, or ADD such an item. Automatic conversion from one usage to another is supplied by the compiler.

Picture. This clause is used with every ELEMENTARY-ITEM of data described in the DATA DIVISION. The purpose of the PICTURE clause is to forewarn the computer about the form of the data-values you plan to give that item of data.

It has the following form:

$$\left[; \left\{ \begin{array}{c} \text{PICTURE} \\ \text{PIC} \end{array} \right\} \text{IS character-string} \right]$$

Generally speaking, the PICTURE clause's character string tells the computer the SIZE of the item and the CLASS of the item.

The size of an item is the maximum number of characters that its data values can be expected to have. PICTURE characters fall into three general categories. The first of these categories is Data Character Symbols, which indicate whether the data-item is alphabetic, numeric, or alphanumeric. Second, there are the Operational Symbols which indicate the operational sign, the assumed decimal position, and the assumed decimal scaling position of a numeric value. Last, there are the Editing Symbols. These characters indicate the editing to be done before printing an elementary item. Two types of editing symbols are available; replacement and fixed insertion.

The replacement symbol specifies that some character in the data item (usually zero) is to be suppressed and replaced by another character (usually the symbol itself). The fixed insertion character is inserted into the data item in addition to those characters already present. The use of editing symbols results in two additional classes of data; alphanumeric edited and numeric edited. These classes are discussed later.

The character string of a PICTURE clause may be made up of one or more of the following characters:

9 V S P X A

You use a 9 to indicate a character position which will contain a digit. Consider this example entry from the DATA DIVISION of a COBOL program:

```
006500 FD  REORDER-LIST LABEL RECORD IS OMITTED
006600     DATA RECORD IS REPLENISH-STOCK-ITEM.
006700 01  REPLENISH-STOCK-ITEM.
006750     08 FILLER PICTURE IS X(5).
006800     08 STK-NUMBER-PRINT PICTURE IS X(6).
006900     08 FILLER PICTURE IS X(5).
007000     08 NO-MFR PICTURE IS 9(3).
007100     08 FILLER PICTURE IS X(7).
007250     08 FLAG-NEW-STOCK PICTURE IS A.
007300     08 FILLER PICTURE IS X(7).
007350     08 MFR-ORDER-NUMBER PICTURE IS X(10).
007400     08 FILLER PICTURE IS X(7).
007450     08 ITEM-DESCRIPTION PICTURE IS X(30).
007500     08 FILLER PICTURE IS X(5).
007550     08 UNITS-ON-HAND PICTURE IS ZZZ9.
007575     08 FILLER PICTURE IS X(5).
007600     08 EMERGENCY-REORDER-FLAG PICTURE IS X(3).
007700     08 FILLER PICTURE IS X(5).
007800     08 MIN-UNITS PICTURE IS ZZZ9.
007900     08 FILLER PICTURE IS X(5).
008000     08 UNIT-COST PICTURE IS $$$$Z.99.
008100     08 FILLER PICTURE IS X(12).
```

Fig. 3-5. Note the use of FILLER to format the output information into an easily readable table.

03 ZIP-CODE PICTURE 99999.

Here the computer has been forewarned that the data name ZIP-CODE will have data values given to it, all of which will be five digits long. Consider a second example:

03 PHONE-NUMBER PICTURE 9999999.

There we have told the computer that all PHONE-NUMBERs will be made up of seven digits. This is an equivalent "short-hand" way of writing the last example:

03 PHONE-NUMBER PICTURE 9(7).

Whenever you have repeated characters in a PICTURE clause, you may indicate the repetition with that sort of parenthetical notation.

The PICTURE clause characters V and P are used in connection with numeric data-values that are not integers, and are discussed later. The character S is used with numeric data values that could possibly be negative.

The character string of an alphabetic PICTURE clause may be made up only of A's. Similar in use to the 9 in a numeric PICTURE clause, the A is used to indicate a character position which will contain a letter or a space. For example, this entry appearing in the DATA DIVISION:

03 MONTH-NAME PICTURE AAA.

would forewarn the computer that all MONTH-NAMEs will be made up of three letters. The way the programmer could do that would be to decide to abbreviate all month names.

If he wanted to spell out the month names, he'd have to provide enough room for the longest name, SEPTEMBER, and use an entry like this:

03 MONTH-NAME PICTURE AAAAAAAAA.

or

03 MONTH-NAME PICTURE A (9)

Having promised the computer that all MONTH-NAMEs would be nine letters long, he will have to make good his promise by spelling the seven-letter name JANUARY with two spaces following it, FEBRUARY with one space, MARCH with four spaces, and so on.

Note that although the space is technically a special character, it is the only special character that may occur in a character position described by an A.

In an alphanumeric PICTURE clause the 9 is used in exactly the same way as it was in the numeric clause. Likewise, the A is used for exactly the same purpose as it was with the alphabetic clause. The X is used to indicate a character position which could be occupied by any character in the COBOL set.

Here is an example of the use of the clause. A leading department store uses catalog numbers of this form:

23XW92746F   35XG30428C

(two digits, two letters, five digits, and one letter). A program which uses catalog numbers of that form as one of its items of data would probably include this DATA DIVISION entry:

04 CATALOG-NUMBER PICTURE 99AA9(5)A.

Editing. The following list shows all of the symbols that can be used for editing purposes:

* 0 , $ - CR Z B . + DB

Each of these symbols will be described in more detail

*-specifies that before a data item is printed asterisks should replace leading zeros as indicated by the PICTURE clause. For example:

PICTURE	DATA ITEM	EDITED ITEM
****	0000	****
****	8730	8730
****	0087	**87
****	8736	8736
***9	0087	**87
**99	0087	**87
*999	0087	*087

An asterisk can never appear in a PICTURE with Z, A, X, or S or more than one currency, minus, or plus sign. It cannot be preceded by a 9, V, or P.

0-specifies that a zero is to be inserted in the item in the character position corresponding to that of the 0 in the PICTURE.

PICTURE	DATA ITEM	PRINTED
990099	8936	890036
$999.00	0736	$736.00

,-specifies a character position into which a comma is to be inserted unless the preceding character has been suppressed. A comma cannot occur in a PICTURE containing any A or X characters.

PICTURE	DATA ITEM	PRINTED
99,999	87362	87,362
	87000	87,000
ZZ,ZZZ	00873	873
	20000	20,000

$-may be used as either a fixed insertion character or as a replacement character. If only one $ is used in a PICTURE, then it is a fixed insertion character and will occur in the specified position within the data item when that item is printed. For example:

PICTURE	DATA ITEM	EDITED ITEM
$9999	1234	$1234
$ZZZ9	0000	$ 0
$ZZZZ	0000	

If more than one consecutive currency sign is used in the high-order end of a PICTURE, the currency sign becomes a replacement symbol. It suppresses all leading zeros as dictated by the PICTURE and inserts $ in place of the rightmost zero suppressed. However, if the value of the data is zero, then the edited item will contain spaces. For example:

PICTURE	DATA ITEM	EDITED ITEM
$$$9999	001234	$1234
$$$	000	
$$$$$	0008	$8
$$99	123	$123

The currency sign may never appear in a PICTURE with A, X, or more than one plus or minus sign.

− or +-may be used as either fixed insertion or replacement characters. If the plus or minus sign is written as an insertion character in either the first character or last character of a PICTURE, a displayed sign (as opposed to an operational sign) is inserted into the indicated position.

When the minus sign is inserted, a minus sign will appear if the item is negative; a blank will appear in the specified position if the item is positive or unsigned. When the plus sign is used, a plus sign appears if the item is positive; a minus sign appears if the item is negative. Unsigned items are considered positive. For example:

DATA ITEM	PICTURE	EDITED ITEM
+33	−99	33
−33	99−	33−
−33	−99	−33
00	−99	00
+22	+99	+22
−22	+99	−22
20	99+	20+

If either the minus or plus sign is used as a replacement symbol, it will suppress leading zeros as dictated by the PICTURE. The rightmost zero suppressed is replaced according to the following rules:

1. If a floating minus sign is used and the data item is negative, then a minus sign will replace the rightmost zero suppressed. If the item is positive or zero, a blank will replace it. For example:

PICTURE	DATA ITEM	EDITED ITEM
−−99	123	123
−−−99	−012	−12
−−−−	000	

2. If a floating plus sign is used and the data item is positive, then a plus sign will replace the right-most zero suppressed. If the item is negative, then a minus sign will replace it. For example:

PICTURE	DATA ITEM	EDITED ITEM
++99	012	+12
+++9	−006	−6
++++	000	
++99	123	+123

DB-specifies that two character positions of the item are to contain the characters DB if the value of the data item is negative. DB can only occur as the last characters (except for P) of a PICTURE. DB cannot be used in a PICTURE containing A, X, -, +, S, or CR characters.

PICTURE	DATA ITEM	PRINTED
$$$$.99 DB	24567	$245.67
$$$$.99 DB	−00138	$1.38 DB

Z-specifies that before the data item is printed, as many leading zeros as there are Z's are to be suppressed (replaced by a blank or space).

PICTURE	DATA ITEM	PRINTED
ZZZZ	0000	
ZZZZ	8730	8730
ZZZZ	0087	87
ZZZZ	8736	8736
ZZZ9	0087	87
ZZ99	0087	87
Z999	0087	087

B-specifies that a blank or space is to be inserted in the item in the character position corresponding to that of the B in the PICTURE.

PICTURE	DATA ITEM	PRINTED
99B9B9	8736	87 3 6
9BB999	8736	8 736

.-specifies a character position into which a decimal point is to be inserted unless the succeeding character positions have been suppressed. It cannot be used in a PICTURE clause containing any A, X, P or V characters.

CR-specifies that two character positions of the item are to contain the characters CR if the value of the data item is negative. CR can only occur as the last characters (except for P) of a PICTURE. CR cannot be used in a PICTURE containing A, X, -, +, S, or DB characters.

P-is used to hold a position when you are not sure where the decimal point will be. If needed, zeros will fill where a P is placed, and if not needed, they are ignored.

V-is an editorial mark that instructs the computer to place a decimal point at the indicated position, even though one does not appear there in the stored value. Both P and V are used for output, not input. Thus, you would not tell the computer to read a data card with a number whose picture is

VPP99. If you used this for output however, it could print any number from .01 to .0099. For instance, if LITERS equalled .28 it would print .28, if LITERS equalled .028 it would print .028, .0028 would print .0028, and .00028 would print .0003.

Justified. This clause is used to right justify alphabetic or alphanumeric data within an area set aside to hold that particular elementary item. Standard positioning for this type of data is left justification with space fill on the right. When this statement is used the data is right justified and the unused positions are space filled. Left truncation occurs when the receiving data area is smaller than the data being moved into it. For example:

DATA ITEM	RECEIVING AREA SIZE	NORMAL POSITIONING	JUSTIFIED RIGHT POSITIONING
A9BQ7	7 characters	A9BQ7ΔΔ	ΔΔA9BQ7
MUTUAL	4 characters	MUTU	TUAL

"Δ" indicates space

The format of this clause is:

$$\left[; \left\{ \begin{array}{c} \underline{\text{JUSTIFIED}} \\ \text{JUST} \end{array} \right\} \text{RIGHT} \right]$$

This clause may not be used with numeric data since such data is either aligned by decimal point with zero fill on either end as required, or right justified in the absence of a decimal point with zero fill on the left.

Synchronized. This clause permits unpacked data storage by placing each elementary item in the least number of computer words required to contain it. The data is packed in order to conserve storage space, and must be unpacked before it can be used. The format of this clause is:

$$\left[; \left\{ \begin{array}{c} \underline{\text{SYNCHRONIZED}} \\ \text{SYNC} \end{array} \right\} \left\{ \begin{array}{c} \underline{\text{LEFT}} \\ \underline{\text{RIGHT}} \end{array} \right\} \right]$$

When SYNCHRONIZED LEFT is specified, the item starts at the leftmost boundary of the computer word. Similarly, when SYNCHRONIZED RIGHT is specified, the data is positioned so that it terminates at the rightmost boundary of the computer word. The words SYNC and SYNCHRONIZED are logically equivalent.

Items specified at the 01 level are automatically synchronized (numeric items to the right, alphabetic items to the left). In the following examples, each computer word has a capacity of four characters, and the word boundaries are indicated by the symbol |.

Consider three adjacent data items in a word with the following PICTURE descriptions:

9(5), A(2), 9.

If no synchronization is specified they are stored in packed form, i.e.,

|9999|9AA9|

However, if synchronization is specified for any or all of the items, they may be represented in memory as follows:

	9(5)	A(2)	9	MEMORY
Synchronized	Right	Right	Right	|0009|9999|ΔΔAA|0009
	Right	Left	N.S.	|0009|9999|AAΔΔ|9000|
	N.S.	Left	Right	|9999|9000|AAΔΔ|0009|
	N.S.	Right	Right	|9999|9AAΔ|0009|

(N.S. means no synchronization; Δ means space.)

Value Is. This clause is used to either define the value of a condition name or to specify the initial value of a working storage area. The literal may be any literal or figurative constant. The VALUE clause may be used in the WORKING-STORAGE SECTION to either specify the value, or range of values, of a condition name or the value of an item to be contained therein. In the File Section, it may only be used to define the value of condition name and any other use of this clause in that section is for documentation purposes only. With the exception of a condition name entry, the VALUE IS clause must not be used in an entry that either contains a REDEFINES clause or is subordinate to an entry containing a REDEFINES clause. The VALUE clause must not contradict the PICTURE clause in either length or class (numeric or nonnumeric). Further, when an item has editing symbols specified by the PICTURE clause, the literal in the VALUE clause must be nonnumeric and in edited form. A numeric literal used in this clause must have a value within the range specified by the PICTURE clause. For example, if the PICTURE of a numeric item is VPPP99, the literal specified in the VALUE clause must be within the range .00000 to .00099.

If the VALUE clause is used at a group level within the WORKING-STORAGE SECTION, it must not appear in the entries within the group. The group will be initialized without regard to the individual items or other groups within that group. The general format of this clause is:

; { VALUE IS / VALUES ARE } literal-1 [THRU literal-2][, literal-3 [THRU literal-4]]...

When used in a conditional variable, one VALUE clause must be supplied for each condition-name at an 88 level. No further entries need be specified. The form would appear in the following manner:

level number data name
        88 condition-name-1 VALUE IS literal-1
        88 condition-name-2 VALUE IS literal-2
        .
        .
        .
        88 condition-name-n VALUE IS literal-n

Example:

    77 PAY PICTURE IS 9(8) USAGE IS COMPUTATIONAL.
    88 FICA-MAX VALUE IS 00660000 THRU ALL 9.

The effect of this clause is that FICA-MAX is a condition-name, dependent upon the value of PAY. If PAY is within the range of values described by the VALUE clause, the condition-name FICA-MAX becomes "true".

Blank. Format: [; <u>BLANK</u> WHEN <u>ZERO</u>].

This clause is used to set an item to blanks when its value is zero. If the asterisk is used as the zero suppression symbol and the BLANK WHEN ZERO clause appears in the same entry, the zero suppression editing overrides the function of the BLANK WHEN ZERO clause.

PICTURE	DATA ITEM	BLANK WHEN ZERO SPECIFIED?	EDITED ITEM
$ZZZ9	0000	No	$ 0
$ZZZ9	0000	Yes	
****	0000	No	****
****	0000	Yes	****

REDEFINES Format: level-number <u>data-name-1</u> ;REDEFINES <u>data-name-2</u>.

The REDEFINES clause allows the same computer storage area to contain different data times at different times; i.e., to "overlay" items in storage. For example, suppose a work area called MONTH-TABLE is needed in a program, and another work area, MONTH-LOOK, is used later in the same program. Normally, each area would be described separately in the WORKING-STORAGE SECTION, and each would occupy different portions of storage. However, if the programmer knows that MONTH-TABLE is never used when MONTH-LOOK is used, he may use the REDEFINES clause enabling both items to occupy the same physical area in storage. Example:

```
03 QUANTITY
    04 TONS PICTURE IS S9(4)V99 SYNCHRONIZED RIGHT.
    04 BASE-BOXES PICTURE IS S9(5) SYNCHRONIZED RIGHT.
    04 BASE-SYM REDEFINES BASE-BOXES.
        05 FIRST-DIGIT PICTURE IS 9.
        05 BASE-BOX-REST PICTURE IS S9(4).
```

The REDEFINES clause must immediately follow the entries controlled by data-name-1 (i.e., the sublevel to data-name-1). This is the only descriptive clause which must occur in a fixed place in an item description. The level-numbers of data-name-1 and data-name-2 must be identical, and must not be 66 or 88. Also, the REDEFINES clause must not appear in 01 level entries in the File Section; implicit redefinition is provided by the DATA RECORDS clause in the File Description entry.

When an area is redefined, all descriptions of the area remain in effect. If B and C are two separate items sharing the same storage area, the procedure statements MOVE X TO B or MOVE Y TO C could be executed at any point in the program. In the first case, B would assume the value of X and take the form specified by the description of B. In the second case, the same physical area would receive Y according to the description of C. A redefinition does not cause any data to be erased and does not supersede a previous description.

In using the REDEFINES clause, the programmer must be extremely careful especially when either the SYNCHRONIZED clause or the SIGNED option is used. If the areas utilized by each of the data names are not equal, program errors are likely to occur. Except for condition name entries, the entry describing the new storage area must not contain a VALUE clause.

Renames. Format: 66 <u>data name-1</u>; <u>RENAMES</u> data-name-2 [<u>THRU</u> data-name-3]

The RENAMES option permits an item or items established by a record description entry to be assigned a new name. Unlike REDEFINES, this clause does not redefine existing data descriptions but merely allows data to be accessed and/or grouped under alternative names while maintaining the previously defined data description. For example, assume that a record is laid out in the following manner (this does not constitute a complete record description):

```
01 A
   02 B
      03 G
      03 H
   02 C
      03 I
      03 J
   02 D
   02 E
   02 F
```

The items may be renamed as follows:
   66 K RENAMES G Thru I.
   66 M RENAMES B Thru C.
   66 N RENAMES E.

In this case, any reference to K would access items G, H, and I. Groups B and C would be accessed by a reference to M, and E would be referenced as N.

One or more RENAMES entries may be written for a record and must directly follow the last data description entry of the specific record. Data name-1, 2, and 3 must be either elementary items or groups within the associated record and may not be the same data name. The RENAMES clause may not be used for other 66 level entries nor can it be used for a 01, 77, or 88 level entry.

When data name-3 is not specified, data name-2 can either be a group item or an elementary item. When data name-2 is a group item, data name-1 is treated as a group item, and when data name-2 is an elementary item, data name-1 is treated as an elementary item. Data name-2 must precede data name-3 in the RECORD DESCRIPTION. Data-name-3 cannot be contained within data name-2. Data name-1 cannot be used as a qualifier, and can only be qualified by names at the 01 level or FD entries.

Qualification of Data

Generally, the use of duplicate names in COBOL is absolutely forbidden. There may not be duplicate paragraph names, section names, file names, or record names. However, duplicate data names are allowed, but to use them in the PROCEDURE DIVISION you must specify which one you mean by using a qualifying clause.

The form of a qualifying clause is as follows:

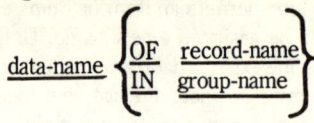

The following rules must be obeyed when using qualification:

1. The qualifier must be of a higher level and within the same heirarchy as the name it is qualifying.
2. The same name may not appear at two levels in a hierarchy so that it would appear to qualify itself.
3. Any data-name requiring qualification must be qualified every time it is referenced. In the absence of qualification, the COBOL compiler cannot determine the logical reference.
4. If a data-name or condition-name is assigned to more than one data item in a program, it must be qualified in all references to it in the program.
5. A name can be qualified even though it does not need qualification. The use of more names for qualification than are actually required for uniqueness is permitted. If there is more than one combination of qualifiers which ensure uniqueness, then any set can be used.
6. A conditional variable can be used as a qualifier for any of its condition-names.
7. A section-name is the highest and only qualifier for a paragraph-name. A paragraph-name must not be duplicated within a section. When a paragraph-name is qualified by a section-name, the word SECTION must not appear in the entry. A paragraph-name need not be qualified when the reference to it is made from within the same section.
8. The length of a qualified data-name is set by the specific implementation (generally, no more than 200 characters).

For example, suppose that you had two records in your program called CUSTOMER-RECORD and PART-RECORD, and that they were organized as shown here:

```
01 CUSTOMER-RECORD
    02 NAME
    02 ADDR
        05 ACCT-NR
```

```
008200 WORKING-STORAGE SECTION.
008300 77 DIVIDEND PICTURE IS 9(6) VALUE IS ZERO.
008400 77 PERCENTAGE PICTURE IS 9999 VALUE IS 0000.
008500 77 SWITCH PICTURE IS 9 VALUE IS ZERO USAGE IS COMPUTATIONAL.
008610 77 LINE-NO VALUE IS 0 PICTURE IS 99.
008700 01 1-REPLENISH-REPORT-HEADING.
008800    10 FILLER PICTURE IS X(116) VALUE SPACES.
008900    10 PAGE.
009100       15 PAGEKON VALUE IS 'PAGE' PICTURE IS X(5).
009110       15 PAGE-NO PICTURE IS 999 VALUE ZERO.
009150    15 FILLER PICTURE IS X(8) VALUE SPACES.
009300 01 2-REPLENISH-REPORT-HEADING.
009350    02 ONE-THRU-SIXTY-ONE PICTURE X(61) VALUE IS '         STOCK
009400-   '  MFR     NEW     CATALOG                           ITE'.
009450    02 SIXTY-TWO-THRU-132 PICTURE X(71) VALUE IS 'M - UNIT
009500-   '   UNITS   EMERG     MIN                UNIT          '.
009700 01 3-REPLENISH-REPORT-HEADING.
009750    02 ONE-THRU-71 PICTURE X(71) VALUE IS '  NUMBER    NUMBER
009800-   '  STOCK      NUMBER                      DESCRIPTION'.
009900    02 SEVENTY-ONE-THRU-132 PICTURE X(61) VALUE
010000                  ON HAND    REORD     UNITS              COST'.
```

Fig. 3-6. While the FILE DESCRIPTION area describes the format of input and output data, the WORKING STORAGE section describes the format of data while it is in memory, being worked on.

```
       02 AGE
          03 YR
          03 MO
01 PART-RECORD
       02 NUMBER
       02 UNIT-PRICE
       02 MFG-DATE
          03 MO
          03 YR
```

If you then wanted to MOVE the customer's name to a receiving field called NAME-OUT, you could say:
    MOVE NAME IN CUSTOMER-RECORD TO NAME-OUT.
If you wanted to move the year that the part was manufactured to a receiving field called YEAR-OUT, you'd have to say:
    MOVE YR OF MFG-DATE TO YEAR-OUT.

THE WORKING-STORAGE SECTION

The WORKING-STORAGE SECTION is used to describe areas of memory which are to contain intermediate results of processing and other temporarily stored data at object running time. These areas may be specified in any one of three ways:

1. As single item areas containing data that is unrelated to any other data contained in the working-storage area.

2. As record areas containing items of data that are interrelated and organized into records.

3. As conditional item areas mapped to contain variables and their associated condition names.

Generally, programmers use this section for four purposes. First, it is used to store the intermediate results of arithmetic calculations. Second, it is used to build lines of output file for printing. A third use is to safeguard data which if left in an input record would be prematurely destroyed. Last, the section is used to build and manipulate tabular data of the sort involved in income tax calculations.

The WORKING-STORAGE SECTION begins with a section header followed by descriptions of both the single item and the conditional item areas. The descriptions for record areas then follow. The general format is as follows:

```
WORKING-STORAGE SECTION
77 (name and description of single item areas)
              .
              .
              .
77 (name and description of conditional variables)
      88 (condition-name-1)
      88 (condition-name-2)
```

01 (name and description for record area)

Single Item Areas. These areas are complete files which are not subdivided and are not themselves subdivisions of some other item. They are always assigned the level number 77. Each single item file must be described in a separate data description entry consisting of the level number 77, a data name, and a PICTURE clause. Other record description clauses are optional and can be used to complete the description of the item, if necessary. When writing an area for them in the WORKING-STORAGE SECTION, entries for all single items are placed before the entries describing record items.

Independent items are used only in the WORKING-STORAGE SECTION. They are essentially elementary items with one additional restriction; they may not be a part of a group item. They must stand entirely alone. In all other ways independent items are exactly like elementary items.

Independent items are coded at Margin A using level number 77. If you use any 77 level entries in your WORKING-STORAGE SECTION, they must be placed at the beginning of the section, prior to any other entries.

These areas are frequently used for the temporary storage of intermediate results pending completion of a calculation. For example, suppose that the programmer wishes to total several items in order to obtain an average, and he wishes to retain the total for some future calculation. In this case, the total would have to be stored temporarily. Unless it were to be used as part of a larger grouping of items, it would often be convenient to store it in an independent item area of working storage.

Record Areas. Data elements in working storage which bear a definite relationship to one another must be grouped into records according to the rules for formation of record descriptions. All clauses which are used in normal input or output record descriptions, can be used in a WORKING-STORAGE Record Description. Each working-storage record name (01 level) must be unique since it cannot be qualified by a file name. Subordinate data-names need not be unique if they can be made unique by qualification.

Condition-Item Areas. Any working storage item may constitute a conditional variable with which one or more condition names may be associated. Entries defining condition names must immediately follow the item to which they relate. Both the conditional variable entry and the associated condition name entries may contain VALUE clauses.

Initial Values for Working-Storage Areas. The initial value of any item in the Working-Storage Section may be specified by using the VALUE clause of the record description. If VALUE is not specified, the initial value may be unpredictable. All the rules for the expression of literals and figurative constants apply. The size of the literal value can be equal to or less than the size specified in the PICTURE clause of the associated data entry,

```
004700 FD  DETAIL-TRANSACTION-CARDS DATA RECORD IS TRANSACTIONS
004800     LABEL RECORDS OMITTED.

005000 01  TRANSACTIONS.
005100     05 STOCK-CONTROL-NUMBER PICTURE IS X(6).
005110     05 NO-TRANSACTOR PICTURE IS 999.
005120     05 ORDER-NUMBER PICTURE IS X(10).
005200     05 DTL-DESCRIPTION PICTURE IS X(30).
005300     05 TYPE-TRANSACTION PICTURE IS 9 USAGE IS COMPUTATIONAL.
005500     05 QUANTITY PICTURE IS 9(4).
005600     05 UNIT-COST PICTURE IS 9(4)V99.
006010     05 FILLER PICTURE IS X(20).
```

Fig. 3-7. The remaining FILE SECTION code for our sample program. The number at the far left indicates sequence. By putting all of these examples in numeric order, you will have a complete program, properly formatted for the COBOL compiler.

but it cannot be greater. When the size is less, normal rules for data positioning apply.

SAMPLE PROBLEM

In the sample problem two input files and two output files were used. These were the input master inventory file, the input detail transaction file, the output (updated) master inventory file, and the output reorder list file. Descriptions of the files are shown below, first in English prose and then in COBOL. The records contained in these files are described in the next section.

Master Inventory (Input and Output)

The input and output master inventory files are identical in format, the latter being an updated version of the former. For this reason, their file descriptions are identical except for file name. Each is physically stored on magnetic tape, fifty master records to a physical block with a standard label that contains a tape identifier, MSTINVTP. Both files contain a logical master record for each individual stock item in the inventory. See Fig. 3-2.

Detail Transaction File (Input)

The detail transaction file consists of records contained on punched master record for each individual stock item in the inventory. See Fig. 3-2.

Stock Reorder-List File (Output)

The stock Reorder-List file is printed during runtime. The record area is called Replenish-Stock-Item, the elements of which are as shown in the next section. See Fig. 3-5.

Data records which comprise the files are described in detail below, first using English descriptions and then the COBOL equivalent.

Master Inventory File

The input and output master inventory files are each described by the same File Description; their record formats are also identical. Figure 3-3 shows the breakdown of the record format, including its mnemonic name in the program.

Reorder List File

The table in Fig. 3-4 shows the format of the Reorder List Record, with the description of the record format, written in COBOL, appears in Fig. 3-5.

The working storage data is used in the sample to support the performance of various procedures. See Fig. 3-6 for the actual working storage section.

Chapter 4

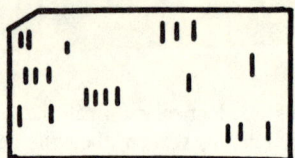

The Procedure Division

The PROCEDURE DIVISION is the last of the four divisions that make up COBOL programs. It is in this final division that the computer is told exactly what it is supposed to do. In this chapter the various elements that make up the division are explained.

The basic unit of the PROCEDURE DIVISION is the sentence which consists of one or more statements and/or expressions. A procedure is formed by combining one or more sentences into a paragraph and one or more paragraphs into a section. A procedure, then, is a paragraph, a group of successive paragraphs, or a section within the PROCEDURE DIVISION. Only sections and paragraphs may be named, and therefore, are the only elements with which communication may be made.

EXPRESSIONS

An expression in the COBOL language may be defined as a meaningful combination of data names, literals, and operators which may be reduced to a single value. In procedural statements, two types of expressions may be specified; the arithmetic expression and the conditional expression.

Arithmetic Expressions

Arithmetic expressions are data names, identifiers, or numeric literals or a series of data names, identifiers, and literals separated by arithmetic operators which define or can be reduced to a single numeric value. The format of arithmetic expressions using arithmetic operators in COBOL procedure is as follows:

or

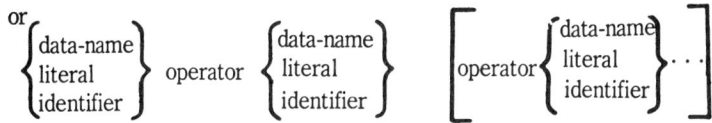

Five arithmetic operators are available for use in an arithmetic expression:

OPERATOR	MEANS
+	Addition
−	Subtraction
*	Multiplication
/	Division
**	Exponentiation

When arithmetic expressions are evaluated by the COBOL compiler, each term is examined and evaluated in a precise order of precedence established by the arithmetic operators. Normal precedence from high to low is as follows:

1. Exponentiation
2. Multiplication and division
3. Addition and subtraction

The following examples illustrate the effect this ordering has on the result of an expression as opposed to a simple left to right evaluation. In these examples, let A=4, B=6, C=2, D=3, and E=12.

	LEFT TO RIGHT	COBOL EVAULATION
A + B * C ** D	8000	52
A + B * C	20	16
E − A / C	4	10

Conditional Expressions

Conditional expressions are used in situations where the outcome of a test will determine the next logical steps to be performed. Like the arithmetic expression which reduces to a single numeric value, the conditional expression may also be thought of as reduced to a single value-in this case, true or being false. In general, truth or falseness is determined by a relation test either between a data name and a literal, or among several data names.

The following list names the six relational operators available in COBOL and their meanings:

RELATIONAL OPERATOR	MEANING
>	
IS GREATER THAN	Is greater than
NOT >	Is not greater than-
IS NOT GREATER THAN	Is less than or equal to

RELATIONAL OPERATOR	MEANING
<	Is less than
IS LESS THAN	
NOT <	Is not less than-
IS NOT LESS THAN	Is greater than or equal to
=	
IS EQUAL TO	Equals
NOT =	Does not equal
IS NOT EQUAL TO	

Characters are compared and evaluated on the basis of a computer collating sequence in which the characters have a specified order of magnitude. This order is built into the machine, and every character meaningful to the computer has its position in this ordering. The result of a comparison depends on the relative position of each character in the machine's collating sequence.

The comparison of numeric items is based on the respective values of the items considered purely as algebraic values. The item length, in terms of the number of digits, is not itself significant. Zero for example, represents a unique value regardless of the length, sign, or implied decimal point location of an item.

A comparison of a data item which has a value of +000003 with a data item which has a value of +03 will result in an "equal" condition. Similarly, the value of 000000 is equal to the value +0000. Following the rules of algebra, +01 is greater than −155.

For two nonnumeric items, or one numeric and one nonnumeric item, a comparison results in the determination that one of the items is LESS THAN, EQUAL TO, or GREATER THAN the other with respect to the ordered character set. If a signed, computational item is compared with a nonnumeric item, the sign is ignored. There are two cases to consider, equal length items and unequal length items. In a comparison of two nonnumeric items, the character in an item is compared with the corresponding character of the other item. The comparison begins with the high order (leftmost) character of each item. If these two characters are equal, the next two are compared and so on. As soon as the unequal condition is noted, the comparison stops and the result is recorded.

If the items are of equal length, comparison proceeds by comparing characters in corresponding character positions starting from the high order end and continuing until either a pair of unequal character is encountered or the low order (low end) of the item is reached. The items are determined to be EQUAL when the low-order end is reached, and no equal pair of characters was detected. The first encountered pair of unequal characters is compared for relative location in the ordered character set. The item which contains the character which is positioned higher in the ordered sequence is determined to be the GREATER item.

If the items are of unequal length, comparison proceeds as described above. If this process exhausts the characters of the shorter item without detection of a difference, then the shorter item is LESS THAN the longer item unless the remainder of the longer item consists solely of spaces.

CONDITIONS

A simple condition reducing to the value true or false may be expressed by any of the following:

- a relation
- a condition name
- a sign condition
- a class condition
- a switch status condition.

Any of the above may be used in a decision-making operation to select different paths of control in a program.

Relational Condition

A relational condition causes a comparison of magnitude between two quantities (or operands). Each quantity may be either an identifier, a literal, or an arithmetic expression. The general form of the relational expression is as follows:

$$\left\{\begin{array}{c} \underline{\text{data-name-1}} \\ \text{literal-1} \\ \text{arithmetic-expression-1} \end{array}\right\} \text{relational-operator} \left\{\begin{array}{c} \underline{\text{data-name-2}} \\ \text{literal-2} \\ \text{arithmetic-expression-2} \end{array}\right\}$$

The first quantity is called the subject of the condition. The second is referred to as the object. The subject and object in a relational expression may not both be literals. The relational operators listed specify the type of comparison to be made between the two quantities. A relational operator must be preceded and followed by a space.

Condition Names

A condition name is a name assigned in the Data Division to one of the values a conditional variable may assume. In a condition name condition, the variable is tested to determine whether or not it is equal to a value associated with a particular condition name. If the condition name is associated with a range of values, the variable is tested to determine if the value falls within this range. This includes both the upper and lower values.

Sign Conditions

Sign conditions take this form:

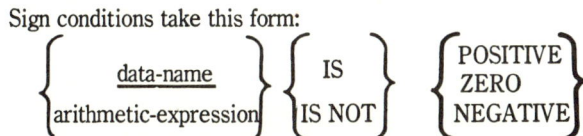

This condition determines whether a numeric quantity is less than, equal to, or greater than zero. Any condition that can be expressed in a numeric status test may also be expressed by a relational expression. For example, A + B * C IS POSITIVE, may also be expressed in a relational expression as A + B * C IS GREATER THAN 0.

Class Conditions

The format of the class condition is as follows:

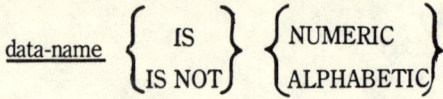

This form of condition is provided for your use when you want to check data being input to be sure it is of the correct form. Some computers make less rigorous checks than others to see if data values being input conform with PICTURE clauses describing them. If your computer is one of the less rigorous ones, you want to check especially those fields that are going to be involved in arithmetic calculations to be sure they contain only numeric data-values.

Switch Status Condition

The switch status condition is used to determine whether a particular hardware switch is off or on. The implementor name and its associated ON or OFF value must be named in the SPECIAL-NAMES paragraph of the Environment Division, which will be discussed later. The result of the test is true when the switch is set to the specified position corresponding to the condition name.

STATEMENTS AND SENTENCES

Statements form the basic functional components of COBOL procedures. Just as clauses make up sentences in normal English language construction, so statements make up COBOL language sentences. A sentence may contain one or more statements. There are three basic types of statements and sentences permitted in COBOL:

- Imperative
- Conditional
- Compiler-directing

The following rules govern the construction of sentences:
1. Each sentence may be made up of one or more statements.
2. Each sentence is terminated by a period.
3. Separators may be used to enhance readability. They are optional.
4. The allowable separators in a COBOL sentence are a space, a semicolon, or a comma.
5. Two contiguous separators are not permissible.
6. Separators may be used between statements, between a condition and statement-1 in a conditional sentence and between statement-1 and ELSE in a conditional statement.

Imperative Sentences

Imperative sentences and statements are explicit and direct commands to the computer.
For example:
>ADD TEMP1 TO TEMP2.
>MULTIPLY PAY-RATE BY HOURS-WORKED GIVING GROSS-PAY; GO TO FICA- COMPUTATION.
>ADD A TO B GIVING C; PERFORM 321 THRU 328.
>MOVE 1050 TO REORDER-POINT.

After an imperative statement is executed, control is passed on to the the next statement in sequence unless a GO TO or STOP RUN verb is present. If either is used, it must be the last statement in the sequence since control will be immediately transferred.

Conditional Sentences

Conditional statements and sentences are vital to any data processing problem. In effect, they specify alternative courses of action depending upon the outcome of a test or comparison. The format of a conditional statement is as follows:

$$\underline{IF}\ condition;\ \left\{\begin{array}{c}statement\text{-}1\\ \underline{NEXT\ SENTENCE}\end{array}\right\};\ \underline{ELSE}\ \left\{\begin{array}{c}statement\text{-}2\\ \underline{NEXT\ SENTENCE}\end{array}\right\}$$

Here, a conditional expression (either simple or compound) is evaluated and determined to be either true or false. If the condition is true, then statement-1 is executed. If it is not a GO TO or STOP RUN, then control is transferred to the next sentence. If condition is false, then statement-2 is executed, if it is not a GO TO or STOP RUN, control is passed on to the next sentence. If NEXT SENTENCE is specified instead of statement-1, control passes to the next sentence if the statement is true. If no false path is specified and the true side contains NEXT SENTENCE, for example:

>IF condition NEXT SENTENCE

then control passes to the next sentence regardless of whether the statement is true or false thereby having the effect of a skip-to-next-instruction operation.

PROCEDURE FORMATION

Procedures are formed by combining one or more sentences into a paragraph and one or more paragraphs into a section. Each paragraph or section must be preceded by a procedure name. These names may be either numeric, alphabetic, or alphanumeric. If numeric, leading zeros are significant. All procedure names must start at position A (column 8) on the COBOL Programming Form, be a maximum of 30 characters in length, and be followed by a period.

Paragraphs

One or more sentences may be combined to form a paragraph. Essentially, a paragraph expresses a single procedure to be executed in the main program. Each program contains many such paragraphs. Each paragraph must be preceded by a procedure name since reference may only be made to an entire paragraph and not to individual sentences contained therein. If reference is to be made to a single sentence, that sentence must be defined as a complete paragraph and must be preceded by a procedure name.

Sections

One or more paragraphs can be grouped into a section. The section is the largest unit in COBOL to which a procedure name may be assigned. This is done by writing a procedure name, followed by the key word SECTION, followed by a period. The remainder of the line on which it is written must be left blank. The Procedure Division need not be broken into sections if the programmer does not find it convenient.

Procedural Verbs

As in the English language, verbs specify actions to be performed. In COBOL, each verb built into the system causes a specific series of events to occur at object time. Each verb operates within the context of one or more fixed format statements. The formats indicate the arrangement of verb and operand and indicate the particular category of procedure statement. The various verbs inherent in the COBOL language are categorized and will be described in the following manner:

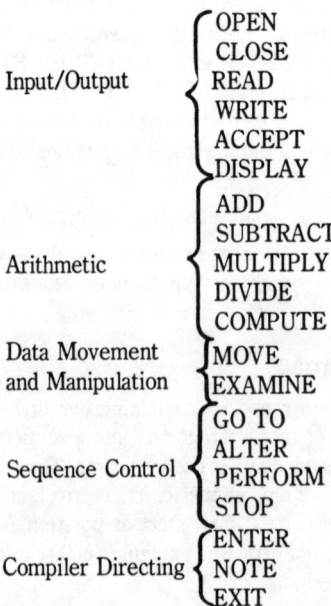

Input/Output	OPEN, CLOSE, READ, WRITE, ACCEPT, DISPLAY
Arithmetic	ADD, SUBTRACT, MULTIPLY, DIVIDE, COMPUTE
Data Movement and Manipulation	MOVE, EXAMINE
Sequence Control	GO TO, ALTER, PERFORM, STOP
Compiler Directing	ENTER, NOTE, EXIT

Input/Output Verbs

In any data processing application, quantities of data pass between the central storage facilities of the computer and external media such as card and tape devices. Control and coordination of the main flow of data is achieved by four input/output verbs; OPEN, CLOSE, READ, and WRITE. These verbs enable the programmer to obtain records for processing and then send the processed record to some external media. The remaining two verbs, ACCEPT and DISPLAY, permit small quantities of data to be either accepted from or produced upon some external input/output device. The following pages explain the format and uses of each of these verbs.

OPEN [INPUT { file-name [REVERSED] [WITH NO REWIND] } ...]
     [OUTPUT { file-name [WITH NO REWIND] } ...]

The function of this verb is to initiate the processing of both input and output files. Any FD entry (file) in the Data Division must be OPENed prior to the first READ or WRITE instruction directed to that particular file. This applies to the printer, card reader, and card punch as well as tape files.

The key word INPUT must be included for all input files, and the key word OUTPUT must be stated for all output files. If INPUT has been specified, then the execution of an OPEN statement causes the checking of the label record if a label record has been defined in the FD entry. Similarly, if OUTPUT has been specified, the OPEN statement causes the writing of the label record upon the output file.

A file may be repeatedly OPENed and CLOSEd, both for INPUT and OUTPUT, in the same program. The OPEN does not obtain or release the first data record. A READ or WRITE, respectively, must be executed to obtain or release the first data record. When the external medium is tape, the following rules apply:

1. If neither REVERSED nor NO REWIND is specified, the file is repositioned to its beginning point, i.e., the tape is rewound.

2. If either REVERSED or NO REWIND is specified, no repositioning takes place. When REVERSED is specified, the file must be at its end point and subsequent READ statements cause the records to be read in reverse order. The file must be at its beginning point whenever NO REWIND is specified.

Input files OPENed in the REVERSED mode must be single-reel files. The implementor should provide a means of identifying the file to make certain that the correct tape was mounted. The method of implementing this identification is up to the user. One method, and it is probably the easiest to implement, would be to place a beginning-of-file and an end-of-file label record at the beginning and end of each file. In this way, regardless of the direction of tape movement, a label record is available for checking and identification purposes. The REVERSED and WITH NO REWIND options are only applicable to magnetic tape files and are meaningless when operating with card or printer files.

READ file-name RECORD [INTO identifier]
; AT END imperative-statement

The READ verb directs the reading of a record from an input file. If the input file is a data deck then the READ verb causes a single data card to be read. The file name must be that of a file that has been OPENed for INPUT. The file and the arrangement of the data values on each of its records were described in FD and 01 level entries in the FILE SECTION of the DATA DIVISION. READing of a record from that file results in all the data values from that record being moved to and stored in the input buffer in the computer's memory unit.

The AT END clause of the READ sentence has the function of telling the computer what to do if in attempting to read a data card, it finds there are none left, i.e., if it finds that is AT the END of the data deck (or input file). The programmer must insert some imperative statement in the AT END clause that will tell the computer what he wants it to do when that happens. In most cases, this will be a GO TO statement that tells the computer to jump to the end of the program. Here is an example of a complete READ sentence:

READ CARD-FILE RECORD, AT END GO TO LAST-PARAGRAPH

A WRITE statement causes one record to be written on the output file. If the output file is the line printer then the WRITE statement will cause a single line of print to be printed on the line printer paper. The simplest form of this statement is as follows:

WRITE record-name

Notice that in the WRITE statement, you give a record name, while the READ statement you give a file name. Memorize this catch phrase right now and don't forget it for the rest of your COBOL life; READ FILES-WRITE RECORDS.

Recall that record names are 01 level entries in the FILE SECTION of the DATA DIVISION. In order for it to be legal to write a record, that record must be a part of a file that has been OPENed for OUTPUT. If you assume that the file was OPENed for OUTPUT was called EMPLOYEE-FILE, and that following the DATA DIVISION's FD entry for EMPLOYEE-FILE was the 01 level entry EMPLOYEE-LISTING, then a proper WRITE statement would look like this:

WRITE EMPLOYEE-LISTING.

When a WRITE statment is obeyed, the line printer advances the paper one line and then WRITEs (or prints) whatever record you want written. What you get is what you'd call "single spacing" on a typewriter. If you want double spacing, triple spacing, etc., you use the optional ADVANCING clause of the WRITE statement:

WRITE record-name $\left\{\begin{array}{c}\text{AFTER}\\ \text{or}\\ \text{BEFORE}\end{array}\right\}$ ADVANCING $\left\{\begin{array}{c}\text{integer}\\ \text{or}\\ \text{data-name}\end{array}\right\}$ LINES.

You see that you have option of saying AFTER ADVANCE or BEFORE ADVANCING. If you say AFTER ADVANCING, the line printer will advance the paper and then print the record. If you say BEFORE ADVANCING, the line printer will print the record and then advance the paper. Don't forget that data must be MOVEd to the output file buffer before you can WRITE it.

After you are finished with your files you must CLOSE them. The form of the CLOSE statement is as follows:

CLOSE file-name-1, file-name-2, ...

If you were using files named CARD-FILE and PRINT-FILE in your program, then before the end of the program you would have to be sure to say:

CLOSE CARD-FILE, PRINT-FILE.

Notice that there is no need to say anything about whether the files were input or output files. You simply CLOSE them without any regard for how they were used in the program.

Though the CLOSE statement may impress you as a relatively trivial part of the program and something that wouldn't be missed if you forgot it, quite the contrary is true. It is an essential part. It serves as a signal to the computer that it may start some necessary, internal tidying up operations that it must do in order to be ready to handle the next program. On many computer systems, in fact, the computer checks through your program ahead of time to be sure you've included a CLOSE statement, and it will terminate compilation.

ACCEPT identifier [FROM mnemonic-name]

This verb is used to read low volume data from the specified hardware device. The hardware device associated with a mnemonic name must be specified in the SPECIAL-NAMES paragraph of the Environment Division and used when the FROM option is employed.

In many cases, a standard hardware device is used for a particular implementation of COBOL, thereby making the FROM clause unnecessary. Also, a maximum size for the data represented by identifier will be set. The individual supplement manuals for a particular computer system should be consulted for this information. If the data ACCEPTed is less than the maximum size for the particular system, it appears in the leftmost positions of the input area with zero fill if the data is numeric and space fill if alphabetic or alphanumeric.

For example:

DISPLAY "FURNISH DATE" UPON CONSOLE.
ACCEPT PRESENT-DATE FROM CONSOLE.

Previously, the console typewriter was designated as CONSOLE in the SPECIAL-NAMES paragraph of the Environment Division. When the DISPLAY statement is executed, FURNISH DATE appears on the console typewriter. Control passes to the ACCEPT statement and the program waits for the operator to type in the current date, after which the data accepted is stored in location PRESENT-DATE. Control then passes to the statement following the ACCEPT statement.

$$\underline{\text{DISPLAY}} \left\{ \begin{matrix} \text{literal-1} \\ \text{identifier-1} \end{matrix} \right\} \left[, \left\{ \begin{matrix} \text{literal-2} \\ \text{identifier-2} \end{matrix} \right\} \right] \ldots$$
$$[\underline{\text{UPON}} \text{ mnemonic-name}]$$

This verb displays low volume data on an output device. The hardware device associated with a mnemonic name must be specified in the SPECIAL-NAMES paragraph of the Environment Division when the UPON option is employed. A specific peripheral unit may be designated as the standard display device thereby making the UPON clause unnecessary. Maximum length for DISPLAYed data is set by the implementor. Rules for positioning are the same as for the ACCEPT verb.

Literals and identifiers may be used in combination in a DISPLAY statement. Any figurative constants, except ALL, may be used. For example:

DISPLAY "TOTAL AMOUNT IS", TOTAL-AMOUNT

Assume TOTAL-AMOUNT has a value of 4800 at the time the DISPLAY statement is executed. The information that appears on the display device is as follows:

TOTAL AMOUNT IS 4800.

Since "TOTAL AMOUNT IS" is a nonnumeric literal, it is displayed as is.

Arithmetic Verbs

The arithmetic verbs permit basic calculations to be performed on the data that has been moved to the working storage area. Four verbs are provided in COBOL corresponding to the four basic arithmetic operations; ADD, SUBTRACT, MULTIPLY, and DIVIDE. In addition, a fifth verb, COMPUTE, allows the programmer to effect arithmetic calculations through the use of arithmetic expressions. The following rules pertain to the arithmetic verbs:

1. All identifiers used in arithmetic statements must represent numeric data defined in the Data Division. The results are unpredictable if the identifiers contain other than numeric data at run time.

2. All literals used in arithmetic statements must be numeric.

3. The maximum size of any operand (identifier or literal), intermediate result, or receiving item is 18 digits.

4. The formats (PICTURE) of multiple operands in an arithmetic statement may differ from each other. Decimal point alignment is supplied

automatically throughout computations. Conversions of items with unlike usage is automatic.

5. The format of any data item involved in computations (e.g., addends, subtrahends, multipliers, etc.) cannot contain editing symbols. The compiler will indicate an error by an appropriate message when the fields involved are defined in such a way that they would contain editing symbols. This is because the editing symbols only apply to data in the output tile buffer. Operational signs and implied decimal points are not considered editing symbols.

6. If the number of fractional places in a computed result (sum, difference, product, or quotient) exceeds the number of fractional places in the format of the identifier associated with the result (i.e., the identifier that is to take on the value of the result), truncation occurs unless the ROUNDED option has been used.

Truncation is the dropping of excess digits; it is always determined by the PICTURE of the identifier associated with the result. When ROUNDED is specified, however, the least significant digit specified by the format of the result is increased by 1 whenever the most significant digit of the excess is greater than or equal to 5. For example, with a receiving item PICTURE of 9(4)V9, the value 8250V96 becomes 8251V0 if the ROUNDED option is specified, and 8250V9 when ROUNDED is not used.

7. Whenever the number of integral places (i.e., those to the left of the decimal point) in the calculated result exceeds the number of the integral places associated with the resultant identifier, a size error condition arises. In the event of a size error condition, one of two possibilities will occur, depending on whether or not the ON SIZE ERROR option has been specified.

Use of ON SIZE ERROR must be carefully controlled. This clause does not substitute for proper investigation and record design. The testing for size error condition occurs only when the ON SIZE ERROR option is specified in the verb format. In the event that ON SIZE ERROR is not specified, and a size error condition arises, the results are unpredictable. If the ON SIZE ERROR option has been specified, and a size error condition arises, then the value of the resultant identifier is not altered. The imperative statement associated with the ON SIZE ERROR option is executed after the last resultant identifier is considered.

To direct the computer to add two or more values, you use an ADD TO or an ADD GIVING instruction:

    Form I: ADD 1st-item(s) TO receiving-item.
    Form II: ADD 1st-items(s) GIVING receiving-item.

The following rules apply to the use of the verb.
    1. There may be more than one 1st-item.
    2. Any 1st-item may be a data name or numeric literal.
    3. The receiving item must be a data name.
    4. The 1st-item(s) must be numeric.

5. The receiving item must be numeric in Form I and numeric edited in Form II.
(See Fig. 4-1 for examples).

To tell the computer to perform a subtraction operation, you use a SUBTRACT FROM or a SUBTRACT FROM GIVING statement as above. The same rules apply. (See Fig. 4-2 for examples).

The divide verb divides one numeric data item by another and stores the resulting quotient in the last data item specified in the statement. There are three forms:

Form I: DIVIDE 1st-item INTO receiving-item.
Form II: DIVIDE 1st-item INTO 2nd-item GIVING receiving-item.
Form III: DIVIDE 1st-item BY 2nd-item GIVING receiving-item.

The following rules apply:

1. There may not be more than one first item.

2. The first item or second item may be a data name or numeric literal.

3. The receiving item must be a data name.

4. The first item and second item must be numeric.

5. The receiving item must be numeric in Form I and numeric or numeric edited in Forms II and III. (See Fig. 4-3 for examples).

The MULTIPLY verb multiplies two numeric data items and stores the resulting product in the last data item specified in the statement. The two forms are:

Form I: MULTIPLY 1st-item BY receiving-item.
Form II: MULTIPLY 1st-item BY 2nd-item GIVING receiving-item.

The above rules apply. (See Fig. 4-4 for examples).

$$\underline{\text{COMPUTE}} \text{ identifier-1 } [\underline{\text{ROUNDED}}] = \begin{Bmatrix} \text{identifier-2} \\ \text{literal} \\ \text{arithmetic-expression} \end{Bmatrix}$$

[; ON $\underline{\text{SIZE}}$ $\underline{\text{ERROR}}$ imperative-statement]

This verb causes one or more numeric data items (defined and established in the Data Division) to assume a new value derived from either a named or literal numeric data item or an arithmetic expression.
For example:

```
COMPUTE A = (B+C)/D-E)
COMPUTE FICA-ACCUM = TOT-FICA
COMPUTE NET-PAY = GROSS-DED
```

Only identifier-1 may contain editing symbols. Identifier-2 must be an elementary numeric item.

Data Movement and Manipulation

Several COBOL verbs have the ability to move or manipulate data in some manner. Two verbs are provided in COBOL for the specific-purpose of moving or manipulating data. They are the MOVE and EXAMINE verbs.

Statement	Result Field PICTURE IS:	Calculation
ADD A, B TO C.	9999	A+B+C stored in C as xxxx
ADD A, B, C TO D.	$9999.99	Error – operand may not contain editing symbols except with GIVING option.
ADD A, B, C TO D.	S9999V99	A+B+C+D stored in D as + xxxxVxx
ADD A, B, C GIVING D.	$9999.99	A+B+C stored in D as $xxxx.xx
ADD 1, 5, C TO 7.		Error – result cannot be stored in literal.
ADD A, 14 TO C ROUNDED.	99999	A+14+C stored in C as $x_1x_2x_3x_4x_5$; rounded if $x_6 \geq 5$
ADD A, B, 43.6 GIVING D ON SIZE ERROR GO TO O—FLOW.	99V99	A+B+43.6 stored in D; if integer result is greater than 2 digits, SIZE ERROR occurs.

NOTE: *x's show result format.*

Fig. 4-1. ADD and the resulting format.

Statement	Result Field PICTURE IS:	Calculation
SUBTRACT 16, A, B FROM D.	999	D – (16 + A + B) stored in D as xxx.
SUBTRACT A, B FROM D.	$$99.99	Error – operand may not contain edit symbols unless GIVING option is used.
SUBTRACT A, B FROM 126.		Error – result cannot be stored in literal.
SUBTRACT A, B FROM 126 GIVING C.	999	126 – (A+B) stored in C as xxx.

NOTE: x's show result format.

Fig. 4-2. SUBTRACT and the resulting format.

Statement	Result Field PICTURE IS:	Calculation
DIVIDE A INTO B.	9(4)V9(2)	B ÷ A stored in B as xxxx.xx
DIVIDE A INTO B.	$$99.99	Error — editing not permitted except with GIVING option.
DIVIDE A INTO B GIVING C.	S999V99	B ÷ A stored in C as +xxxVxx
DIVIDE A BY B GIVING C.	9(5)	A ÷ B stored in C as xxxxx

NOTE: x's show result format.

Fig. 4-3. DIVIDE and the resulting format.

The primary purpose of the MOVE verb is to transmit data from one file buffer area to another. The EXAMINE verb, however, causes data to be examined and moved only when certain factors are present.

In the course of writing a program, you will find the need to move new data values into memory locations whose data values are no longer correct. Sometimes those new values will already be in one buffer but need to be moved to another, and sometimes they will not be in a memory at all. The MOVE verb is used to direct such movements. In a MOVE statement you can tell the computer to move a data value from one location (called the "Sending Field") to another location (called the "Receiving Field"). There are two forms to choose from:

Option I

$$\underline{\text{MOVE}} \begin{Bmatrix} \text{identifier-1} \\ \text{literal} \end{Bmatrix} \underline{\text{TO}} \{\underline{\text{identifier-2}}\}\ldots$$

Option 2

$$\underline{\text{MOVE}} \begin{Bmatrix} \underline{\text{CORRESPONDING}} \\ \underline{\text{CORR}} \end{Bmatrix} \underline{\text{identifier-1}}\ \underline{\text{TO}}\ \underline{\text{identifier-2}}$$

If the CORRESPONDING option is used, selected items subordinate in hierarchy to identifier-1 are moved, with any required editing, to selected items subordinate in hierarchy to identifier-2. Items are selected on the basis of matching identifiers. Identifiers match if they and all their possible qualifiers are the same. At least one of the pair of selected items must be an elementary item. In determining which identifiers are CORRESPONDING, any identifiers subordinate to identifier-1 or identifier-2 which have REDEFINE clauses are ignored, as well as any identifiers which are subordinate to the REDEFINEd identifiers. This restriction does not preclude identifier-1 or identifier-2 themselves from having REDEFINEs clauses or from being subordinate to identifiers with REDEFINEs clauses. Identifier-1 or identifier-2 cannot have a level number of 66, 77, or 88.

It is illegal to MOVE a group item whose format is such that editing would be required on the elementary items in separate operations. If such a MOVE is desired, each elementary item must be MOVEd and edited individually or the CORRESPONDING option should be used.

When moving group items without the CORRESPONDING option, the move is from left to right. If the item PICTURE or USAGE is not identical, a diagnostic message is given. Truncation of low order positions from the source item occurs if the receiving area is smaller. Space fill of low order positions of the receiving area occurs if the source item is smaller than the receiving field. If the source group is computational and the receiving group is not (or vice versa), a diagnostic message is given and the above rule on size governs the results of the move.

When both the receiving and source areas are elementary items, editing, as specified in the receiving area, is automatically performed for each MOVE command. The rules governing this are:

For Numeric Elementary Items

1. If the source area is larger than the receiving area, truncation occurs. If the receiving area is larger than the source area, the unfilled positions are zero filled. Data from the source area is aligned with respect to the implied or actual decimal point in the receiving area, with truncation or zero fill occurring to either side of the decimal point as illustrated below.

SOURCE AREA		RECEIVING AREA	
Picture	Value	Picture	Value After Moving
9V9	12	99V99	0120
9V999	8765	V99	76

2. Data is converted from the USAGE shown in the source area to the USAGE of the receiving area.

3. Insertion of a currency sign, a decimal point, commas, etc., with proper alignment, is accomplished in accordance with the PICTURE of the receiving area. If these latter characters are in a source area, the field(s) will

Statement	Result Field PICTURE IS:	Calculation
MULTIPLY A BY B.	999	A x B stored in B as xxx.
MULTIPLY HOURS BY 100.		Error — result cannot be stored in literal.
MULTIPLY HOURS BY 100 GIVING GROSS.	9999	HOURS x 100 stored in GROSS as xxxx.
MULTIPLY 12 BY B.	$$9.99	Error — no editing without GIVING option.

NOTE: x's show result format.

Fig. 4-4. MULTIPLY and the resulting format.

be nonnumeric and, thus the MOVEment must conform to the nonnumeric rules.

4. If no decimal point has been specified, either assumed or actual, data is right justified in the receiving area.

5. A numeric edited, alphanumeric edited, or alphabetic data item must not be MOVEd to a numeric or numeric edited data item.

6. A numeric or numeric edited item must not be MOVEd to an alphabetic item.

7. A numeric item whose assumed decimal point is not to the extreme right must not be MOVED to an alphanumeric edited data item.

For Nonnumeric Elementary Items

1. Data from the source area is placed in the receiving area filling from left to right unless specified otherwise.

2. If the receiving area is larger than the source area, the unfilled low-order positions are replaced with blanks (spaces).

3. If the source area is greater in length than the receiving area, the MOVE terminates when the receiving area is filled. A warning is given at compilation time indicating this situation. (See Fig. 4-5 for examples).

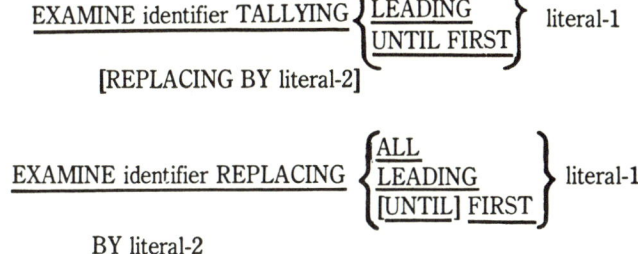

The EXAMINE verb replaces a given character or counts the number of times it appears in a data item. The data-name being EXAMINEd cannot be COMPUTATIONAL. Any literal used in an EXAMINE statement must consist of only one character and it must be the same class as the identifier. Each literal may be any figurative constant except ALL. The literal should be bounded by quote marks. If the description of the identifier in the Data Division specifies a CLASS that uses less than the full character set (e.g., NUMERIC or ALPHANUMERIC), then each literal used in an EXAMINE statement must be one of the characters in the restricted set. Thus, if the CLASS of data name is NUMERIC, each literal used in the statement must be a numeric character.

When an EXAMINE statement is executed, the examination begins with the first (i.e., the leftmost) character of the data item and proceeds to the right. Each character in the item represented by data name is examined in turn. If the data item being examined is numeric and signed, examination excludes the operational sign.

SOURCE AREA		RECEIVING AREA	
Picture	Data in source area	Picture	Data in receiving area
9999V99	567891	9999V99	567891
9999V99	567891	9999V9	56789
9V9	78	999V99	00780
XXX	M8N	XXXXX	M8N
99V99	6789	999.99	067.89
AAAAAA	WARREN	AAA	WAR
99V99	6789	$$$99.99	$67.89

Fig. 4-5. Centering on the edit marks.

The TALLYING option creates an integral count (i.e., a tally) which replaces the value of a special data location called TALLY. The count represents the number of:

- Occurrences of literal-1 when the ALL option is used.
- Occurrences of literal-1 prior to encountering a character other than literal-1 when the LEADING option is used.
- Characters not equal to literal-1 encountered before the first occurrence of literal-1 when the UNTIL FIRST option is used.

When either of the REPLACING options is used (i.e., with or without TALLYING) the replacement rules are as follows:

- When the ALL option is used, then literal-2 is substituted for each occurrence of literal-1.
- When the LEADING option is used, the substitution of literal-2 terminates as soon as a character other than literal-1 or the right hand boundary of the data item is encountered.
- When the UNTIL FIRST option is used, the substitution of literal-2 terminates as soon as the first literal-1 or the right hand boundary of the data item is encountered.
- In Option 2, when the FIRST option is used, the first occurrence of literal-1 is replaced by literal-2.

Sequence Control

Normally, each statement in the Procedure Division is executed consecutively in order of their appearance. This is also true of the execution of each paragraph and section. However, it is often necessary to alter this normal sequence of operations and to jump to a different point in the program to execute a number of lines of coding before the next statement in sequence can logically be operated upon. Two verbs, GO TO and PERFORM, are used to fulfill this function. In addition, two supplementary control verbs are also provided; STOP and ALTER. The STOP verb controls the termination of the program, whereas ALTER permits the GO TO statement to be modified to permit control to be transferred to different points in the program.

Option 1:
<u>GO TO</u> [procedure-name]
Option 2:
<u>GO TO</u> procedure-name-1 [, procedure-name-2] . . ., procedure-name-n
<u>DEPENDING</u> ON identifier

This verb permits a departure from the normal sequence of procedures by specifying a transfer of control to another point in the program. If the GO TO statement is to be ALTERed when using Option 1, the paragraph in which the GO TO statement is contained must consist solely of the GO TO statement. The paragraph name assigned to the GO TO statement is referred to by the ALTER verb in order to modify the sequence of the program.

In Option 2, the identifier must refer to a positive integral value. The branch will be to the 1st, 2nd, . . ., nth procedure name, as the value of identifier is 1, 2, . . ., n. When no transfer is executed, control passes to the next statement in the normal sequence for execution. Example:

CALCULATE
GO TO CK-FOR-TIN-WKS.

The example shown is an unconditional transfer of control to CK-FOR-TIN-WKS. Any GO TO statement which is a paragraph unto itself and is in the format of Option 1, however, may be ALTERed.

CHANGE-CALC.
ALTER CALCULATE TO PROCEED TO CALCULATE-TONS.
GO TO CALCULATE-TONS.

The above instruction changes CALCULATE (the paragraph name of the GO TO sentence in the first example) to GO TO CALCULATE-TONS, and then, unconditionally, transfers control to the routine named CALCULATE-TONS. Thus, the next time that CALCULATE is executed, control passes to CALCULATIONS.

The above operation could have been accomplished in another manner. At CALCULATE, we could have had this sentence:

GO TO CK-FOR-TIN-WKS, CALCULATE-TONS
DEPENDING ON WKS-HIGHER-THAN-TIN.

WKS-HIGHER-THAN-TIN would be a Working-Storage area defined with a value of 1 at compilation time. Each time this instruction was executed and WKS-HIGHER-THAN-TIN contained a 1, control would pass to CK-FOR-TIN-WKS. If control should pass to CALCULATE-TONS, a MOVE 2 TO WKS-HIGHER-THAN-TIN instruction would effect such a transfer whenever CALCULATE was executed. A subsequent MOVE 1 TO WKS-HIGHER-THAN-TIN would cause control once again to pass to CK-FOR-TIN-WKS. If anything other than 1 or 2 was moved to WKS-HIGHER-THAN-TIN, then control would fall through to the statement following CALCULATE.

<u>ALTER</u> procedure-name-1 TO [<u>PROCEED TO</u>] procedure-name-2 [procedure-name-3 TO [<u>PROCEED TO</u>] procedure-name-4] . . .

This verb modifies the effect of a GO TO statement thereby changing the predetermined sequence of instructions. Procedure-name-1, procedure-name-3, . . ., are names of paragraphs which each contain a single sentence consisting of only a GO TO statement as defined under Option 1 of the GO TO verb.
Examples:

EX-HDR.
  GO TO SET-MON.
SET-MON.
  .
  .
  .
EX-HDR-A.
  GO TO EX-HDR-REST.
EX-HDR-REST.
  ALTER EX-HDR-A TO PROCEED TO SET-UP-EX EX-HDR TO PROCEED TO EX-HDR-MV.

The two GO TO paragraphs might have been switches originally set to fall through to the next paragraph in sequence. After being ALTERed, they go to EX-HDR-EX instead of EX-HDR-REST. Upon completion of a specified routine, EX-HDR-A may then be ALTERed back to its original status, or to some other operand by subsequent ALTER verbs. Note that EX-HDR and EX-HDR-A are one sentence paragraphs containing a GO TO statement. Control is transferred to the next statement in sequence, following the execution of the ALTER statement.

Option 1:
  <u>PERFORM</u> procedure-name-1 [<u>THRU</u> procedure-name-2]

Option 2:
  <u>PERFORM</u> procedure-name-1 [<u>THRU</u> procedure-name-2]
  $\begin{Bmatrix} \text{identifier} \\ \text{integer} \end{Bmatrix}$ <u>TIMES</u>

Option 3:
  <u>PERFORM</u> procedure-name-1 [<u>THRU</u> procedure-name-2]
  <u>UNTIL</u> condition

Option 4:
  <u>PERFORM</u> procedure-name-1 [<u>THRU</u> procedure-name-2]
  <u>VARYING</u> identifier-1 <u>FROM</u> $\begin{Bmatrix} \text{literal-1} \\ \text{identifier-2} \end{Bmatrix}$
  <u>BY</u> $\begin{Bmatrix} \text{literal-2} \\ \text{identifier-3} \end{Bmatrix}$ <u>UNTIL</u> condition

This verb allows a temporary departure from the normal sequence of procedures in order to execute one statement or a sequence of statements a specified number of times or until a condition is satisfied and provides automatic return to normal sequence. The first statement of procedure-name-1 is the point to which control is transferred by PERFORM. The return mechanism is automatically inserted as follows:

● If procedure-name-1 is a paragraph name, and procedure-name-2 is not specified, then the return mechanism is inserted after the last statement of the procedure-name-1 paragraph.

● If procedure-name-1 is a section name, and procedure-name-2 is not specified, then the return mechanism is inserted after the last statement of the procedure-name-1 paragraph.

● If procedure-name-2 is specified and is paragraph name, then the return mechanism is inserted after the last statement of the procedure-name-2 paragraph.

● If procedure-name-2 is specified and is a section name, then the return mechanism is inserted after the last statement of the last paragraph of the section.

When procedure-name-2 is specified, the required relationship between procedure-name-1 and procedure-name-2 is that of logical sequence; i.e., execution sequence must proceed from procedure-name-1 to the last statement of the procedure-name-2 paragraph or section. GO TO statements and other PERFORM statements are permitted between procedure-name-1 and the last statement of procedure-name-1, provided the sequence ultimately returns to the final statement of procedure-name-2. If the logic of a procedure requires a conditional exit prior to the final sentence, the EXIT verb is used in order to comply with the foregoing requirements. In this case, procedure-name-2 must be the name of a paragraph consisting solely of the verb EXIT; all paths must lead to this point.

When ELSE NEXT SENTENCE appears as the last sentence that is to be executed, control returns to the statement following the PERFORM statement. A procedure referenced by one PERFORM statement can be referenced by other PERFORM statements. PERFORM may reference a NOTE; no action is taken and the automatic return to the proper line is generated.

In all cases, after the completion of a PERFORM, a bypass is automatically created around the return mechanism which had been inserted after the last statement. Therefore, when no related PERFORM is in progress, sequence control will pass around the return mechanism to the following statement as if no PERFORM has existed. A simplified illustration of the bypass is presented below. For discussion purposes, the bypass and the return mechanism are one and the same. Procedure names have been placed on the same line as procedural sentences for brevity.

Procedure-Name	Procedural-Sentence
1 SUBROUTINE-1	READ . . .
2	MOVE . . .
3	MULTIPLY . . .
	GO TO SUBROUTINE-2 BYPASS-1
4 SUBROUTINE-2	SUBTRACT
	GO TO SUBROUTINE-3 BYPASS - 2

Procedure-Name	Procedural-Sentence
5 SUBROUTINE-3	WRITE . . .
.	.
.	.
.	.
22 MAIN-ROUTE	PERFORM SUBROUTINE-1
23	ADD . . .
.	.
.	.
56 GO-AGAIN	PERFORM SUBROUTINE-1 THRU SUBROUTINE-2.
57	GO TO . . .
58 ABLE	MOVE . . .
.	.
.	.
74	PERFORM SUBROUTINE-1 THRU SUBROUTINE-2.

Upon execution of MAIN-ROUTE, the following steps occur:

● The line number of the statement following the PERFORM (i.e., line 23) is placed in BYPASS-1.

● Control is transferred to SUBROUTINE-1.

● At the completion of SUBROUTINE-1 (lines 1 through 3), BYPASS-1 is reset to its initial status after control has transferred to line 23.

● Similarly, upon execution of GO-AGAIN, BYPASS-1 will retain its GO TO SUBROUTINE-2 status, but BYPASS-2 will be changed, in effect, to GO TO line 57, i.e., the statement immediately following GO-AGAIN. (The programmer does not concern himself with these bypasses as they are automatically created by the compiler.) At times, it is necessary to give a sentence a procedure name in order to control the number of instructions to be executed by a PERFORM sentence.

One important point should be noted in the use of the PERFORM verb: the last statement referred to in procedure-name-1, procedure-name-2, etc., must not contain a GO TO statement or unconditional (GO TO) transfers of control within conditional (IF) statements. For example, if line 3 of the illustration had GO TO ZILCH instead of MULTIPLY, then any attempt to PERFORM SUBROUTINE-1 would not be successfully concluded since control would always be transferred at line 3 to ZILCH; the bypass would never be entered and a return to the statement following the PERFORM (i.e., line 23) could never be accomplished.

Essentially then, the programmer has the facility to use conditional (IF) statements within a range of instructions referenced by a PERFORM verb. He must be governed by the fact that the bypass is only reset (i.e., returned to its original status) after the last sentence in the range has been executed. Therefore, if control is passed from the routine and never returned back into the range, the bypass will not be reset, but rather, will be set to transfer to the sentence following the last PERFORM that affected the routine. By closing the routine containing such a condition, the proper setting of the bypass can be assured.

Option 1:

In the previous example, MAIN-ROUTE and GO-AGAIN are examples of Option 1, the simple PERFORM. Briefly stated, a procedure referenced by the simple PERFORM statement is executed once and then control passes to the next statement after the PERFORM.

Example:
>   WR-EX.
>   WRITE EXCEPTIONS.
>   MV-1-EX-PG.
>   PERFORM WR-EX.

The PERFORM WR-EX causes paragraph WR-EX to be executed once and control passes to the line after PERFORM WR-EX. All necessary program steps to accomplish this are generated by the compiler.

Option 2:

The TIMES option provides a means of repeating a procedure a specified number of times. The number of times, whether stated as integer or as identifier, must be a positive integer and can be zero. If zero, no execution will occur. The PERFORM mechanism sets up a counter and tests it against the specified value before each jump to procedure-name-1. The return mechanism after the last statement steps the counter and then sends control to the test. The test cycles control to procedure-name-1 the specified number of times, and after the last time sends control to the statement following the PERFORM. Example:

>   PERFORM INCREASE-WORKS 4 TIMES.
>   PERFORM INCREASE-WORKS CALCULATE TIMES.

Both of the above illustrations would give the same result assuming that CALCULATE contained the value of four. The paragraph INCREASE-WORKS is executed four times and then control passes to the statement following the PERFORM.

Option 3:

The UNTIL option is essentially the same as the TIMES option, except that the PERFORM evaluates a specified conditional expression instead of counting and testing the count against a specified integer.

Condition may be any conditional statement; that is, the condition may involve relations and tests. Condition is evaluated before execution of procedure-name-1. If the condition is false, control passes to procedure-name-1, the procedure is executed once, and control returns for another evaluation of condition. This is repeated until the condition is satisfied (i.e., true), at which time control passes to the sentence following the PERFORM. Should the conditional expression be true when the PERFORM is entered, no transfer of control to procedure-name-1 takes place and control falls through the PERFORM instruction to the next sequential sentence.

Example:

PERFORM READ-MASTER-ROUTINE UNTIL WORKS-CODE
OF MASTER IS EQUAL TO WORKS-CODE IN DETAIL.

READ-MASTER-ROUTINE will be performed until an equality is found between the two designated WORKS, at which time control will pass to the sentence following the PERFORM.

Option 4:

The VARYING option is used to PERFORM a procedure repetitively, increasing or decreasing the value of identifier-1 for each repetition, until a specific conditional expression (condition) is satisfied. Option 4 is arithmetic in nature and the arithmetic rules apply.

The PERFORM mechanism first sets the value of identifier-1 equal to its starting value (the FROM value), then evaluates the conditional expression (the UNTIL condition) for truth or falseness. If the expression is true at this point, no execution of the procedure takes place. Instead, control is transferred to the next statement after the PERFORM. If the condition is false, procedure-name-1 through procedure-name-2 are executed once, after which the PERFORM alters the value of identifier-1 by specified increment of decrement (the BY value) and again evaluates the condition for truth or falseness.

This cycle continues until the conditional expression becomes true, at which time control passes to the sentence following the PERFORM. The value of the BY and FROM clauses must be numeric, but not necessarily integral (e.g., may be 25 or V25 or .25). The initial value (FROM) must be positive or zero but the BY value may be positive, negative, or zero. After the condition is found to be true, identifier-1 will be one increment (or decrement) greater (or less) than its last used value unless the starting value (FROM value) is zero.

$$\underline{STOP} \begin{Bmatrix} literal \\ \underline{RUN} \end{Bmatrix}$$

The STOP verb terminates the object program either permanently or temporarily. The format must specify a literal, or the key word RUN must be used with STOP. If a literal is employed it is displayed by the object program at the time STOP occurs either on the console printer or a substitute medium, such as console lights.) If the operator should elect, continuation of the object program begins with the execution of the next statement in sequence.

STOP RUN automatically activates the standard ending routine of the operating system. Therefore, it should be used only as the final executable statement of the program.

Some examples of the use of STOP are:

    STOP 3.
    STOP 127.
    STOP "INPUT SHOULD BE DESCRIPTIONS".
    STOP RUN.

Whenever numeric literal is used, as in the first two examples, it is customary to specify a different number for each STOP. These numbers are then catalogued with their respective definitions, for use with the object program. The literal used may be numeric or nonnumeric or any figurative constant except ALL.

Compiler Directives

Certain verbs direct the compiler to perform some specific action and do not directly produce any object coding. These are called compiler directing verbs. Two of the verbs, ENTER and EXIT, only affect the object program indirectly, whereas the verb NOTE has absolutely no effect on the object program.

The EXIT verb provides an end point for a procedure being executed by a PERFORM verb. EXIT must be the only word within a paragraph. The EXIT verb is necessary only if there is more than one common ending point to the subroutine; in this case, each of these points should come together at the EXIT in order to provide one ending point path.

EXIT should contain a transfer of control to the first sentence of the paragraph following the PERFORM paragraph. If the EXIT paragraph is referenced by some procedure other than a PERFORM, control passes through the EXIT point to the first sentence of the paragraph following the EXIT paragraph. For example:

REORDER-STOCK
    WRITE REPLENISH-STOCK-ITEM BEFORE ADVANCING 3 LINES.
    ADD 1 TO LINE-NO.
    IF LINE-NO IS GREATER THAN 17 PERFORM HEADER-PRINT.
    GO TO PARAEXIT.
    HEADER-PRINT
    PARAEXIT.
    EXIT.

PARAEXIT provides the needed common ending point for two alternative paths in the program. If LINE-NO is not greater than 17, the end of the page has not been reached, and the page heading is not required. Control falls through the IF statement to the unconditional GO TO statement and HEADER-PRINT is not performed. Control then transfers back to the statement following the PERFORM, i.e., GO TO PARAEXIT. Control now transfers to PARAEXIT and the program continues.

NOTE permits the programmer to insert comments in his source program for reference purposes. These comments are printed out but have no effect on the object program. If a NOTE sentence is the first sentence of a paragraph (i.e., immediately following a procedure-name), the entire paragraph is considered as commentary. If a NOTE sentence appears as other than the first sentence of a paragraph, the commentary ends with the appearance of a period. Any characters from the COBOL character set may be used excluding the period which is used to terminate the comment.

ENTER language-name [routine-name].

This verb allows the inclusion of object code produced by some assembler or compiler other than COBOL into the object program. The language name may refer to any other language allowable on that particular computer. The language statements are executed in the object program as if they had been compiled immediately following the ENTER statement.

If the statements of the entered language cannot be written in line (incorporated among the normal COBOL statements), a routine name is specified by the programmer to identify and access the coded portion of the entered language and to execute this coding at the desired point in the procedural sequence. The routine name is a COBOL data name which may only be referenced in an ENTER statement.

If the entered language statements can be written in line, the routine name option is not used. The sentence:

ENTER COBOL

must follow the last statement in the entered language code segment to indicate to the compiler where a return to COBOL source language occurs. The implementor must specify all details as to how the other languages are to be written.

SAMPLE PROBLEM

The data having been defined in a previous chapter, the actions to be taken at run time are now specified. These actions begin with the opening of the several files (i.e., initializing the files so as to make them capable of releasing or accepting data). Data is then read in a specific sequence, with various manipulative, logical, and arithmetic operations performed. This done, the files are closed and the run terminated.

Flow Chart: A flowchart is shown in Fig. 4-6. An interpretation of this chart is now presented. The numbers in parentheses refer to the block keying numbers on the flowchart.

To initiate the run, all files are opened and the first page is printed (1). Follow along on Fig. 4-7. Now the relationship of the current input master inventory record and the current detail transaction is determined. When a detail transaction is read (2) (assuming there are any remaining to be read) (20) the Master-In switch is tested (3).

The Master-In switch is ON, whenever the processing of the last read input master has not yet been terminated and no new master is to be read. If OFF, a new input master must be read (4) because the processing of the last input master read has been terminated prior to the reading of the detail transaction. In either case the Master-In switch is turned off (5) immediately after testing. It is turned on at other points in the program when it develops that the master just read is not to be immediately terminated.

If the stock number in the newly read detail transaction is greater than the input master stock number (6) all detail transactions for this master (if any) have been processed. Complete the processing of the master (D) as

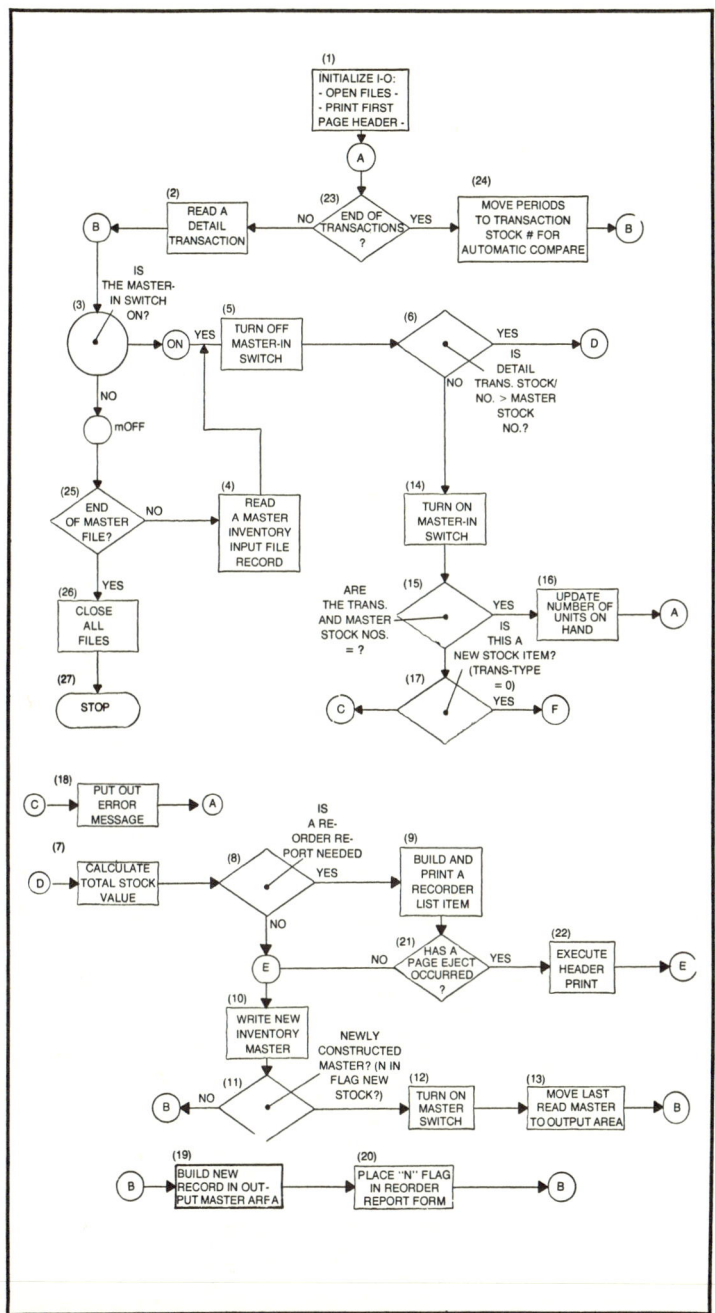

Fig. 4-6. Flowchart.

```
010200 PROCEDURE DIVISION.
010300 INITIALIZE.
010400     OPEN INPUT OLD-MASTER-INVENTORY, DETAIL-TRANSACTION-CARDS.
010500     OPEN OUTPUT NEW-MASTER-INVENTORY, REORDER-LIST.
010700     PERFORM HEADER-PRINT.
010800 GET-NEXT-TRANSACTION.
010900     READ DETAIL-TRANSACTION-CARDS AT END GO TO SET-UP-END-RUN.
020000 READ-INVENTORY-RECORD.
020100     IF SWITCH IS EQUAL TO 1 GO TO RESET-SWITCH.
020200     READ OLD-MASTER-INVENTORY INTO MASTER-RECORD OF
020300     NEW-MASTER-INVENTORY AT END GO TO CLOSE-FILES.
020800 RESET-SWITCH.
020900     MOVE ZERO TO SWITCH.

300300 HEADER-PRINT.
300400     ADD 1 TO PAGE-NO.
300500     WRITE REPLENISH-STOCK-ITEM FROM 1-REPLENISH-REPORT-HEADING
300510     AFTER ADVANCING NEW-PAGE LINES.
300600     WRITE REPLENISH-STOCK-ITEM FROM 2-REPLENISH-REPORT-HEADING.
300610     WRITE REPLENISH-STOCK-ITEM FROM 3-REPLENISH-REPORT-HEADING.
300620     MOVE SPACES TO REPLENISH-STOCK-ITEM.
300630     WRITE REPLENISH-STOCK-ITEM.
300700     MOVE ZEROS TO LINE-NO.
```

```
030000 CHECK-STOCK-NUMBER.
030100     IF STOCK-CONTROL-NUMBER GREATER THAN SEQ-STOCK-NUMBER
030200         OF NEW-MASTER-INVENTORY GO TO FINISH-MASTER.

060100 FINISH-MASTER.
060200     MULTIPLY ON-HAND-UNITS OF NEW-MASTER-INVENTORY BY COST-PER-UN
060300-    IT OF NEW-MASTER-INVENTORY GIVING TOTAL-WHOLESALE-VALUE OF
060400     NEW-MASTER-INVENTORY ON SIZE ERROR DISPLAY 'OVERFLOW ON TOTAL
060410-    ' WHOLESALE VALUE'.
060420     DISPLAY SEQ-STOCK-NUMBER OF MASTER-RECORD IN
060430     NEW-MASTER-INVENTORY.
060500     IF FLAG-NEW-STOCK IS EQUAL TO 'N' MOVE 1 TO SWITCH.
060600     IF MIN-STOCK-UNIT-QUANTITY OF NEW-MASTER-INVENTORY IS GREATER
060700     THAN ON-HAND-UNITS IN NEW-MASTER-INVENTORY OR FLAG-NEW-STOCK
060800     IS EQUAL TO 'N' PERFORM REORDER-STOCK.
070100     PERFORM WRITE-NEW-INVENTORY.
070200     MOVE MASTER-RECORD OF OLD-MASTER-INVENTORY TO MASTER-RECORD
070210     OF NEW-MASTER-INVENTORY.
070300     GO TO READ-INVENTORY-RECORD.
070400 WRITE-NEW-INVENTORY.
070500     WRITE MASTER-RECORD OF NEW-MASTER-INVENTORY.
```

Fig. 4-7. Partial listing of sample problem.

```
030300          MOVE 1 TO SWITCH.
030400          IF STOCK-CONTROL-NUMBER IS EQUAL SEQ-STOCK-NUMBER
030500              OF NEW-MASTER-INVENTORY GO TO UPDATE.

040400      UPDATE.
040600          IF TYPE-TRANSACTION IS EQUAL TO 1 OR 2 GO TO SHIPMENT.
040700          IF TYPE-TRANSACTION IS EQUAL TO 3 OR 4 GO TO RECEIPT.
040800          GO TO ERROR-MESSAGE.
050300      SHIPMENT.
050400          SUBTRACT QUANTITY FROM ON-HAND-UNITS
050500              IN NEW-MASTER-INVENTORY.
050600          GO TO GET-NEXT-TRANSACTION.
050700      RECEIPT.
050800          ADD QUANTITY TO ON-HAND-UNITS IN
050900              NEW-MASTER-INVENTORY.
060000          GO TO GET-NEXT-TRANSACTION.
```

```
030900        IF TYPE-TRANSACTION IS EQUAL TO ZERO GO TO NEW-STOCK-ITEM.
040000    ERROR-MESSAGE.
040100        DISPLAY STOCK-CONTROL-NUMBER ' NOT IN FILE, TRANSACTION
040200-       ' TYPE IS ' TYPE-TRANSACTION.
040300        GO TO GET-NEXT-TRANSACTION.

100100    NEW-STOCK-ITEM.
100500        MOVE SPACES TO MASTER-RECORD OF NEW-MASTER-INVENTORY.
100600        MOVE STOCK-CONTROL-NUMBER TO SEQ-STOCK-NUMBER IN
100700            NEW-MASTER-INVENTORY.
100800        MOVE NO-TRANSACTOR TO NUMBER-MANUFACTURER IN
100900            NEW-MASTER-INVENTORY.
200200        MOVE ORDER-NUMBER TO MFR-CATALOG-NUMBER IN
200300            NEW-MASTER-INVENTORY.

200400        MOVE DTL-DESCRIPTION TO DESCRIPTION IN NEW-MASTER-INVENTORY.
200600        MOVE ZEROS TO ON-HAND-UNITS OF NEW-MASTER-INVENTORY,
200700            TOTAL-WHOLESALE-VALUE IN NEW-MASTER-INVENTORY.
200800        MOVE UNIT-COST OF TRANSACTIONS TO COST-PER-UNIT IN
200900            NEW-MASTER-INVENTORY.
300000        MOVE QUANTITY TO MIN-STOCK-UNIT-QUANTITY IN
300010            NEW-MASTER-INVENTORY.
300100        MOVE 'N' TO FLAG-NEW-STOCK.
300200        GO TO GET-NEXT-TRANSACTION.
```

Fig. 4-7. Partial listing of sample problem. (Continued from page 79).

```
070700 REORDER-STOCK.
080000     MULTIPLY ON-HAND-UNITS OF NEW-MASTER-INVENTORY BY 100
080050         GIVING DIVIDEND ON SIZE ERROR DISPLAY
080060         'OVERFLOW ON MULTIPLICATION'.
080070     DISPLAY SEQ-STOCK-NUMBER OF MASTER-RECORD IN
080080         NEW-MASTER-INVENTORY.
080100     DIVIDE MIN-STOCK-UNIT-QUANTITY OF NEW-MASTER-INVENTORY INTO
080200         DIVIDEND GIVING PERCENTAGE ROUNDED.
080300     IF PERCENTAGE IS LESS THAN 60 MOVE 'EEE' TO
080400         EMERGENCY-REORDER-FLAG.
080500     MOVE SEQ-STOCK-NUMBER OF NEW-MASTER-INVENTORY TO
080600         STK-NUMBER-PRINT.
080700     MOVE NUMBER-MANUFACTURER OF NEW-MASTER-INVENTORY TO NO-MFR.
080900     MOVE MFR-CATALOG-NUMBER OF NEW-MASTER-INVENTORY TO
090000         MFR-ORDER-NUMBER OF REORDER-LIST.
090100     MOVE DESCRIPTION IN NEW-MASTER-INVENTCRY TO ITEM-DESCRIPTION.
090200     MOVE ON-HAND-UNITS IN NEW-MASTER-INVENTORY TO UNITS-ON-HAND.
090400     MOVE MIN-STOCK-UNIT-QUANTITY OF NEW-MASTER-INVENTORY TO
090500         MIN-UNITS.
090600     MOVE COST-PER-UNIT IN NEW-MASTER-INVENTORY TO UNIT-COST
090610         OF REORDER-LIST.
090700     WRITE REPLENISH-STOCK-ITEM BEFORE ADVANCING 3 LINES.
090800     ADD 1 TO LINE-NO.
090810     MOVE SPACES TO REPLENISH-STOCK-ITEM.
090900     IF LINE-NO IS GREATER THAN 17 PERFORM HEADER-PRINT.
```

```
300900 SET-UP-END-RUN.
400000     MOVE '.....' TO STOCK-CONTROL-NUMBER.
400100     GO TO READ-INVENTORY-RECORD.

400200 CLOSE-FILES.
400300     CLOSE OLD-MASTER-INVENTORY, DETAIL-TRANSACTION-CARDS.
400690     CLOSE NEW-MASTER-INVENTORY, REORDER-LIST.
400700     STOP RUN.
```

Fig. 4-7. Partial listing of sample problem. (Continued from page 80).

follows: compute the total stock value (7) by multiplying the number of units on hand times the price per unit. Check whether the number of units on hand has fallen below the reorder level (8), and if so, write a list entry on the stock reorder report (9). Write the updated master inventory record from the output area (10). If the output master was constructed from a new stock item detail transaction (i.e., if new stock flag contains "N") (11), set the Master-In switch ON (12) and move the input area copy of the last input master inventory record to the output area (13). Branch to read the next input master (B).

Assuming the stock number on the detail transaction was not greater, turn the Master-In switch ON (14) and test if the stock numbers are equal (15). If so, update the quantity on hand by the quantity of the shipment or receipt (16). Then go to read the next detail transaction (A).

If the detail stock number is less than the master stock number, test whether the transaction is type 0 (17) (new stock item). If not, display an error message describing the transaction (18). If so, use the detail transaction to build a new master inventory record (19) and set the new-stock-item flag (20) in the output area. In either case, go to read the next transaction (A).

A list, called the stock-reorder list, is printed to reflect newly added stock items, and stock items on which the stock on hand falls below the minimum level. Information pertinent to the current status of the stock is shown, including a flag to indicate a newly added stock item and a flag to indicate when the stock level has fallen below 60 percent of minimum. Following each line printed, a test is made to determine whether a page eject has occurred (21). If so, the page contour is updated and the report header printed.

After all detail transactions have been read and processed (23), the detail transaction input area is modified so that all subsequent input master inventory records to be read will have lower stock numbers than that shown in the detail transaction field (24). Thus, all remaining input master inventory records will be automatically transferred to the output master file without updating.

When the end of the input master inventory file is reached and the last input master record put on the output master inventory (25), all files are closed (26) and the object run is terminated. (27).

Chapter 5

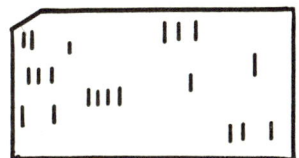

The Environment Division

This is the second division of a COBOL program. It has the purpose of describing the environment in which the program was designed to run. The computer that the program was written for is listed in this division. Also, we tell which input and output devices the program uses and which files of data are going to be on each device.

CONFIGURATION SECTION

The first of these is the CONFIGURATION SECTION, in which three paragraphs are used to detail the overall specifications for the computing systems involved in the COBOL program. The paragraphs are as follows:

- SOURCE-COMPUTER—Defines the computer on which the COBOL language program is to be compiled.
- OBJECT-COMPUTER—Defines the computer on which the compiled object program is to be run.
- SPECIAL-NAMES—Defines problem oriented names for specific pieces of equipment.

SOURCE COMPUTER

This paragraph names the computer upon which the source program is to be compiled and sets up communication with the operating system. Format: <u>SOURCE-COMPUTER.</u> computer name.

OBJECT COMPUTER

This paragraph describes the computer upon which the object program is to be run and specifies the equipment configuration present during object running time. Computer name provides a means for describing equipment configuration. The computer name and its implied configuration are specified by each implementor. If the configuration implied by computer name comprises more or less equipment than is actually needed by the object program, the descriptive clauses following computer name permit the specification of the actual subset of the configuration. The configuration definition contains specific information concerning the memory size.

Format:

OBJECT-COMPUTER. computer-name

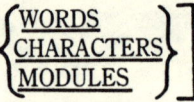

[MEMORY SIZE INTEGER { WORDS / CHARACTERS / MODULES }]

Usually both paragraphs contain the same computer name, but there are occasions when they do not. These computer names are not programmer invented-names; they come from the reserved word list for your particular computer. (See Appendix A.)

SPECIAL NAMES

This paragraph provides a means of relating hardware device names (implementor name) to problem oriented mnemonic names assigned by the user. An example of the use of the SPECIAL-NAMES feature is as follows:

SPECIAL-NAMES. CARD-READER IS READER.

This paragraph is usually not required if the actual hardware names are used in the program. A mnemonic name may only be used in formats which specifically permit their use. If the implementor name is not a switch, the associated mnemonic name may be used in ACCEPT, DISPLAY, and WRITE statements.

If implementor name is a switch, it must be assigned a mnemonic name, a condition name, or both. The status of the switch is interrogated by testing the condition name assigned to it.

The literal, that you specify in the CURRENCY IS clause, must be used in PICTURE clauses to represent the currency symbol. This literal must be a single character and it cannot be any digit (0 through 9) or the Alphabetics A, B, C, D, P, R, S, V, X, Z, or the space. Do not use these characters: * , (+ .) − ; OK ". When the CURRENCY IS clause is not present, only the currency symbol normal to the implementor may be used in PICTURE clauses. The DECIMAL-POINT IS COMMA clause interchanges the function of the comma and period in PICTURE clause character strings and in numeric literals.

This paragraph, specified in the Environment Division, would permit reference to the hardware device CARD-READER to be made in the program in the following manner:

ACCEPT RATE-CHANGE FROM READER.

The individual programmer's reference manual must be consulted for both the permitted use of mnemonic-names, as well as the standard hardware device names for that computer. (See Appendix A.)

INPUT-OUTPUT SECTION

The second section in the Environment Division is the INPUT-OUTPUT SECTION. This section deals with the definition of the external media and provides information needed to create the most efficient transmission of data between the media and the object program. This section is divided into two paragraphs, the FILE-CONTROL which names and associates the files with external media, and the I-O-CONTROL which defines special input/output techniques, rerun, and multiple file tapes.

File-Control

Format:

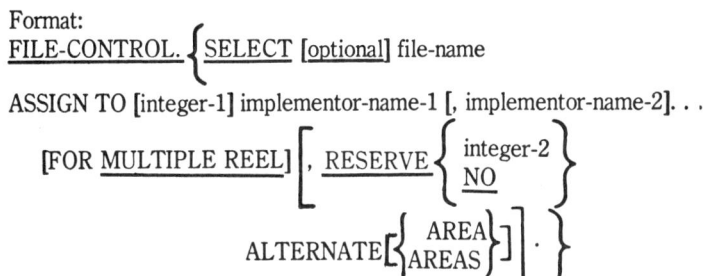

This paragraph is used to name each file, identify the hardware medium which contains it, permit specific hardware assignments for the program, and to specify alternate input-output areas. Each file selected by a FILE CONTROL entry must have a corresponding File Description entry in the Data Division. The keyword OPTIONAL is required for input files that may or may not be present when the object program is run.

Integer-1 indicates the number of input-output units assigned to a file name. If integer-1 is not specified, the compiler determines the number of units to be assigned. All files employed in the program must be ASSIGNed to a specific input/output hardware device (card reader, tape unit, printer, etc.). The exact name for each of these units are covered in the specific programmers reference manual. If a tape file is to use more than one reel, the FOR MULTIPLE REEL option is specified.

The RESERVE clause allows the user to modify the number of input-output areas allocated by the compiler. The option RESERVE ALTERNATE AREAS means that additional areas are to be reserved for the file in addition to the minimum area. The implementation specifies the minimum area and the additional areas for particular hardware. No additional areas are reserved for the file when the NO option is selected.

I-O-Control

Format:
I-O-CONTROL.
$$\underline{\text{RERUN}} \left[\underline{\text{ON}} \left\{ \begin{array}{l} \text{file-name-1} \\ \text{implementor-name} \end{array} \right\} \right]$$

87

$$\left[\text{EVERY} \begin{Bmatrix} \begin{Bmatrix} \text{END OF } \underline{\text{REEL}} \\ \text{integer-1 } \underline{\text{RECORDS}} \end{Bmatrix} \text{ OF } \underline{\text{file-name-2}} \\ \text{integer-2 } \underline{\text{CLOCK-UNITS}} \\ \underline{\text{condition-name}} \end{Bmatrix} \right] \dots$$

[; <u>SAME</u> [<u>RECORD</u>] AREA FOR <u>file-name-3</u> {, <u>file-name-4</u>} ...] ...

[; <u>MULTIPLE FILE TAPE</u> CONTAINS file-name-5 [<u>POSITION</u> integer-3] [, <u>file-name-6</u> [<u>POSITION</u> integer-4]] ...] ....

This paragraph, which is optional, permits the user to specify such things as input-output techniques and points at which rerun is to be established. When either the integer-1 RECORDS or integer-2 CLOCK-UNITS option is selected, the implementor name must be given in the RERUN option. The RERUN clause specifies where the rerun information is recorded and when the memory dump occurs. Memory dumps may be recorded in either of the following ways:

● The memory dump is written on a separate rerun tape or unit, as specified by the hardware device name of the RERUN option.

● The memory dump is written on each reel or unit of an output file with the specified implementation specifying where, on the reel or file, the dump is to be recorded.

The SAME AREA clause specifies that two or more files are to use the same memory area (including alternate areas) during processing. If the RECORD option is specified, only one record can reside in the record area at any one time regardless of the number of files that may be open (see Fig. 5-1). Since only one record can be in the record area, it is the responsibility of the programmer to determine which record of which file is in the record at any point in the program.

If the RECORD option is not specified in the SAME AREA clause, then the area being shared includes all storage assigned to the files specified in the SAME AREA clause. In this case, the programmer must make certain that no more than one file is open at any point in the program.

Since more than one SAME AREA or SAME RECORD AREA clause can be written in the I-O-CONTROL paragraph, certain restrictions are placed on the use of the file names. These restrictions are as follows:

● A particular file-name cannot be specified in more than one SAME AREA clause nor in more than one SAME RECORDS AREA clause.

● If one or more of the file names specified in SAME AREA clause also appears in the SAME RECORDS AREA clause, all file names specified in the SAME AREA clause must be listed in the SAME RECORDS AREA clause. However, any dissimilar file names specified in the SAME RECORDS AREA clause need not be listed in the SAME AREA clause. For example, assume that FILEA, FILEG, and FILEL are to have the same area and that FILEA, FILEB, and FILEZ are to have the same record area. The SAME AREA and SAME RECORD AREA clauses must be written as follows:

SPECIAL NAMES.

implementor-name [IS mnemonic-name].. [, $\left\{ \begin{array}{c} \underline{ON} \\ \underline{OFF} \end{array} \right\}$ STATUS IS condition-name-1 [, $\left\{ \begin{array}{c} \underline{OFF} \\ \underline{ON} \end{array} \right\}$ STATUS IS condition-name-2] ...

[, CURRENCY SIGN IS literal] [, DECIMAL-POINT IS COMA].

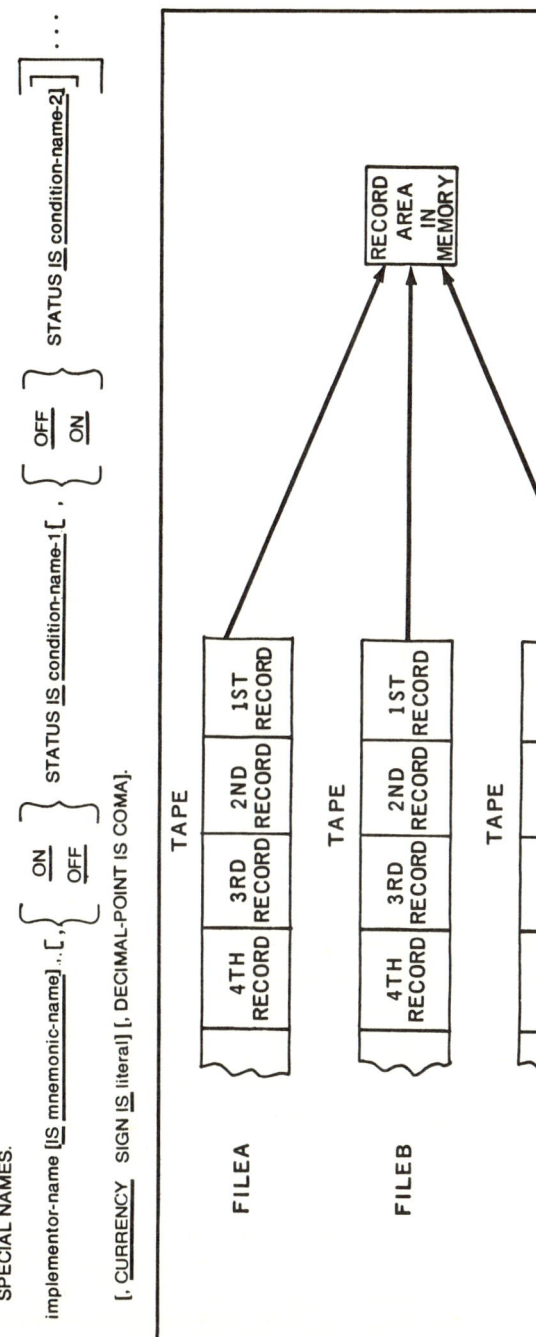

Fig. 5-1. If only one record is defined in working storage, then only one record can be read at a time, regardless of the number of records or files in storage.

SAME AREA FILEA, FILEG, FILEL
SAME RECORD AREA FILEA, FILEB, FILEG, FILEL, FILEZ

● If both a SAME AREA clause and a SAME RECORD AREA clause appear in an I-O-CONTROL paragraph, only one file can be open at any point in the program.

The MULTIPLE FILE option is required when more than one file shares the same physical reel of tape. Regardless of the number of files on a single reel, only those files used in the object program need be specified. The POSITION option is not required if all the files are listed in consecutive order. If any file on the tape is not listed, the position relative to the beginning of the tape must be given for each file listed.

SAMPLE PROBLEM

The Environment Division section of the program describes and centralizes those aspects of the total problem which depend upon the characteristics of the computing equipment. It links the logical concepts of data and records described in the Data Division with the physical aspects of the files on which they are stored. The various information will be shown first in English prose and then in COBOL. The header for this division is:

0001400 ENVIRONMENT DIVISION.
001500 CONFIGURATION SECTION.

The source-computer (the computer on which the compiling operation will be performed) is specified in a format reserved for that particular computer.

001600 SOURCE-COMPUTER. MARK-I.

The object-computer (the computer on which the compiled object program will be executed) is specified, and its equipment configuration and operational mode is described as name of computer, and memory size used (20,000 words).

001700 OBJECT-COMPUTER. MARK-I.
001800 MEMORY SIZE 20000 WORDS.

The Special-Names paragraph specifies mnemonic names which may be equated to standard hardware names or switches. In this case, TOP-OF-NEXT-PAGE could contain the computer manufacturer's symbol which instructs the printer to advance to a new page. The programmer has equated *his* name (NEW-PAGE) with the manufacturer's name.

001800 SPECIAL-NAMES. NEW-PAGE IS TOP-OF-NEXT-PAGE.
0012100 INPUT-OUTPUT SECTION.

Each file is named and is described as to medium and hardware assignment. The files assigned in this program are as follows:

● The old (input) master inventory file is assigned to a tape.

● The new (output) master inventory is assigned to a tape. This file is an updated version of the old (input) master inventory, with an identical file description and record description; therefore, the RENAMING clause may be used. The detail transaction cards input file is assigned to the card reader and the stock reorder output list file is assigned to the printer.

```
002200 FILE-CONTROL.
002300   SELECT OLD-MASTER-INVENTORY ASSIGN TO
         MAGNETIC-TAPE-UNIT.
002400   SELECT NEW-MASTER-INVENTORY ASSIGN TO
         MAGNETIC-TAPE-UNIT.
002600   SELECT DETAIL-TRANSACTION-CARDS ASSIGN TO
         CARD-READER
002610   SELECT REORDER-LIST ASSIGN TO PRINTER.
```

In this instance, the I-O-CONTROL statement is used to obtain a memory dump at the end of each reel of the NEW-MASTER-INVENTORY file. This information is useful when restarting a program that has aborted during a run; the program can be restarted at the last valid rerun point and there is no need to rerun the entire program.

```
                    002640 I-O-CONTROL.
002650 RERUN EVERY END OF REEL OF NEW-MASTER-
                    INVENTORY
```

Chapter 6

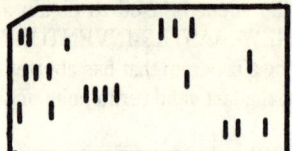

The Identification Division

Every program starts off with this division, the purpose of which is simply to give some information about the program. Unlike the other three divisions, it does not have sections. It has seven paragraphs each with its own special name. These paragraph names are not programmer invented-names; they come from the reserved word list. As mentioned in a previous chapter, the paragraph names are coded at Margin A, and each is followed by a period.

PROGRAM ID

This paragraph is the only paragraph which is required. The other six are optional. The PROGRAM-ID paragraph contains the official name of the program. It is a programmer invented name and must conform to the rules governing the formation of such names. The name given to the program may not be used anywhere else in the program. Example:
> PROGRAM-ID.
> CREDIT-RATING-PROGRAM.

As mentioned above, the remaining six paragraphs are optional. You may include all of them if you like or omit any you wish, but those you use must be in the order presented here. They are not for the use of the computer, but are considered a part of the documentation of a program.

Documentation is a term which describes any purely explanatory information provided with a program for the enlightenment of other humans, but is essentially ignored by the computer. Because of the importance of writing programs so others can understand them, most Data Processing Managers stress the use of documentation, and therefore insist that their programmers include these six optional paragraphs in their IDENTIFICATION DIVISIONS.

Since the content of the remaining paragraphs are ignored by the computer, there is very little restriction on what they may contain. There are really only two restrictions. They may contain only characters from the COBOL character set, and they must end with a period.

AUTHOR
The AUTHOR paragraph provides a place for you to claim your rightful glory as the author of this ingenious program.

INSTALLATION
In this paragraph you can give credit to the employer who showed such wisdom in hiring such an ingenious programmer. Example:
                    INSTALLATION.
                ES+GS COMPUTATION CENTER.

DATE WRITTEN
In this paragraph you record the date on which you wrote the program. Example:
                    DATE-WRITTEN.
                    APRIL 5, 1981.

DATE COMPILED
Although you might run your program on the same day you write it, chances are you'll run it many more times on later dates. If you do not store your compiled object program, but, instead, compile it over again each time you run it, you will not find this paragraph very useful. This is a somewhat unusual paragraph in that no matter what date you might include in it, each time you compile the program the computer will replace your data with the proper date. Suppose you provided a DATE-COMPILED paragraph like this:
                    DATE-COMPILED.
                    APRIL 7, 1981.
When you compiled your program on April 26, this program listing would include this paragraph:
                    DATE-COMPILED.
                    78/04/26.
Note that the computer provides the date in a format of its own choosing. Each computer has its own form, but they are usually not difficult to decipher whatever their form.

SECURITY
The SECURITY paragraph allows you to stipulate what measure of protection the program is to receive. Many companies keep their prize programs from their competitors and from the general public. In such a case, this might be the form of this paragraph:
                    SECURITY.
            ACCESS RESTRICTED TO ES+GS CREDIT DEPT STAFF.
NOTE: This provides no computer oriented security, such as passwords, etc. its sole purpose is for human eyes.

```
000100 IDENTIFICATION DIVISION.
000200 PROGRAM-ID. MASTER-INVENTORY-UPDATE.
000300 AUTHOR. AB. C. DEFGHI.
000350 INSTALLATION. OSHKOSH.
000400 DATE-WRITTEN. JUNE 7 1966.
000450 DATE-COMPILED. JUNE 23 1966.
000500 SECURITY. CLASS B COMPANY CONFIDENTIAL.
000600 REMARKS. MASTER INVENTORY ON TAPE IS RUN AGAINST DETAIL
000700     TRANSACTIONS FOR UPDATING TO CREATE A NEW MASTER
000800     INVENTORY FILE. NEW STOCK ITEMS MAY BE ADDED BY
000900     ZERO-TYPE DETAIL TRANSACTIONS.
001000     STOCK ITEMS ON WHICH THE QUANTITY ON HAND HAS
001100     FALLEN BELOW REORDER LEVEL WILL BE LISTED WITH
001200     PURCHASING INFORMATION ON THE PRINTER, AS WILL
001300     BE ALL NEW STOCK ITEMS.
```

Fig. 6-1. The identification division of the sample program.

REMARKS

In this paragraph you usually make some remark regarding the purpose of the program. For example:

REMARKS.
THIS PROGRAM ASSIGNS CREDIT RATINGS TO CUSTOMERS BASED UPON SUBSCRIBER PROVIDED DATA SUCH AS PAYMENT RECORDS, PAST DUE NOTICES, ETC.

Sentences can begin anywhere, as long as they don't begin to the left of Margin B. Programmers most often take advantage of this leniency when they write the IDENTIFICATION and ENVIRONMENT DIVISIONS where the sentences are so short. Note that for the sake of orderly appearance, all of the sentences have been lined up on the same column. No official requirement exists for you to do this, but if you do it, be sure you provide for at least one space following the period after every paragraph-name.

SAMPLE PROBLEM

This section of the program identifies or labels the program. It may also contain any other documentation information that is desired as to authorship, location of installation, date of writing or compiling, security, and any other comments regarding the functional or peripheral aspects of the program. Information that may be included is shown below, first in English prose and then in the COBOL version (See Fig. 6-1).

- A Program Identification (required).
- Author.
- Installation.
- Date written.
- Date compiled.
- Security level of the program output.
- Remarks. A general functional description of the program.

Chapter 7

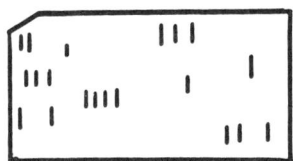

COBOL Reference Format

The standard COBOL Reference Format is, essentially, a format within which the COBOL source program is constructed. This is necessary because the COBOL language must be used very precisely at each level of organization. Extreme care must be used to observe the rules stated in this book.

In addition to observing the rules of sentence formats, a source program must be written such that its various sections and divisions appear in a particular sequence at compilation time. The standard COBOL Reference Format describes the standards by which source program information must be arranged and sequenced on the COBOL coding form for the compiler to interpret the information and convert it to an object program that will perform the intended functions.

This chapter will define the purposes of the Reference Format and the rules governing its use in each of the four divisions of the COBOL source program. In doing this, the various rules and principles previously stated in this book will be summarized.

PURPOSE OF REFERENCE FORMAT

The Reference Format has three main purposes:

● It provides a convenient form for the programmer to use. The COBOL Programming Form helps both the programmer and the person who punches cards from this format to arrange the program in the proper form.

● It provides a medium by which the programmer may specify those items that the compiler needs to create the object program.

● It provides a standard form for the printed listing of the source program which could serve, with modification, as the input form to a COBOL compiler on another computer.

STANDARD PROCEDURE

The rules that follow for the use of the Reference Format take precedence over any other rules stated in this book with respect to spacing of formats.

The Reference Format Programming Form is shown in Fig. 7-1. Each line of coding represents the information that is to be keypunched on one 80-column card, as indicated in the following paragraphs.

Sequence Number

Columns 1 through 6 contain the sequence number. Sequence numbers are optional, and are intended to aid the programmer in making corrections and changes in the source program by establishing a linear card sequence.

Continuation Indicator

Column 7 is used as a continuation indicator. Whenever a paragraph or entry requires more than one line of coding, and the break in the line occurs in the middle of a literal or word, the continuation is shown by a hyphen in column 7 of the line in which the broken word or literal is completed.

If no hyphen appears at the start of any given line, the last word of the preceding line is assumed to have ended. No space is required at the end of any line. If the hyphen is used, the first character of the hyphenated line is considered a continuation of the last word of the preceding line.

A word or numeric literal may be interrupted in any column (and the rest of the line space filled) if there is a hyphen in column 7 of the next succeeding line. If a nonnumeric literal extends beyond the end of a line, there must be a hyphen in column 7 of the next line. Also, the continuation of the nonnumeric literal must start with a quotation mark. Until the final quotation mark terminates the nonnumeric literal, it is assumed that each card column up to and including column 72 is part of the literal.

Text

Columns 8 through 72 are used to contain text, i.e., the information from which the data and instructions, which comprise the object program, are compiled. Two margins are used to align this information; Margin A and Margin B. An item aligned with Margin A has its first character in column 8; an item aligned with Margin B has its first character in column 12.

Names of divisions, names of sections, names of paragraphs, and all main entries of the Data Division (i.e., file descriptions and record descriptions) are placed at Margin A. Division and section names must appear on a single line. Subordinate items, continuations, and procedural statements are placed at Margin B.

Identification

Columns 73 through 80 are used for card deck identification at the discretion of the programmer. The contents are shown in the source program listing, but do not affect the compilation operation.

SEQUENCE NUMBER		A	B	TEXT
1 6	7	8 11	12	20
		A. LOO	P. S	ECTION.
		B. LOO	P. S	ECTION 1.1.

Fig. 7-1. A formatted coding sheet.

USING THE REFERENCE FORMAT

There are four divisions to the Reference Format; the Identification Division, the Environment Division, the Data Division, and the Procedural Division, appearing in the Reference Format in that order. The remainder of this section explains the format usage rules of these four divisions.

The Identification Division

The Identification Division provides a means of identifying or labeling a COBOL source program. The only information required in this division is the PROGRAM-ID paragraph. Other information follows a standard format, but its inclusion is optional. Thus, the division may be composed of from one to seven paragraphs. The PROGRAM-ID paragraph must always appear as the first paragraph. Thereafter, any or all of the remaining fixed name paragraphs may appear.

The name of the division, and the names of the paragraphs within it, start under Margin A. The first line of this division contains its name, followed by a period; i.e.,

IDENTIFICATION DIVISION.

The text of each paragraph may start on the same line as the paragraph name, or on the next line, as preferred. Any paragraph which occupies more than one line must be continued by starting at Margin B on the next line.

The Environment Division

This division specifies those elements of a COBOL program that are dependent upon physical aspects or limitations of the specific equipment. The first line of the division consists of its name, followed by a period, i.e.,

ENVIRONMENT DIVISION.

The section names CONFIGURATION SECTION and INPUT-OUTPUT SECTION must also be single entries, each on a line by itself and followed by a period. Paragraph names, like the division name and section name, must each start at Margin A and must be followed by a period. However, the clauses which comprise each paragraph may follow the paragraph immediately, on the same line. The I-O-CONTROL and the FILE-

CONTROL paragraphs may each be comprised of several sentences, whereas the paragraphs of the CONFIGURATION section are each composed of one sentence only.

The Data Division

The basic unit in the Data Division is an entry. Each entry begins with a level indicator or level number that is followed by a data name, or the word FILLER and then by a set of descriptive clauses. The first line of the Data Division is the division name, followed by a period; i.e.,

DATA DIVISION.

The Data Division is separated into two distinct sections; the FILE SECTION and WORKING-STORAGE SECTION. Each section is begun with the appropriate section name; the section name is on a line by itself followed by a period. In the File Section, each file description is begun with its appropriate level indicator at Margin A, followed by the file name at Margin B. File-description clauses may then follow on the same line, and continue until a period ends the File Description entry.

All Record Description entries for label records or data records that pertain to a given file must follow the File Description for that file. After all the File Section entries are completed, the Working-Storage Section entries are made. These entries must be preceded by the words WORKING-STORAGE SECTION on a line by themselves. The level number of the entry is aligned with Margin A, while the entry itself starts at Margin B. In the Working-Storage Section, all 77 level entries, and their subordinate 88 level condition name entries, must precede any record description entries.

In any section of the Data Division, various entries may be indented for the purpose of displaying a hierarchal data structure within a given Record Description. The choice between left justification or indentation of entries according to level number is left to the discretion of the programmer. Under no circumstances does indentation affect the magnitude of a level number or the result of a compilation operation.

The 01 level number which begins a record description is placed at Margin A, after which the data name for the record is placed at Margin B. All entries subordinate to the record description are begun with the level number at Margin B, with the data name separated from the level number by one or more spaces. If a single entry requires more than one line, the left margin limit for each line within the entry is the same; i.e., the position under the first character of the data name. When level numbers are indented each new level number is placed four spaces to the right of the starting position of the previous level number.

The Procedure Division

The first line of the division consists of its name, followed by a period, starting at Margin A, as follows:

PROCEDURE DIVISION.

The section name is followed by a space, the word SECTION, and a period. However, the use of segmentation requires a priority number, and a period. In either case, the remainder of the line is left blank. See Fig. 7-1.

A paragraph consists of one or more successive sentences, the first of which must be preceded by a paragraph name. The paragraph name starts at Margin A and is followed by a period. A new paragraph is determined by the appearance of another paragraph name.

All lines in a paragraph which follow the paragraph-name must start at Margin B. If a word or literal must be split over two lines, this will be indicated by placing a hyphen in the seventh character position of the second line. If the user prefers not to split a word or literal, he may leave the remainder of the line space filled and then start the word or literal on the next line.

Chapter 8

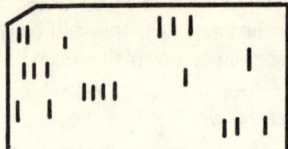

Segmentation

COBOL segmentation allows object program overlay to be accomplished through the compiler. This is necessary with programs that cannot be contained in memory at one time. Segmentation does not deal with data, so only the Procedure and Environment Divisions are considered. The compiler has no way of determining the need for segmentation, so it is the responsibility of the programmer. Normal practice is to restrict the number of overlay segments to a minimum and then only to infrequently used functions.

ORGANIZATION

The Procedure Division of a source program is usually written in sections. Each section normally represents a set of closely related operations designed to perform a particular function. Normally, sectional division is not mandatory however, when segmentation is used, the entire Procedure Division must be sectioned, and each section must be classified as either a fixed portion or as the independent or overlay segment.

Fixed Portion

This is the part of the object program that is treated as if it were always in memory. It is made up of two types of segments, the first of which is a permanent segment. This type of segment cannot be overlaid by any other part of the program. The second type of segment is the overlayable fixed segment, which can be overlaid, if necessary, by another segment to optimize memory utilization. However, such a segment, if called for by the program, always contains the object code loaded there last.

Independent Segment

This is part of the object program which can overlay, and be overlaid by, either an overlayable fixed segment or another independent segment. It differs from an overlayable fixed segment in that it is always loaded with its variables and constants re-initialized.

Segment Classification

This is accomplished by means of priority numbers in the section header. The priority is written as follows:

section-name SECTION [priority-number].

The priority number must be an integer in the range 0 through 99. If omitted, a priority of zero (0) is assumed. Generally, the more often a segment is referred to, the lower its priority number.

Sections which must always be available or which are referenced very frequently, will have a priority number of 0. All segments with priority number 0 through 49 belong to the fixed portion. Sections which frequently communicate with one another should be given the same priority number.

Sections which are to be independent overlay segments will have priority numbers 50 through 99. All sections that have the same priority number constitute members of the same segment.

SEGMENTATION CONTROL

The logical sequence of the program is the same as the physical sequence. The compiler provides all necessary transfers of control from segment to segment, and provides control necessary for a segment to operate when that segment is called upon to be used. The segment under reference will be brought in before program continuation unless it is already in memory.

SEGMENT LIMIT

The memory area reserved for containing independent overlay segments is equal to the size of the largest overlay segment. However, when there is insufficient memory to contain all permanent segments plus the largest independent overlay segment, it is necessary to decrease the number of permanent segments. The SEGMENT-LIMIT feature provides the user with a method of reducing the number of permanent segments, while retaining the logical properties of fixed segments.

The SEGMENT-LIMIT clause appears in the OBJECT-COMPUTER paragraph and has the following format:

[, SEGMENT-LIMIT IS priority-number]

Priority number is an integer in the range 1 through 49. When the SEGMENT-LIMIT clause is specified, all fixed position segments with a priority number equal to, or greater than, the segment limit are thus defined as overlayable fixed segments. All fixed segments with priority number 0 and up to, but not including, the segment limit constitute the permanent segment. All sections with priority number 0 must always be part of the permanent segment, which means that segment-limit cannot be less than 1.

When the SEGMENT-LIMIT clause is not specified, all segments with priority numbers under 50 are permanent segments which cannot be overlaid. Not all compilers support SEGMENT-LIMIT. SEGMENT-LIMIT affects the restrictions that are placed on the use of the ALTER and PERFORM statements.

ALTER Statement

A GO TO statement in any fixed segment can be ALTERed by an ALTER statement located in any other segment of the program. A GO TO statement in an overlayable or independent segment can only be ALTERed by an ALTER statement located in the same segment as the GO TO statement. So if you use both the SEGMENT-LIMIT clause and the ALTER statement, watch your priority numbers.

PERFORM Statement

The permissible range of a PERFORM statement is dependent upon whether the segment priority number is less than the SEGMENT-LIMIT, or equal to or greater than the SEGMENT-LIMIT.

If the PERFORM statement has a priority number less than the SEGMENT-LIMIT, the range of the PERFORM statement is restricted to the fixed segment of the program. If the PERFORM statement is located in an overlayable or independent segment, its range is restricted to the segment in which it appears.

If the priority number is equal to the SEGMENT-LIMIT, its range is restricted to the segment in which it appears plus those segments having a priority number that is less than the SEGMENT-LIMIT. Remember that the segment limit is 50 if the SEGMENT-LIMIT clause is not used.

When a procedure name that is in an overlayable or independent segment is referred to from within a PERFORM statement that is in a segment with a different priority number, the segment referred to is made available in its initial state for each iteration of the PERFORM statement.

Chapter 9

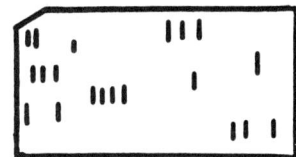

The COBOL Library

The COBOL library contains routines available to a source program at compilation time through the use of the COPY statement. The effect of the compilation of library entries is the same as if the text were actually written as part of the source program. The COBOL library may contain three types of routines as follows:

- Routines for the Environment Division consisting of equipment oriented information.
- Routines for the Data Division consisting of information pertaining to file and data description entries.
- Routines for the Procedure Division consisting of sequences of procedure paragraphs and sections.

The format of the COPY statement is as follows:

<u>COPY</u> library name

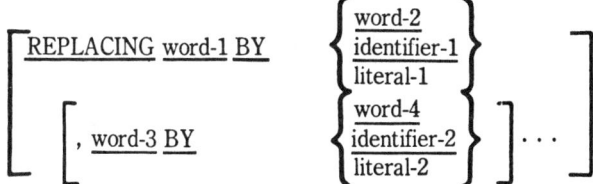

The COPY statements permit the incorporation of existing library routines into the Environment, Data, and Procedure Divisions. A library routine is a segment of COBOL source code. By specifying the appropriate library name an appropriate format, the programmer can cause a routine to be copied from the library during compilation, and the result is the same as if the programmer had written the entry as part of his source program. In this format, word represents any of the following:

   data name

103

procedure name
condition name
mnemonic name
file name

No other statement or clause may appear in the same entry as the COPY statement, and the library text to be COPYed must not contain any COPY statements. The COPYing process is terminated automatically when the end of the library text is reached. The COBOL implementor must specify whether the COPY statement itself or the statements of the library text to which it refers, or both, is to appear on the output listing. When both are to be listed, the relationship between them must be clearly indicated.

If the REPLACING option is used, each of the library words or identifiers is replaced by the word or identifier specified in the format. This replacement does not alter the material as it exists in the library, and the entry may be called again in the same program with different replacements. Words specified in the REPLACING option may be any COBOL word except reserved words. The replacement of an identifier includes the replacement of all associated qualifiers, subscripts, and indexes.

USE IN THE ENVIRONMENT DIVISION

There are five types of entries in the library that may be associated with the Environment Division; entries for the Special Names, Source Computer, Object Computer, File Control, and I-O Control paragraphs.

To use an entry contained in the COBOL library, the COPY clause must follow the appropriate paragraph-name and indicate the statement (library name) of the entry to be copied from the library. The formats are as follows:

SOURCE-COMPUTER. copy-statement.
OBJECT-COMPUTER. copy-statement.
SPECIAL-NAMES. copy-statement.
FILE-CONTROL. copy-statement.
I-O-CONTROL. copy-statement.

For example:
I-O-CONTROL. COPY LIB-IOC9.

If this entry is used, the library must contain an I-O-CONTROL paragraph with the name LIB-IOC9.

USE IN THE DATA DIVISION

There are two types of entries associated with the Data Division:

● Entries pertaining to the File Description portion of the Data Division.

● Entries pertaining to record descriptions in the Record Description or Working-Storage portions of the Data Division.

Each File Description paragraph described in the COBOL Library must have a level indicator associated with its first entry. This separates the information contained within the individual File Descriptions from adjacent File Descriptions. This information may be copied by use of the COPY option in the File Section, however, the Record Description entry associated with the FD entries is not copied from the library.

Data description entries differ from the File Description entries in that they are associated with level numbers rather than level indicators. The first entry in each set of contiguous data descriptions must carry level number 01. Thus this set is separated from adjacent sets. A COPY clause causes all entries subordinate to the specified statement (library name) to be copied from the library.

When copying a data description, the level number in the library must be the same as the COPY clause in the source program. In the File Section of the Data Division, the COPY clause takes the following formats:

<u>FD</u> file-name copy-statement.
<u>01</u> data-name copy-statement.

For example, suppose that the following FD entry exists in the library:
FD EDITED-SHIPMENTS LABEL RECORD IS . . .
This entry could be called from the library by the COPY clause as follows:
FD MASTER-EDITED-SHIPMENTS COPY EDITED-SHIPMENTS.
Note that EDITED-SHIPMENTS is the statement (library name) and MASTER-EDITED-SHIPMENTS is the file name given in the Data Division of the source program. The FD entry would then be placed in the source program as follows:
FD MASTER-EDITED-SHIPMENTS LABEL RECORD IS . . .
Note also that the COPY clause copied only the File Description entry, not the associated Record Description entries.

The effect of the 01 data name form of the COPY clause is to extract an entry or series of entries from the library and insert that information into the source program where the COPY clause appears. Thus the level number and data name are not replaced by the copied information. For example:
01 SHIPMENTS-NOT-COSTED COPY DETAIL-SHIPMENTS.
In this case, the COBOL Library must contain a 01 level Record Description with the name DETAIL-SHIPMENTS. All data description entries from that point on are inserted into the source program in place of the COPY clause.

USE IN THE PROCEDURE DIVISION

Each routine in the COBOL Library is composed of either one paragraph, identified by a paragraph name, or one section, identified by a section name. For purposes of copying this routine from the library, the paragraph name or section name is called a procedure name.

Routines are retrieved from the library and copied into the source program through the use of the COPY statement in the Procedure Divison. Then, at compile time the procedure name that identifies the COPY statement replaces the library procedure name that identifies the library routine, and all references to the routing procedure name as it appears within the library routine are replaced by references to the procedure name of the COPY statement. The format of a COPY clause written in the Procedure Division is as follows:

<u>procedure-name.</u> copy-statement.

Chapter 10

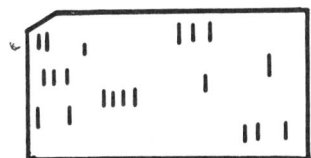

Table Handling

Data processing problems frequently involve the handling of sets of values which can be most readily represented and interpreted when shown in table form. A table is a named set of data items. These items are arranged in some meaningful order, and are functionally homogeneous in some way. There are three basic reasons for arranging data in table form:

● From a documentational standpoint, it is often desirable to arrange a body of data items such that the underlying order of the several items is readily apparent.

● Each item in a table occupies a definite physical position relative to the beginning of the table. Thus each item in the table is addressed relative to the table name, rather than by a unique data name.

● The number of occurrences of a table element may be specified as fixed or variable.

DEFINING TABLE

COBOL tables are defined structurally by including the OCCURS clause in the data description entry. The OCCURS clause specifies the number of times an item is to be repeated. An item described by an OCCURS clause is called a table element, and the name and description of the table element applies to each repetition or occurrence. To define a one dimensional table, an OCCURS clause is written as a part of the data description of the item to be repeated. Example 1 shows a one-dimensional table defined by the item TABLE-ELEMENT.

Example 1:
```
    01   TABLE-1.
         02   TABLE-ELEMENT OCCURS 20 TIMES
              03   SAM . . .
              03   JOE . . .
```

Each 03 level entry occurs in each Table-Element, so in this example each of the twenty TABLE-ELEMENTS contains one SAM and one JOE. To address any individual TABLE-ELEMENT it is necessary to specify the occurrence number of the TABLE-ELEMENT. The complete set of occurrences of TABLE-ELEMENT has been assigned the name TABLE-1. However, it is not necessary to give a group name to a table unless a means of addressing the entire table is desired.

Defining a one-dimensional table within each occurrence of an element of another one dimensional table gives rise to a two dimensional table, as shown in Example 2.

Example 2:
    02   LENGTH OCCURS 30 TIMES; . . .
       05   WIDTH OCCURS 10 TIMES;
       05   FACTOR . . .

LENGTH is an element of a one dimensional table. But within each LENGTH occurrence there are 10 occurrences of WIDTH. Thus WIDTH is an element of a two dimensional table. However, FACTOR occurs only once within each LENGTH, so that it is an element of a one dimensional table. Pictorially, this table might be represented as in Figure 10-1.

In general to define an n dimensional table, the OCCURS clause must appear in the data description of the table element and also appear in n−1 group items which contain that table element as a subordinate item. In COBOL tables, up to three dimensions are permitted.

REFERENCE OF TABLE ITEMS

When referencing a table item it is necessary to indicate either explicitly (by subscripting) or implicitly (by indexing) which occurrence of the table item is intended. The table item can be one of the following:

● a table element,
● an item that is within a group item table element,
● a condition name associated with a table element, or
● a condition name associated with an item that is within a group item table element.

When subscripting or indexing is used to reference a table-item, the subscript or index (or set of subscripts of indices) is enclosed by parentheses. It is written immediately following the data name, or table item to which the subscripting or indexing is applied in that particular reference. The form is:

<u>Data-name-1</u> (a_1[,a_2[,a_3]])

where each "a" represents an occurrence number of a dimension of the table, expressed either in the form of an index name or a subscript. Subscripts are integer values, expressed either by numeric literals or data names which contain integer values. An index name is a word which contains at least one alphabetic character, that names as index (pointer) associated with a specific table.

One to three subscript or index levels may appear in the reference, depending upon how many dimensions are in that table of which the data name has been defined to be an element. There must be one subscript or index level for each OCCURS clause in the defined hierarchy that contains data-name-1, including that for data-name-1. When more than one subscript or index is used in a reference, each must be separated within the parentheses by a comma and a space.

Multiple subscripts and indices are written left to right in descending order of inclusiveness, higher to lower. A multi-dimensional table may be thought of as a group of nested single dimensional tables, with the outermost table the most inclusive and the innermost table the least inclusive. The example below shows a typical multi-dimensional table and explains the manner in which its elements are addressed. Complete data description entries are not shown.

Example:
```
01  TABLE
02    CLASS OCCURS 12 TIMES
    03  RATE . . .
    03  LIMIT OCCURS 7 TIMES
        04  HIGH . . .
        04  LOW . . .
        04  FACTOR OCCURS 4 TIMES
```

In the above example reference to CLASS or RATE (which is within the table element CLASS) requires only one subscript or index because CLASS is the most inclusive table-element, and RATE occurs only once for each

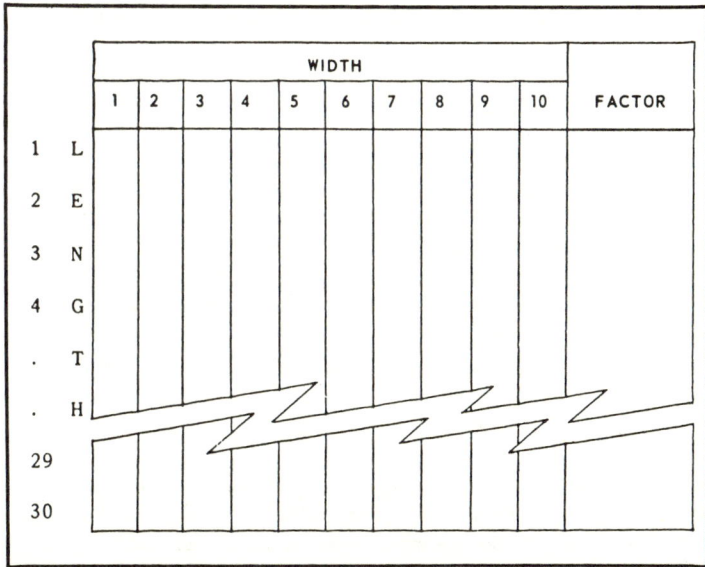

Fig. 10-1. Each item in length has 10 width items and one factor item.

CLASS. References to LIMIT, HIGH and LOW require two subscripts, since the proper occurrence number of CLASS must be specified and so must be the proper occurrence of LIMIT. Similarly, since there are several FACTORS within each LIMIT, reference to FACTOR requires three subscripts; one to specify the proper CLASS, one to show the proper LIMIT, and one to show the proper FACTOR. However, only one HIGH and one LOW occur within each LIMIT, and references to HIGH or LOW require the specification of only two subscripts; for CLASS and for LIMIT.

Subscripting

One method by which occurrence numbers may be specified is to append one, two, or three subscripts to the data name. A subscript is an integer value which specifies the occurrence number of the table element to which the data name refers, within the group item that has the next lower level number. The subscript can be represented either as a numeric literal or as a data name that is defined elsewhere as an elementary numeric data item.

The lowest valid subscript is 1. The highest valid subscript is the maximum occurrence number of the item, as specified in the OCCURS clause. A subscript is invalid if the item it references is neither an element of a defined table nor an item or condition name within an element of a defined table:

Data names may be used freely in place of numeric literal subscripts, and may be mixed with literal subscripts within an item reference; e.g., FACTOR (7, A-KEY, 3), where data name A-KEY contains an integer indicating which occurrence of RANGE is intended. A single data name may be used to refer to items in more than one table, and the tables need not have elements of the same size. Also, the same data name may be the only subscript with one item reference, while being one of two or three subscripts with another item reference.

Indexing

In addition to subscripting, individual items in a table may be referred to by indexing. With this technique, the programmer assigns one or more index names, using the optional INDEXED BY clause, to an item whose data description includes an OCCURS clause. No separate data description entry is needed to describe the index name because the size and radix of each index name is predetermined by the hardware.

At run time the value of an index name corresponds to an occurrence number for the dimension of the table to which the index name was assigned. The manner of correspondence is determined by the specific implementation. The index name must be initialized by a SET statement before it can be used as a table reference. References are made to individual items within a table of homogeneous elements by specifying the name of the item, followed by its related index name, the index name acting as a subscript.

An index can be modified only by the PERFORM, SEARCH, and SET statements. Data items described by the USAGE IS INDEX clause permit storage of the values of index names as data, without conversion. Such data items are called index data items. Direct indexing is the use of an index name in the form of subscript. Relative indexing may also be specified by following the index name with an operator (+ or −) and an integer. The occurrence number, then, is the same as if the integer were added to or subtracted from the occurrence number to which the setting of the index name corresponds. Relative indexing does not cause any altering of the index name value.

For example:

LIMIT (XLZONE + 2)

The index name XLZONE does not change in value, but if the value of XLZONE is set at, say, the third occurrence of LIMIT, the fifth occurrence will actually be addressed.

An index name cannot be defined as part of a file, and therefore cannot be directly modified by use of input/output statements. However, a data item in a file can be described by a USAGE IS INDEX clause, and this data item value can be transferred, without conversion, to an index name by means of the SET statement. A reference to an item may be indexed only by an index name which has been defined (through the use of the INDEXED BY clause) as being associated with the table of which that item is an element.

SUMMARY OF GENERAL RULES FOR SUBSCRIPTING AND INDEXING

- The use of a data name subscript in any reference to a table element or to an item within a table element will not cause any index name to be altered by the object program.
- Index names may not be combined with subscripts in a single data name reference.
- Where subscripting is not permitted, indexing is also not permitted.
- Tables may have one, two, or three dimensions. Thus, a reference to a table element may require one, two, or three indices.
- A data name may be neither subscripted nor indexed when the data name is itself used as a data name subscript or index name in that particular reference.
- An occurrence number specified by a subscript or implied by an index name must not be less than 1 nor greater than the highest permissible occurrence number for the table element.
- When indexing is used to reference a table, the INDEXED BY option must be employed in each OCCURS clause used to define the table. The SEARCH and SET statements appear in the Procedure Division only in connection with indexed table references.

SUBSCRIPTING AND INDEXING: A COMPARATIVE SAMPLE PROBLEM

To clarify the difference between the subscripting and indexing techniques, a simple table handling problem will be solved by each method.

Consider the following two tables:
01 LIABILITY-RATED
    02 TERRITORY-L OCCURS 9 TIMES.
        03 BASE-PREM PICTURE IS 9(3).
        03 CLASS-DIFFERENTIAL OCCURS 7 TIMES.
            04 LIMIT-FACTOR OCCURS 5 TIMES PICTURE IS 9(4).

01 PHYS-DAM-RATES.
    10   TERRITORY-P OCCURS 9 TIMES.
        15   COMP-ACV-BASE PICTURE IS 9(3).
        15   COMP-50D-BASE PICTURE IS 9(3).
        15   COLL-50D-BASE PICTURE IS 9(3).
        15   COLL-100D-BASE PICTURE IS 9(3).
        15   COMPOSITE-FACTOR OCCURS 196 TIMES PICTURE IS 9(4).

These two tables are simplified versions of what might be used in developing automobile insurance premiums. If it is known that the territorial definition is the same for both liability (TERRITORY-L) and automobile physical damage (TERRITORY-P) premiums, then the same data-name subscript can be used in determining the appropriate set of territorial values for each table. Assume that an input file record of an individual policy is to be updated, and the input record includes the following elementary data:

TERR-IN
LIAB-CLASS-CODE-IN
LIAB-LIMIT-IN
CLASS-IN
SYMBOL-IN
AGE-IN

TERR-IN is the territory number. LIAB-CLASS-CODE-IN represents a class code in the range 1 to 7. LIAB-LIMIT-IN represents a coverage limit code number in the range 1 to 5. CLASS-IN, SYMBOL-IN, and AGE-IN represent three code numbers which, when multiplied, produce an occurrence number which points to 1 of 196 composite factors (effectively, a table within a table, although not formally treated as such).

Although the two tables have different numbers of dimensions and different element sizes, TERR-IN can be used to refer to the proper territorial occurrence in either table.

For example:
    LIMIT-FACTOR (TERR-IN, LIAB-CLASS-CODE-IN, LIAB-LIMIT-IN)
    TERRITORY-P (TERR-IN)
are both valid uses of the TERR-IN contents as a subscript. Also, the following procedure:
    MULTIPLY CLASS-IN BY SYMBOL-IN GIVING SCRATCH.
    MULTIPLY AGE-IN BY SCRATCH.
    MULTIPLY COMPOSITE-FACTOR (TERR-IN, SCRATCH) BY COLL-50D-BASE (TERR-IN) GIVING COLL-PREMIUM.

The first two multiplications put the appropriate occurrence for COMPOSITE-FACTOR into SCRATCH. Then the proper COMPOSITE-FACTOR is multiplied by the COLL-50D-BASE ($50-deductible base premium) of the particular territory to get the final collision coverage premium into COLL-PREMIUM (a field in the output billing file for this hypothetical application). This illustrates some of the organizational and technical aspects of handling tables by the subscripting technique.

Using the same table formats, if indexing were used rather than subscripting, the files might be defined as follows:

```
01  LIABILITY-RATES
    02  TERRITORY-L OCCURS 9 TIMES INDEXED BY XTL.
        03  BASE-PREM PICTURE IS 9(3).
        03  CLASS-DIFFERENTIAL OCCURS 7 TIMES IN-
            DEXED BY XCD.
            04  LIMIT FACTOR OCCURS 5 TIMES INDEXED
                BY XLF PICTURE IS 9(4).

01  PHYS-DAM-RATES
    10  TERRITORY-P OCCURS 9 TIMES INDEXED BY XTP.
        15  COMP-ACV-BASE PICTURE IS 9(3).
        15  COMP-50D-BASE PICTURE IS 9(3).
        15  COLL-50D-BASE PICTURE IS 9(3).
        15  COLL-100D-BASE PICTURE IS 9(3).
        15  COMPOSITE-FACTOR OCCURS 196 TIMES PICTURE IS
            9(4) INDEXED BY XCF.
```

Indexing cannot be used to reference a table element (i.e., an item described by an OCCURS clause) unless the INDEXED BY clause appears in the data description of the item and in any table group items to which the table element is subordinate. For example, COMPOSITE-FACTOR must be indexed also.

The handling of tables by indexing is similar to subscripting, except that indices must be modified and controlled by means of SET, SEARCH, and PERFORM statements. Data items that were used as subscripts in the subscripting example (such as TERR-IN, LIAB-LIMIT-IN, SCRATCH, etc.) would have to be converted by means of a SET statement.
For example:
SET XTL, XTP TO TERR-IN.
If the data name TERR-IN is described by a USAGE IS INDEX clause, the compiler interprets the value in TERR-IN as a subscript value which must be converted to the appropriate index value.

COBOL TABLE HANDLING FEATURES

This section describes the specific formats and usage in COBOL for the definition and referencing of tables.

The Data Division

The COBOL Table Handling feature provides two additional facilities for the Data Division of the COBOL program; the OCCURS clause, and the USAGE IS INDEX format option of the USAGE clause.

Option 1:

OCCURS integer-2 TIMES $\left[\left\{\begin{array}{l}\underline{\text{ASCENDING}}\\ \underline{\text{DESCENDING}}\end{array}\right\}\text{KEY IS }\underline{\text{data-name-2}}\right.$
$\left.[\text{, data-name-3}]\ldots\right]\ldots[\underline{\text{INDEXED}}\text{ BY }\underline{\text{index-name-1}}[\text{, }\underline{\text{index-name-2}}]\ldots\right]$

Option 2:

OCCURS integer-1 $\underline{\text{TO}}$ integer-2 TIMES [$\underline{\text{DEPENDING}}$ ON data-name-1]

$\left[\left\{\begin{array}{l}\underline{\text{ASCENDING}}\\ \underline{\text{DESCENDING}}\end{array}\right\}\text{KEY IS }\underline{\text{data-name-2}}\text{ [, }\underline{\text{data-name-3}}]\ldots\right]\ldots$

[$\underline{\text{INDEXED}}$ BY index-name-1 [, index-name-2] . . .]

The OCCURS clause is used for defining sets of repeated homogeneous data such as tables, thus eliminating the writing of separate entries for repeated data. It also supplies information required for the application of subscripts or indices in the handling of tables. All data description clauses associated with an item whose description includes an OCCURS clause apply to each repetition of the item so described.

The OCCURS clause must not be specified in a data description entry that:

- has an 01 or a 77-level number; or
- describes an item whose size is variable. The size of an item is defined as variable whenever the data description of an item subordinate to it contains an Option 2 OCCURS clause.

Integer-1 and integer-2 are positive integers. When both are used, integer-1 must be numerically less than integer-2, and may be zero. In Option 1 integer-2 represents the exact number of occurrences, and in Option 2 the maximum number of occurrences. Data names described by an OCCURS clause must be subscripted or indexed whenever used as an operand, regardless of the number of occurrences.

Data-name-2 must be either the name of the entry that contains the OCCURS clause or the name of an entry subordinate to the entry containing the OCCURS clause. Data-name-3, etc., applies only in the latter case.

The KEY IS option is used to indicate whether repeated data is arranged in ASCENDING or DESCENDING order, according to values contained in data-name-2, data-name-3, etc. Data names are listed in descending order of hierarchal significance (i.e., most inclusive through least inclusive). If data-name-2 is not the subject of this entry, then:

- All entries identified by data-name-2, data-name-3, etc., must be subordinate to the group item which is the subject of this entry.

- None of the data names appearing in the KEY IS option can contain an entry that contains an OCCURS clause nor may they be subordinate to an entry containing an OCCURS clause.

The DEPENDING option is required only when the end of the occurrences cannot be otherwise determined. Data-name-1 can be qualified. Its data description must define it as a positive integer representing the occurrence count, and its value must not exceed that of integer-2. The implementor must specify whether the unused character positions that result from the use of the DEPENDING option are to appear on the external media.

The INDEXED BY clause is required if the subject of the entry to which this clause refers, or an item within it (if a group item), is to be referred to by means of indexing. The index name is not defined elsewhere, since it does not constitute a data name.

Reference to data names described by the OCCURS clause must always be either subscripted or indexed, except when the reference is done by means of a SEARCH statement. Also, any items subordinate to data names so described must be subscripted or indexed.

If data-name-1 is an entry in the record described by this OCCURS clause, data-name-1 must not be the subject of, or subordinate to, an entry whose description contains an Option 2 OCCURS clause. An entry which contains or has a subordinate entry which contains Option 2 cannot be the object of a REDEFINES clause.

Except for condition name entries, a VALUE clause must not be used in a Record Description entry which either contains an OCCURS clause or is subordinate to an entry that contains an OCCURS clause.

USAGE IS INDEX

The USAGE clause specifies the format of a data item in computer storage. The USAGE IS INDEX option can be written at any level. When it is used to describe an elementary item, the item is called an index data item. This item contains a value which corresponds to the occurrence number of a table element.

If the USAGE IS INDEX clause describes a group, the elementary items that comprise the group are all index data items. However, the group itself is not an index data item and it must not be specified in SEARCH or SET statements or in a relation condition.

The actual value assigned to an index data item may be dependent upon the description of the table element. In any case, the method of representation of this value (with respect to its manner of correspondence with the occurrence number) is determined by the specific implementation. The index data item cannot be a conditional value.

An index data item can be referred to directly only by means of a SEARCH or SET statement or in a relation condition with an index name. An index data item can be part of a group that is referred to as an operand in a MOVE or input/output statement, in which case no conversion takes place.

The SYNCHRONIZED, JUSTIFIED, PICTURE, VALUE, or editing clauses must be used to describe group or elementary items described by a USAGE IS INDEX clause.

The Procedure Division

COBOL Table Handling provides three features for the Procedure Division in addition to those of the basic language; the VARYING option of the PERFORM statement, the SEARCH statement, and the SET statement.

$$\underline{\text{PERFORM}} \text{ procedure-name-1 } [\underline{\text{THRU}} \text{ procedure-name-2}]$$

$$\underline{\text{VARYING}} \left\{ \begin{matrix} \text{index-name-1} \\ \text{identifier-1} \end{matrix} \right\} \underline{\text{FROM}} \left\{ \begin{matrix} \text{index-name-2} \\ \text{literal-1} \\ \text{identifier-2} \end{matrix} \right\}$$

$$\underline{\text{BY}} \left\{ \begin{matrix} \text{literal-2} \\ \text{identifier-3} \end{matrix} \right\} \underline{\text{UNTIL}} \text{ condition-1}$$

$$\left[\underline{\text{AFTER}} \left\{ \begin{matrix} \text{index-name-3} \\ \text{identifier-4} \end{matrix} \right\} \underline{\text{FROM}} \left\{ \begin{matrix} \text{index-name-4} \\ \text{literal-3} \\ \text{identifier-5} \end{matrix} \right\} \right.$$

$$\left. \underline{\text{BY}} \left\{ \begin{matrix} \text{literal-4} \\ \text{identifier-6} \end{matrix} \right\} \underline{\text{UNTIL}} \text{ condition-2} \right]$$

$$\left[\underline{\text{AFTER}} \left\{ \begin{matrix} \text{index-name-5} \\ \text{identifier-7} \end{matrix} \right\} \underline{\text{FROM}} \left\{ \begin{matrix} \text{literal-5} \\ \text{index-name-6} \\ \text{identifier-8} \end{matrix} \right\} \right.$$

$$\left. \underline{\text{BY}} \left\{ \begin{matrix} \text{literal-6} \\ \text{identifier-9} \end{matrix} \right\} \underline{\text{UNTIL}} \text{ condition-3} \right]$$

This format of the PERFORM statement is an extension of the VARYING data name option discussed previously. A maximum of three subscript names or index names can be varied in this option. When only one subscript (or index) is being varied, the mechanism is exactly the same as that of the VARYING data name option. When two subscripts (or indices) are varied, the value of identifier-4 goes through a complete cycle (FROM, BY, UNTIL) each time that identifier 1 is augmented with its BY value. The PERFORM is completed as soon as condition-2 is found to be true. When three subscripts are varied, the value of identifier-7 goes through a complete cycle each time that identifier-4 is augmented with its BY value. Further, identifier-4 goes through a complete cycle each time that identifier-1 is augmented with its BY value. The PERFORM is completed as soon as condition-1 is found to be true. Regardless of the number of subscripts being varied, as soon as condition-1 is found to be true, control is transferred to the next statement after the PERFORM statement. The FROM value must be a positive, nonzero integer. The BY value must be a nonzero integer but may be negative. No two identifiers may reference the same item. See Figures 10-2 and 3 for this mechanism.

After the completion of the PERFORM, identifier-4 and identifier-7 will each have a value equal to their respective initial settings, while identifier-1 will have a value which differs from its last used setting by one increment (or decrement).

Option 1:

$$\underline{\text{SEARCH}} \text{ identifier-1} \left[\underline{\text{VARYING}} \left\{\begin{array}{l}\text{index-name}\\ \text{identifier-2}\end{array}\right\}\right]$$

[; AT END imperative-statement-1]

$$; \underline{\text{WHEN}} \text{ condition-1} \left\{\begin{array}{l}\text{imperative-statement-2}\\ \underline{\text{NEXT SENTENCE}}\end{array}\right\}$$

$$\left[;\underline{\text{WHEN}} \text{ condition-2} \left\{\begin{array}{l}\text{imperative-statement-3}\\ \underline{\text{NEXT SENTENCE}}\end{array}\right\}\right] \ldots$$

Option 2:

$$\underline{\text{SEARCH ALL}} \text{ identifier-1} \;\; [;\text{AT } \underline{\text{END}} \text{ imperative-statement-1}]$$

$$; \underline{\text{WHEN}} \text{ condition-1} \left\{\begin{array}{l}\text{imperative-statement-2}\\ \underline{\text{NEXT SENTENCE}}\end{array}\right\}$$

The execution of a SEARCH statement causes a table to be searched for a table element that satisfies a condition specified within the WHEN clause. When the condition is satisfied, the index name associated with the table is adjusted so as to reflect the location of the located element.

In either format, identifier may not be subscripted or indexed, but must contain an OCCURS clause and an INDEXED BY clause. In addition, the description of identifier in Option 2 must contain the KEY IS option in its OCCURS clause.

Option 1 causes a serial type of search, as follows:

● If, at the start of the SEARCH, the current index setting of the index name associated with identifier-1 corresponds to an occurrence number that is greater than the highest permissible occurrence number of identifier-1, the SEARCH is terminated immediately. Then if the AT END clause is

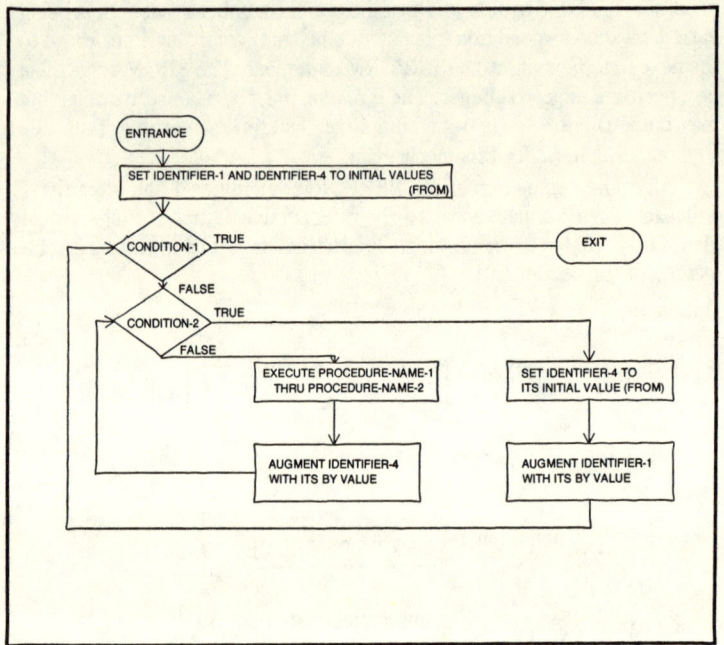

Fig. 10-2. Flowchart of a SET loop.

specified imperative-statement-1 is executed; if the AT END clause is not specified control passes to the next statement in sequence.

● If, at the start of the Search, the current index setting of the index name associated with identifier-1 corresponds to an occurrence number that is not greater than the highest permissible occurrence number for identifier-1 the SEARCH proceeds by evaluating the conditions in the order in which they are written. Index name values, where specified, determine the occurrence of the items that are to be tested. If none of the stated conditions are satisfied, the index name is incremented to obtain reference to the next occurrence. The process is repeated, using new index name settings, unless the index name setting for identifier-1 indicates an occurrence number which exceeds the last element limit of the table by one or more occurrences. In this case the SEARCH operation terminates as explained above.

The SEARCH operation terminates when one of the conditions is satisfied. The index name or identifier remains set at the occurrence on which the condition was satisfied, and the imperative statement associated with that condition is executed. Identifier-2, when specified, must be described as USAGE IS INDEX or else be the name of a numeric elementary item of integer value.

Option 2, or the SEARCH ALL option, causes a nonserial type of search to be employed as follows:

The initial index setting is ignored; it is varied during the SEARCH operation as determined by the implementor. At no time is it set such that the occurrence number to which it corresponds exceeds the occurrence number of the last element of the table, nor is it less than the value corresponding to the first element of the table.

If condition-1 cannot be satisfied for any setting of the index within the permitted range, control passes to imperative-statement-1, if the AT END clause is present. If the AT END clause is not present, control passes to the next statement in sequence. In either case, the final setting of the index is not predictable.

If condition-1 is satisfied at some point, the index setting corresponds to the occurrence number of the table element that satisfies condition-1. Control then passes to imperative-statement-2 of the WHEN clause, if specified. Otherwise control passes to the next statement in sequence.

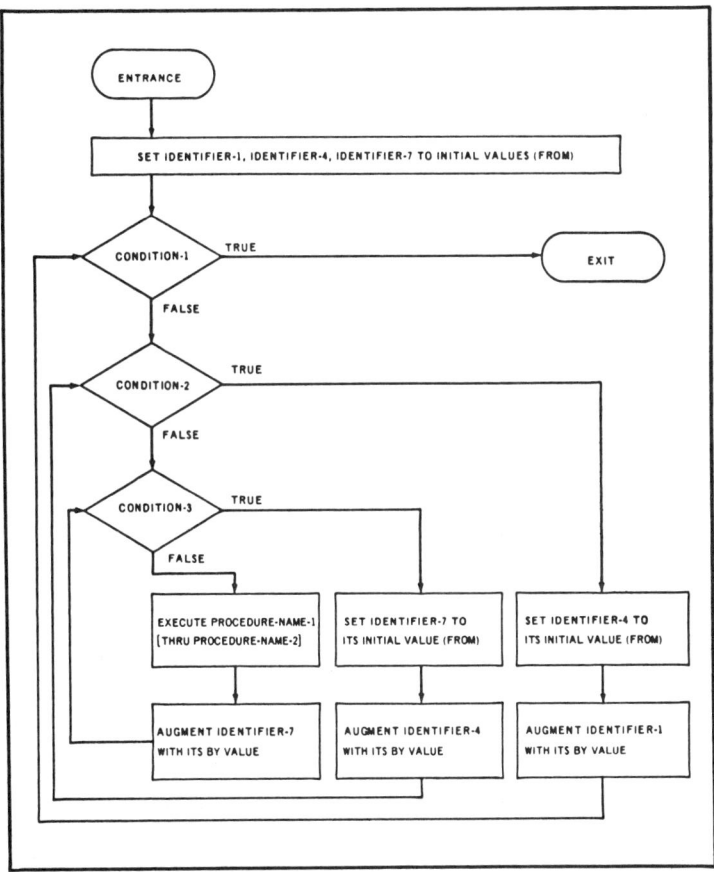

Fig. 10-3. Flowchart of a subscripted SET loop.

In the VARYING option of Option 1, identifier-2 when specified must be described as USAGE IS INDEX, or as the name of an elementary data item integer. Identifier-2 is incremented at the same time and by the same amount as the occurrence number represented by the index name associated with identifier-1. Index name, when specified, is used for the search if index name appears in the INDEXED BY clause of identifier-1. Otherwise, the first (or only) index name given in the INDEXED BY clause of identifier-1 is used.

If index name also appears in the INDEXED BY clause of another table entry, the occurrence number represented by this index name is incremented along with the occurrence number represented by the index name associated with identifier-1.

If identifier-1 belongs to a hierarchy of groups, each described by an OCCURS clause, then each of those groups must also have an associated index name. The settings of these index names are used throughout the execution of the SEARCH statement to refer to identifier-1 or items contained within it. However, only index-name-1 is actually modified. Only the index name associated with identifier-1 and the item identifier-2 or index-name-1 is incremented by the SEARCH. In Option 1, condition-1, condition-2, etc., may be any condition described previously.

In Option 2, condition-1 may consist of a relative condition incorporating EQUALS or EQUAL TO, or a condition name. Condition-1 may also be a compound condition composed of the types just mentioned, with AND as the only connective. Any data name that appears in the KEY option of identifier may be the subject of a test or it may be the name of a conditional variable with which the tested condition name is associated. All preceding data names in the KEY option must also be tested within condition-1. No other tests can appear within condition-1.

Option 1:

$$\underline{SET} \left\{ \begin{array}{l} \text{index-name-1} \\ \text{identifier-1} \end{array} \right\} \left[, \left\{ \begin{array}{l} \text{index-name-2} \\ \text{identifier-2} \end{array} \right\} \right] \ldots \underline{TO} \left\{ \begin{array}{l} \text{index-name-3} \\ \text{identifier-3} \\ \text{literal} \end{array} \right\}$$

Option 2:

$$\underline{SET} \; \underline{\text{index-name-1}} \; [, \underline{\text{index-name-2}}] \ldots \left\{ \begin{array}{l} \underline{\text{UP BY}} \\ \underline{\text{DOWN}} \; \underline{BY} \end{array} \right\} \left\{ \begin{array}{l} \text{identifier} \\ \text{literal} \end{array} \right\}$$

The SET statement establishes reference points for table handling operations by setting index names to values with respect to table elements. Each object of a SET statement must be one of the following:

- an index name,

- an index data item described by a USAGE IS INDEX clause, or
- an elementary data item of integer value. However, in Option 2, identifier may not be an index data item.

Option 1, index-name-1 (and index-name-2, etc.) is set to a value which corresponds to the same occurrence number as that to which either index-name-3, identifier-3, or literal corresponds. No conversion takes place if identifier-3 is an index data item, or if index-name-3 is related to the same table as index-name-1.

Identifier-1 (and identifier-2, etc.), if specified, and if an index data item, may be set equal to either the contents of index-name-3 or identifier (if identifier-3 is also an index data item). Literal cannot be applied in this case.

If identifier-1 is not an index data item, it may be set only to an occurrence number corresponding to the value of index-name-3. Neither identifier-3 nor literal can be applied in this case.

In Option 2, the contents of index-name-1 (and index-name-2, etc.) are incremented (UP BY) or decremented (DOWN BY) by a value corresponding to the number of occurrences represented by the value of literal or identifier.

Examples:

SET IX-TABLE TO 3.

The index name IX-TABLE is set to an index value which corresponds to occurrence number 3 for that table. If IX-TABLE is not defined via an INDEXED BY clause this statement is illegal.

SET LOOKUP TO KEY-POINT

If LOOKUP is an index name, it is set to the occurrence number which corresponds to KEY-POINT. If KEY-POINT is an index name that is not related to the same table as LOOKUP, an appropriate conversion is performed; otherwise, no conversion takes place. If LOOKUP is an index data item, (i.e., defined by a USAGE IS INDEX clause) it is set to the actual contents of KEY-POINT. KEY-POINT must be either an index data item or an index name, or this statement is illegal. If LOOKUP is neither an index name nor an index data item, KEY-POINT must be an index name. LOOKUP is then set to the occurrence value to which index name KEY-POINT corresponds.

SET DEPT-INDEX UP BY KEY-JUMP

The index name DEPT-INDEX is incremented by a value that corresponds to the number of occurrences indicated by KEY-JUMP; i.e., if the value of KEY-JUMP is 3, DEPT-INDEX is incremented by a value that is equivalent to three occurrences.

COMPARISONS INVOLVING INDEX NAMES AND/OR INDEX DATA ITEMS

The comparison of two index names is the same as if the corresponding occurrence numbers were compared. Similarly, when an index name is compared with a data item (other than an index data item) or literal, it is the same as if their corresponding occurrence numbers were compared. When a comparison between an index name and an index data item is made, the actual values are compared without conversion. Any other comparison involving an index data item is invalid and will cause unpredictable results.

Chapter 11

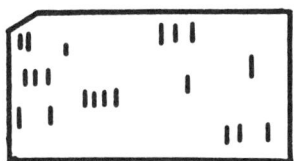

Sorting

Like any other file, the sort file is a set of records. It is described in the Data Division by means of a special type of file description called a Sort File Description. The sort file is an internally contained, intermediate representation of the file, which follows the initial input of unsorted records and precedes the final output of sorted records.

SORT OPERATION

In general, a SORT operation proceeds as follows:

1. Control passes to a SORT statement. The SORT statement specifies:

    a. the sort file to be created

    b. the keys on which the records are to be sorted and

    c. the input and output procedures or names the source of the unsorted input records and those files which are to receive the sorted output records.

2. The input procedure, if named in the SORT statement, is executed. If no input procedure is specified, the USING option of the SORT statement must be used to name the input file. The effect of either option is to make input records available to the SORT operation.

3. The records are sorted in accordance with the keys specified in the KEY clause of the SORT statement.

4. In this phase of the operation, the sorted records are moved from the sort file to the output file. This can be accomplished in either of two ways:

    a. By the output procedure, if one is named in the SORT statement. Control is passed to this procedure by the SORT statement.

        or

    b. If no output procedure is named, the GIVING option of the SORT statement must be used to specify the output file.

5. The operation of the SORT statement terminates and control passes to the next statement in sequence.

INPUT AND OUTPUT PROCEDURES

Whenever an input or output procedure is in control, all control transfers (by ALTER, GO TO, or PERFORM statements) occurring within these procedures must refer to procedures contained within that input or output procedure. Conversely, control cannot be transferred into an input or output procedure from points outside the physical limits of the given input or output procedure. Neither the input nor the output procedure may contain a SORT statement.

TYPES OF SORT PROGRAMS

There are two types of sort programs:

● Basic-In a basic SORT program the Procedure Division contains one SORT statement and a STOP RUN statement in the first nondeclaratives section. Other sections consist exclusively of input and output procedures.

● Extended-An extended SORT program may contain more than one SORT statement. These SORT statements can be located anywhere in the Procedure Division except in the DECLARATIVES section or in the input and output procedures identified within a SORT statement.

When control passes to the SORT statement the SORT operation is completely automatic, affected only by the KEY parameters and the file or record parameters contained in the SORT statement. The input and output procedures may contain any necessary statements for special processing procedures that will add, delete, select, alter, or otherwise modify records.

Special procedures in the input procedure may be used to modify key parameters. Such modifications will occur prior to the actual sort, and can be made to affect the final sequence of the records in the output file, following the SORT operation. Record modifications in the output procedures will appear in the sorted output but do not affect the final sequence.

PROGRAMMING CONSIDERATIONS

The remainder of this chapter discusses the specific formats in the COBOL language used in writing a source program which includes a SORT operation. Formats in the Environment, Data, and Procedure Divisions are described.

The Environment Division

The COBOL SORT feature may require the use of the following additional facilities in the Environmental Division of a COBOL source program.

Option 1:

FILE-CONTROL. {SELECT file-name}

ASSIGN TO [integer] implementor-name-1
[, implementor-name-2] . . .} . . .

Option 2:
FILE-CONTROL. {SELECT file-name ASSIGN TO implementor-name-1
  [, implementor-name-2] . . . OR implementor-name-3
  [, implementor-name-6]
  [FOR MULTIPLE REEL] .} . . .

Options 1 and 2 are similar to the FILE-CONTROL paragraph shown and discussed in a previous chapter of this book. This information will not be repeated here. Option 1 must be specified for sort files described in the Data Division. Option 2 must be used when the GIVING option of the SORT statement is specified. When sorting, the programmer cannot reserve alternate areas in memory.

In Option 1, the sort file will appear on each hardware device specified by implementor-name-1, implementor-name-2, etc. The OR clause in Option 2 enables the programmer to specify several alternate hardware devices and the sort file will appear on only one of the designated hardware devices. After the SORT operation is completed, the COBOL SORT feature provides an indication as to which hardware device contains the sort file. The hardware device containing the sort file is automatically addressed when this file is OPENed for input.

I-O-Control

The basic format of the I-O-CONTROL paragraph is shown and discussed in a previous chapter of this book. Note that only in sorting is it permissible to specify a sort-file-name as the object of a RERUN or MULTIPLE FILE clause. The use of the SAME AREA clause in connection with a sort file is discussed below.

$$\left[\text{SAME} \left\{ \begin{array}{l} \text{RECORD} \\ \text{SORT} \end{array} \right\} \text{AREA FOR file-name-1} \{, \text{file-name-2}\} \ldots \right] \ldots$$

The SAME AREA clause names two or more files that are to share the same main storage area. If the RECORDS option is selected, then:

• All specified files can be open during any phase of the SORT operation.

• All specified files, including sort files, share the same record area.

• This record area may contain only one logical record at any one time, and this record is the record currently being processed. It is the programmer's responsibility to determine which record of which file is in the record area at any point in the program.

If the SORT option is selected, then:

• All specified sort files share the same buffer storage area.

• Only the sort files associated with the particular phase (input procedure, sort, or output procedure) of a SORT operation can be open during the execution of that particular phase. It is the programmer's responsibility to make certain that only the sort files named in this clause are open and that all other files are closed.

● Those specified files, which are not sort files, do not share the same storage area as the sort files but will be assigned their own storage areas by the compiler.

If the RECORDS option is chosen, the action is similar to that described in the I-O-CONTROL paragraph discussion in a previous chapter of this book.

Assume that the SORT option is selected and that the SAME SORT AREA clause specifies four files, three of which are sort files (files A, B, and C) and the fourth file (file G) is a nonsort file. The diagram below illustrates the storage configuration that the compiler will set up in memory. (Figure 11-1.)

The storage area shared by the sort files is the area that will be used by the open sort file for storage. The FILE G area and any other area assigned to files not named in the SAME SORT AREA clause may also be allocated as needed for sorting the sort files named in the SAME SORT AREA clause. The extent of such allocation must be specified by the implementor.

The Data Division

The COBOL SORT feature requires the use of a special type of file description called a Sort File Description, the format and rules of which are explained below.

Option 1:

<u>SD</u> file-name <u>COPY</u> library-name

Option 2:

<u>SD</u> file-name

[; <u>RECORD</u> CONTAINS [integer-1 <u>TO</u>] integer-2 CHARACTERS]

[; DATA $\left\{ \begin{array}{l} \underline{\text{RECORD}} \text{ IS} \\ \underline{\text{RECORDS}} \text{ ARE} \end{array} \right\}$ data-name-1 [,data-name-2] . . .].

The Sort File Description furnishes information concerning the physical structure, identification, and record names of the file to be stored. Option 1 is used only when the COBOL library contains the full Sort File Description entry; otherwise Option 2 must be used. The level indicator SD must precede the file-name to identify the beginning of the Sort File Description entry. All semicolons shown are optional, although the entry must be terminated by a period. The clauses which comprise the Sort File Description entry also comprise a Standard File Description. Such clauses are optional except for the DATA RECORDS clause, and the order of their appearance is immaterial.

The Procedure Division

The COBOL sort feature makes use of three verbs in the Procedure Division, in addition to the verbs of the basic language; RELEASE, RETURN, and SORT.

RELEASE record-name [FROM identifier]

The RELEASE statement transfers the records from the input file to the initial phase of a SORT operation. One record is transferred each time a RELEASE statement is executed. RELEASE may be used only within the range of an input procedure associated with a SORT statement. This SORT statement must refer to a sort file whose DATA RECORD clause contains the same record-name as the RELEASE statement. The record must be read into memory before it can be released to the SORT program.

Record name and identifier must not be the same storage area in memory. The contents of identifier are moved to record name, then the contents of record name are released to the sort file. After the transfer, information in the record area is no longer available, but information in the data area associated with identifier is available. Moving is effected by the same rules as govern the MOVE statement without the CORRESPONDING option. After the RELEASE statement is executed, the contents of record name are no longer available. When control passes from the input procedure, the sort file contains all the records placed in the sort file by the RELEASE statements.

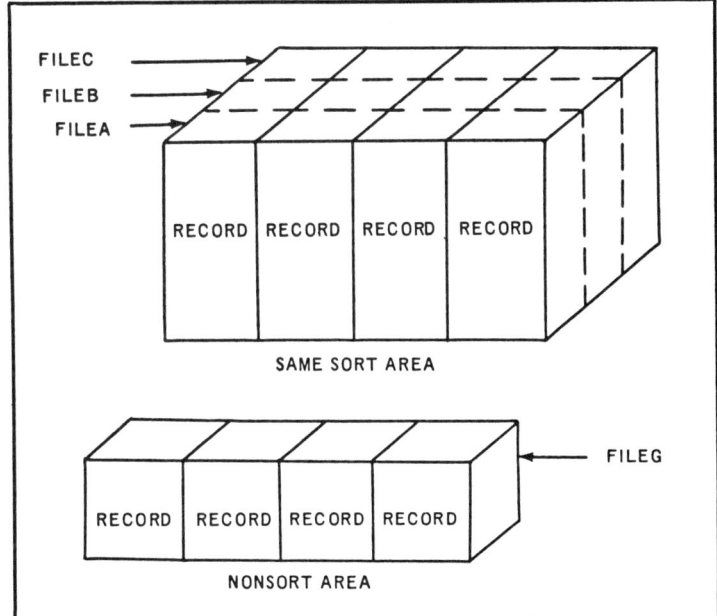

Fig. 11-1. Sort file areas being shared.

<u>RETURN</u> file-name RECORD [<u>INTO</u> identifier]
; AT <u>END</u> imperative-statement

The RETURN statement is a request for the next ordered record from a sort file. It may appear only within an output procedure associated with a SORT statement for file-name, (i.e., file name must be a sort file described by an SD entry).

The execution of the RETURN statement causes the next record, in the order specified by keys listed in the SORT statement, to be made available for processing. The record is located in the record area associated with the sort file. When a file consists of more than one type of logical record, the shared storage area is implicitly redefined for each record and only the information present in the current record is accessible.

When the INTO option is used, the data record is available in both the input record area and the data area associated with identifier. This option may be used only when the input file contains just one type of record. Identifier and the record area associated with the file must not be the same storage area in memory. Moving is effected according to the rules governing the MOVE statement without the CORRESPONDING option. When the SORT key indicates the end of the sort file, the imperative statement in the AT END phrase is executed. After this, no RETURN statements may be executed within the current output procedure.

<u>SORT</u> file-name-1 ON $\left\{ \dfrac{\underline{DESCENDING}}{\underline{ASCENDING}} \right\}$ KEY $\{$identifier$\}$ ...

[; ON $\left\{ \dfrac{\underline{DESCENDING}}{\underline{ASCENDING}} \right\}$ KEY $\{$identifier-2$\}$ ...] ...

$\left\{ \dfrac{\underline{INPUT} \ \underline{PROCEDURE} \ IS \ \underline{section\text{-}name\text{-}1} \ [\underline{THRU} \ \underline{section\text{-}name\text{-}2}]}{\underline{USING} \ file\text{-}name\text{-}2.} \right\}$

$\left\{ \dfrac{\underline{OUTPUT} \ \underline{PROCEDURE} \ IS \ \underline{section\text{-}name\text{-}3} \ [\underline{THRU} \ \underline{section\text{-}name\text{-}4}]}{\underline{GIVING} \ file\text{-}name\text{-}3.} \right\}$

The SORT statement creates the sort file in a three-phase operation:

- Phase 1-Executes an input procedure or transfers the unsorted records directly from another file (by means of USING option).
- Phase 2-Sorts the records in accordance with specified keys.
- Phase 3-Executes output procedure or transfers sorted records directly to an output file (by means of GIVING option).

File-name-1 must be a sort file described by a Sort File Description in the Data Division, and each KEY identifier must be a data item described in records associated with file-name-1.

Section-name-1 is the name of an input procedure, and section-name-3 is the name of an output procedure. File-name-2 and file-name-3 must be described by a File Description (not a Sort File Description) in the Data Division.

Upon encountering a SORT statement specifying input and output procedures, by means of the USING/GIVING options, the compiler automatically inserts the control mechanisms needed to execute the three phases of a SORT operation, and to pass control to the statement following the SORT statement after the SORT operation is completed.

Each input and output procedure must consist of one or more consecutively written sections, no part of which can be common to both procedures. The input procedure must include at least one RELEASE statement in order to transfer records to the sort file. The output procedure must include at least one RETURN statement to transfer sorted records to the output file. Control must not be passed on to an input procedure or to an output procedure except by a SORT statement because RELEASE and RETURN statements have no meaning unless controlled by a SORT statement.

Input and output procedures may consist of any procedures needed to select, modify, create, or copy records. Three restrictions must be observed in writing the procedural statements that comprise such procedures:

- No SORT statement may be written as part of an input or output procedure.
- Neither an input nor an output procedure may contain any transfer of control (by means of ALTER, GO TO, and PERFORM statements) to points outside the procedure.

Sort sequence depends on the use of the ASCENDING or DESCENDING option:

- When ASCENDING is used, the sort sequence is from the lowest value of the key to the highest value according to the ordered character set specified by the implementor.
- When DESCENDING is used, the sort sequence is from the highest value of the key to the lowest value.

The record description for every record listed in the DATA RECORDS clause of the sort file must contain the KEY items identifier-1, identifier-2, etc. The following rules apply to KEY items:

- They may not be variable length items.
- When a KEY item appears in more than one record, the relevant data descriptions must be equivalent in each record.
- The KEY item must be the same number of character positions from the beginning of each record.
- They may neither contain an OCCURS clause nor be subordinate to entries that contain an OCCURS clause.

If the USING option is specified, all the records in file-name-2 are transferred automatically to file-name-1. File-name-2 must not be open since the SORT statement automatically performs the necessary OPEN, READ, USE and CLOSE functions for file-name-2.

If the GIVING option is specified, all the sorted records in file-name-1 are automatically transferred to file-name-3 as the implied output procedure for this SORT statement. When the SORT statement is executed, file-name-3 must not be open. The SORT statement automatically opens file-name-3 before transferring the records and automatically closes the file after the transfer is completed.

EXAMPLES OF A SORT PROGRAM

The two examples which follow illustrate the two basic organizational approaches that may be adopted by the programmer in writing a SORT program in COBOL. Only those functions that are necessary for illustrating the COBOL SORT feature are shown.

Example 1:
ENVIRONMENT DIVISION.
.
.
.
INPUT-OUTPUT SECTION.
FILE-CONTROL.
    SELECT TO-BE-SORTED ASSIGN TO MAG-TAPE-D.
    SELECT AFTER-THE-SORT ASSIGN TO MAG-TAPE-E.
    SELECT WORK-ING ASSIGN TO MAG-TAPE-A, B, C.
    SELECT FOR-THE-PRINTER ASSIGN TO PRINTER.
.
.
.
DATA DIVISION.
FILE SECTION.
FD TO-BE-SORTED . . . DATA RECORD IS A-FILE
    RECORD CONTAINS 80 CHARACTERS.
01   A-FILE.
    02   1-ACCOUNT PICTURE IS X(4).
    02   1-TYPE PICTURE IS X.
    02   1-AREA PICTURE IS XXX.
.
.
.
FD AFTER-THE-SORT . . . DATA RECORD IS A B-FILE
    RECORD CONTAINS 80 CHARACTERS.
01   B-FILE PICTURE IS X(80).
.
.
.

```
       SD WORK-ING FILE . . . DATA RECORD IS C-FILE
       01   C-FILE.
              02   3-ACCOUNT PICTURE IS X(4).
              02   3-TYPE PICTURE IS X.
              02   3-AREA PICTURE IS XXX.
       FD FOR-THE-PRINTER . . . DATA RECORD IS D-FILE.
       01   D-FILE PICTURE IS X(80).
       PROCEDURE DIVISION.
       OPENING.
              OPEN INPUT TO-BE-SORTED.
              OPEN OUTPUT AFTER-THE-SORT FOR-THE-PRINTER.
       A-SORT SECTION.
              SORT WORK-ING ON ASCENDING KEY 3-ACCOUNT 3-TYPE
              3-AREA.
              INPUT PROCEDURE IS B-SORT THRU B1-SORT.
              OUTPUT PROCEDURE IS C-SORT THRU C1-SORT.
              GO TO OK-PRINT.
       B-SORT SECTION
              READ TO-BE-SORTED AT END GO TO B1-SORT
              RELEASE C-FILE FROM A-FILE.
              GO TO B-SORT.
       B1-SORT SECTION.
              CLOSE TO-BE-SORTED.
       C-SORT SECTION.
              RETURN WORK-ING RECORD INTO B-FILE AT END GO TO
              C1-SORT.
              WRITE B-FILE
              GO TO C-SORT.
       C1-SORT SECTION.
              CLOSE AFTER-THE-SORT.
       OK-PRINT SECTION.
              OPEN INPUT AFTER-THE-SORT.
       A-LOOP.
              READ AFTER-THE-SORT AT END GO TO A-1-MOVE.
              MOVE SPACES TO D-FILE.
              PERFORM A-MOVE.
              WRITE D-FILE.
              GO TO A-LOOP.
       A-MOVE.
              MOVE B-FILE TO D-FILE.
       A-1-MOVE.
              EXIT.
       ALL-DONE SECTION.
              CLOSE AFTER-THE-SORT FOR-THE-PRINTER.
              STOP RUN.
```

In the preceding example, the files defined by FD entries are opened before the SORT statement is executed. The SORT statement sets the sorting mechanism in motion by transferring control to the INPUT PROCEDURE. The files can be opened within the INPUT PROCEDURE, but of course the programmer must take care that he does not attempt to OPEN the input file more than once or CLOSE the input file before input is completed.

Sorting is conducted on an ASCENDING KEY. Note that the KEY elements are in the sort file WORK-ING, not the input file TO-BE-SORTED. The INPUT PROCEDURE is completed when the entire input file has been transferred to the sort file. The mechanism then transfers control to the OUTPUT procedure, and records are written on the file AFTER-THE-SORT in the order specified by the KEY parameters. The sorted records are then listed after the SORT function has been accomplished.

Example 2:

.
.
.

DATA DIVISION.
FILE SECTION.
FD TO-BE-SORTED . . . RECORD CONTAINS 80 CHARACTERS.
    DATA RECORD IS A-FILE.
01 A-FILE
    02 1-ACCT PICTURE IS X(4).
    02 1-DEPT PICTURE IS X(4).
    02 1-BODY PICTURE IS X(72).
FD AFTER-THE-SORT RECORD CONTAINS 80 CHARACTERS.
    . . . DATA RECORD IS B-FILE.
01 B-FILE.
    02 2-ACCT PICTURE IS X(4).
    02 2-DEPT PICTURE IS X(4).
    02 2-BODY PICTURE IS X(72).
SD WORK-ING FILE . . . DATA RECORD IS C-FILE.
01 C-FILE.
    02 3-ACCT PICTURE IS X(4).
    02 3-DEPT PICTURE IS X(4).
    02 3-BODY PICTURE IS X(72).
FD FOR-THE-PRINTER . . . DATA RECORD IS D-FILE.
01 D-FILE.
    02 4-ACCT PICTURE IS X(4).
    02 4-DEPT PICTURE IS X(4).
    02 4-BODY PICTURE IS X(72).

.
.
.

```
PROCEDURE DIVISION.
OPENING.
    OPEN OUTPUT FOR-THE-PRINTER.
A-SORT SECTION.
    SORT WORK-ING ON ASCENDING KEY.
    3-ACCT   3-DEPT.
    USING TO-BE-SORTED GIVING AFTER-THE-SORT.
OK-PRINT SECTION.
    OPEN INPUT AFTER-THE-SORT.
A-LOOP.
    READ AFTER-THE-SORT AT END GO TO A-1-MOVE.
    MOVE SPACES TO D-FILE.
    PERFORM A-MOVE.
    WRITE D-FILE.
    GO TO A-LOOP.
A-MOVE.
    MOVE B-FILE TO D-FILE.
A-1-MOVE.
    EXIT.
ALL-DONE SECTION.
    CLOSE AFTER-SORT FOR-THE-PRINTER.
    STOP RUN.
```

In this second example, the files that are directly involved in the sort must not be open at the time the SORT statement is encountered. This is because the USING and GIVING options perform the functions of the INPUT PROCEDURE and OUTPUT PROCEDURE (i.e., OPEN, READ RELEASE, RETURN, USE, WRITE, and CLOSE) automatically. Although the use of the GIVING and USING options requires a minimum amount of coding, it is not possible to add, delete, or modify individual records of the sort file in any way (i.e., no special processing procedures may be incorporated into a SORT function when this technique is adopted).

Chapter 12

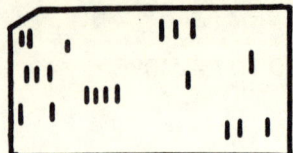

Mass Storage

The terms mass storage, random access, and direct access refer to storage devices capable of accessing data directly by reference to a physical location on the device, as opposed to devices such as magnetic tape which require time to scan sequentially located records until the desired record is reached.

The Mass Storage feature (Random Access module) of COBOL is provided to permit utilization of the non-sequential file organization and random access capability of the direct access device.

FILE HANDLING

The COBOL Mass Storage feature provides two techniques for handling files:

- Sequential access with sequential processing
- Random access with sequential processing

When sequential access with sequential processing is used, the logical records of a file are accessed sequentially in the order in which they were created and processed in that same order (sequentially). This technique is implemented by the COBOL language primarily for use with tape, printer, and card devices, but may also be used with mass storage devices. However, there is a substantial difference between file processing on non-mass storage and mass storage devices.

During processing, a magnetic tape file is either an input file or an output file; it cannot be both at the same time. After a record is read from tape, the reel is automatically in proper position for the next sequential READ. Any writing on tape that may occur before the reading of the next record can only be done on another (output) file. The contents of an input file remain unchanged by a READ.

In contrast, a mass storage file may be used for both input and output. A read operation may be performed on the same physical file as a write operation. The usual technique for updating a mass storage file is to read a record, process it, and then overwrite the original record with the updated version.

The actual location of a mass storage record is specified by an actual key similar to the ACTUAL KEY clause used in random access/sequential processing however, the actual key is updated solely by the operation system to permit access of subsequent records. Therefore, the programmer does not write the ACTUAL KEY clause when sequential access is used.

The imperative statement in the AT END phrase associated with the next READ statement in order of execution is executed when the logical end of the mass storage file is detected. For WRITE statements, the detection of the logical end of a mass storage file before the execution of the CLOSE statement causes the actual key to contain an address outside the logical limits of the file. As this value represents an erroneous location in the file, the INVALID KEY path associated with a particular WRITE statement is executed when that verb is executed.

With the Random Access technique, records are accessed in the order specified by the programmer in the ACTUAL KEY clause and processed sequentially (in the order in which they were accessed). The function of location the data record in the file for subsequent reading or writing is accomplished by the SEEK statement. The SEEK statement is performed implicitly by a READ or WRITE if no immediately preceding SEEK has been executed, or if the SEEK and READ or WRITE refer to different records. The contents of the ACTUAL KEY are used by the compiler as the desired record's location identifier at the time of execution of the explicit of implicit SEEK statement.

Other procedural statements may be executed during the physical seeking operation if they have been written between the SEEK statement and the READ or WRITE statement for a particular file. The READ or WRITE of a particular record of a file cannot be executed until an explicit or implicit seek operation has been completed.

Until a READ statement is executed, any references to data items within the record description of the record being sought will refer to the contents of the last record obtained from the file. Therefore, if the program is written to take advantage of the ability to execute statements during the seek operation, this internal lag of one record must be taken into account by the programmer.

When random access is specified for a mass storage file, there is no logical end to the file. Thus, the INVALID KEY phrase must be specified for both the READ and WRITE statements. If, during execution of either a READ or a WRITE statement, the ACTUAL KEY points to a location outside the logical limits for a file, the imperative statement in the INVALID KEY phrase is executed.

File Organization

The manner in which files are organized is usually a function of the individual mass storage system. The programmer need only select the access mode. However, since a general knowledge of file organization may prove helpful to the programmer, the following discussion is given.

Various types of file organization are possible for direct access devices. Since file organization can vary considerably with the individual implementation, only a general description of a few types can be given here. Before discussing individual methods, it is important to distinguish between a physical record and a logical record.

A COBOL logical record is a group of related information, uniquely identifiable, and treated as a unit. In a COBOL program, an input or output statement refers to one logical record. A logical record may be contained within a single physical unit, or several logical records may be contained within a single physical unit, or a logical record may require more than one physical unit to contain it. The ACTUAL KEY refers to the physical location of a logical record in mass storage unit.

A physical record is a physical unit (or block) of information. Its size and recording mode are convenient to a particular computer for the storage of data on an input or output device. The size of a physical record is hardware-dependent and bears no direct relationship to the size of the file of information contained on a device.

There are three types of data organization; sequential, relative, and direct. When sequential organization is used, the logical records of a file are written sequentially (physically contiguous) in the order in which they are created. Readback is also sequential, that is, before a particular logical record can be accessed, all its predecessors must be read. This type of data organization is normally used for tape and card files, but can also be used for mass storage files.

Relative data organization uses relative logical record addressing. When this addressing scheme is used, the position of the logical records in a file is determined relative to the first record of the field. The maximum record number is defined by the size of the file. A unique key (relative record address) identifies a record, enabling the user to access records in any sequence.

Files with relative data organization must be assigned to direct access devices. Note that entries in this type of file consist entirely of data. No record identification entries are required for system recognition, thereby giving the user access to the contents of the entire file. Two levels of classification are required with this type of organization in order to access a particular record; file name, and record.

Direct data organization is characterized by use of relative physical record (block) addressing. With this method, the location of each logical record in a file is determined by keys supplied by the programmer. These keys specify two things:

- the block (relative to the first block of the file) at which the search is to begin
- the record sought

Record is the minor classification of data within a Block and contains both data and record identification information. Block and record identification information are for system use only and are not available to the programmer.

This type of organization permits the use of both fixed and variable length records and/or blocks. However, it requires three levels of classification; file name, block, and record. Files with direct data organization must be assigned to direct access devices.

Glossary

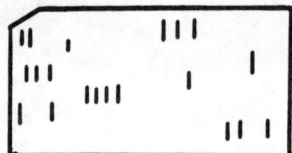

COBOL

access random—(1) Pertaining to the process of obtaining information from or placing information into storage where the time required for such access is independent of the location of the information most recently obtained or placed in storage; (2) pertaining to a device in which random access, as defined in definition 1, can be achieved without effective penalty in time.

access, sequential—An access mode in which any logical record in a file (except the first record) can be accessed only after its logical predecessor has been accessed. The first access to a file after an OPEN statement makes the first logical record in that file available.

actual decimal point—*See* decimal point, actual.

actual key—*See* key, actual.

alphabetic character—*See* character, alphabetic.

alphanumeric character—*See* character, alphanumeric.

area, saved—A storage area, specified in the Data Division, that is composed of one or more data records.

area name—A data name that names a saved area.

arithmetic expression—*See* expression, arithmetic.

arithmetic expression character—*See* operator, arithmetic.

arithmetic operator—*See* operator, arithmetic.

ascending key—*See* key, ascending.

assumed decimal point—*See* decimal point, assumed.

asynchronous control system—*See* control system, asynchronous.

asynchronous processing—*See* processing, asynchronous.

block—(1) A group of computer words considered as a unit by virtue of their being stored in successive storage locations. (2) The set of locations or tape positions in which a block of words, as defined above, is stored or recorded. (3) A circuit assemblage which functions as a unit; e.g., a circuit building block of standard design, and the logic block in a sequential circuit.

character, numeric—A character from the set: 0 1 2 3 4 5 6 7 8 9.
character, punctuation—A character from the set:

Character	Meaning
,	comma
;	semicolon
.	period
"	quotation mark
(	left parenthesis
)	right parenthesis
	space

character, relation—A character from the set:

Character	Meaning
>	greater than
<	less than
=	equal

character, special—A character from the set:

Character	Meaning
+	plus
−	minus
*	asterisk
/	stroke (virgule, slash)
=	equal to
$	currency sign
,	comma (decimal point)
;	semicolon
.	period (decimal point)
"	quotation mark
(	left parenthesis
)	right parenthesis
>	greater than
<	less than

character, set—An agreed set of representations, called characters from which selections are made to denote and distinguish data. Each character differs from all others, and the total number of characters in a given set is fixed; e.g., a set may include the numerals 0 to 9, the letters A to Z, punctuation marks and a blank or space. Clarified by alphabet.

character string—Contiguous characters that form a literal, a word, a PICTURE in the Data Division, or a NOTE in the Procedure Division.

characters, standard—A character string that comprises a data item whose size is measured in accordance with standard data format.

class condition—*See* condition, class.

clause—An ordered set of COBOL words that specifies an attribute of an entry.

clause, data—A clause within a data description entry in the Data Division that describes an attribute of a data item.

clause, environment—A clause within an Environment Division entry.

clause, file—A clause within any of the following Data Division entries:

File Description	(FD)
Sort File Description	(SD)
Report Description	(RD)

character—(1) One symbol of a set of elementary symbols such as those corresponding to the keys on a typewriter. The symbols usually include the decimal digits 0 through 9, the letters A through Z, punctuation marks, operation symbols, and any other single symbols which a computer may read, store, or write. (2) The electrical, magnetic, or mechanical profile used to represent a character in a computer, and its various storage and peripheral devices. A character may be represented by a group of other elementary marks, such as bits or pulses.

character, alphabetic—A character from the set: A through Z, and the space.

character, alphanumeric—Any character in the computer's character set.

character, arithmetic expression—*See* operator, arithmetic.

character, editing—A single character or a fixed two-character combination belonging to the set:

Character	Meaning
B	space
0	zero
+	plus
−	minus
CR	credit
DB	debit
Z	zero suppress
*	check protect
$	currency sign
,	comma (decimal point)
.	period (decimal point)

COBOL object program—*See* object program, COBOL.

COBOL source program—*See* source program, COBOL.

collating sequence—*See* sequence, collating.

column—(1) A character or digit position in a positional information format, particularly one in which characters appear in rows, and the rows are placed one above another; e.g., the rightmost column in a five decimal place table, or in a list of data. (2) A character or digit position in a physical device, such as punch card or a register, corresponding to a position in a written table or list; e.g., the rightmost place in a register; or the third column in an eighty column punch card.

comment—An expression which explains or identifies a particular step in a routine, but which has no effect on the operation of the computer in performing the instructions for the routine.

compile time—*See* time, compile.

compiler directing statement—*See* statement, compiler directing.

condition—The status of one or more variables or statements within a program for which a truth value can be determined; a simple condition, or a syntactically correct combination of simple conditions and logical operators, for which a truth value can be determined.

condition, class—The proposition, for which a truth value can be determined, that the content of an item is wholly alphabetic or is wholly numeric.

condition, condition name—The proposition, for which a truth value can be determined, that the value of a conditional variable is a member of the set of values attributed to a condition name associated with the conditional variable.

condition, invalid key—A condition at object time where the value of the actual key associated with a mass storage file is determined to lie outside the limits of the file being accessed.

condition, relation—The proposition, for which a truth value can be determined, that the value of an arithmetic expression or data item has a specific relationship to the value of another arithmetic expression or data item. See operator, relational.

condition, sign—The proposition, for which a truth value can be determined, that the algebraic value of a data item or an arithmetic expression is either less than, greater than, or equal to zero.

condition, simple—Any condition from the set:

> relation condition
> class condition
> condition-name condition
> switch status condition
> sign condition
> NOT condition

condition, switch status—The proposition, for which a truth value can be determined, that a hardware switch has been set to a specific status (ON or OFF).

conditional statement—*See* statement, conditional.

conditional variable—*See* variable, conditional.

condition name—The data name assigned to a value, set of values, or range of values, within the complete set of values that a conditional variable may possess, or the name assigned to a status of a hardware device.

condition name condition—*See* condition, condition name.

CONFIGURATION SECTION—*See* section, configuration.

connective—A word, or a punctuation character that:
  (a) associates a data name or a paragraph-name with its qualifier;
  (b) links two or more operands written in a series; or
  (c) forms conditional expressions (logical connectives). See operator, logical.
constant, figurative—A reserved word that represents a numeric value, a character, or a string of characters.
constant, literal—*See* literal.
contiguous items—*See* items, contiguous.
control break—The recognition of a change in the contents of a control data item resulting in specific actions taken in respect to presentation of a report group.
control data item—The item of data, one or more of which is used to identify, select, execute or modify another routine, record, file, operation or data value.
control footing—*See* footing, control.
control group—*See* group control.
control heading—*See* heading, control.
control hierarchy—A designated order of control data items.
control system, asynchronous—An operating system that directs or schedules the execution of asynchronous processing cycles.
control system, mass storage—An input/output control system that directs or schedules the processing of mass storage files.
counter—A device, register, or location in storage for storing numbers or number representations in a manner which permits these numbers to be increased or decreased by the value of another number, or to be changed or reset to zero or to an arbitrary value.
cycle, processing—*See* processing cycle.

data clause—*See* clause, data.
Data description entry—See entry, data description.
Data item—Any elementary item, a named group of elementary items within a record, or a record.
data item, index—A data item in which the value associated with an index name can be stored in a form specified by the implementor.
data name—A word that names an entry in the Data Division. It must contain at least one alphabetic character. When used in the general formats (options), data name represents a word which can neither be subscripted, indexed, nor qualified unless specifically permitted by the rules for that option.
data name, indexed—An identifier composed of a data name followed by one or more index names enclosed in parentheses.
Data name, qualified—An identifier composed of a data name followed by one or more sets of either of the connectives OF and IN followed by a data name qualifier.

data name, subscripted—An identifier composed of a data name followed by one or more subscripts enclosed in parentheses.

decimal point, actual—The physical representation of the decimal point position in a data item using either of the decimal point characters, period (.) or comma (,).

decimal point, assumed—A decimal point position which does not exist as an actual character in a data item. Rather, it is an assumed decimal point which has logical meaning but no physical representation.

declaratives—A set of one or more special purpose sections, written at the beginning of the Procedure Division, the first of which is preceded by the header DECLARATIVES and the last of which is followed by the header END DECLARATIVES. Each declarative operates under the control of either the inline procedure, the implementor's input/output system, or the Report Writer. It is composed of a section header, followed by a COPY or a USE compiler directing sentence, followed by a set of one or more associated paragraphs.

descending key—*See* key, descending.

division—One or more sections or paragraphs formed and combined in accordance with a specific set of rules. There are four divisions in a COBOL program:
  IDENTIFICATION
  ENVIRONMENT
  DATA
  PROCEDURE

division header—*See* header, division.

editing character—*See* character, editing.

element, table—A data item within the set of repeated items comprising a table.

elementary item—*See* item, elementary.

end of procedure division—The physical position in a source program after which no further procedures appear.

entry—(1) A statement in a programming system, in general each entry is written on one line of a coding form and punched on one card, although some systems permit a single entry to overflow several cards. (2) A member of a list.

entry, data description—An entry in the Data Division that contains a level number and a data name (if required) followed by a set of data clauses.

entry, file description—An entry in the file Section of the Data Division that contains the level indicator FD, followed by a file name, followed by a set of file clauses.

entry, object of—A set of operands and reserved words, in a Data Division entry, that immediately follows the subject of the entry.

entry, report description—An entry in the Report Section of the Data Division that contains the level indicator RD, followed by a report name (if required) followed by a set of report clauses as required.

entry, saved area description—An entry in the File Section of the Data Division that contains the level indicator SA, followed by a set of file clauses as required.

entry, sort file description—An entry in the File Section of the Data Division composed of the level indicator SD, followed by a file-name, followed by a set of file clauses as required.

entry, subject of—An operand or reserved word immediately following the level indicator or the level number in a Data Division entry.

environment clause—*See* clause, environment.

execution time—*See* time, object.

expression, arithmetic—An identifier of a numeric elementary item, a numeric literal, such identifiers and literals separated by binary arithmetic operators, an arithmetic expression in parentheses, or an arithmetic expression preceded by the unary arithmetic operator.

figurative constant—*See* constant, figurative.

file—An organized collection of information directed toward some purpose. The records in a file may or may not be sequenced according to a key contained in each record.

file, mass storage—A file assigned to a mass storage medium.

file, report—An output file used by the Report Writer to present a report.

file, sort—A collection of records to be sorted by a SORT statement. The sort file is an intermediate, internal representation of an initial input of unsorted records that precedes the final output of sorted records.

file clause—*See* clause, file.

file description entry—See entry, file description.

file limit—A set of logical boundary locations for a mass storage file that are within the physical boundary locations of a mass storage medium.

FILE SECTION—*See* section, file.

FILE-CONTROL—The name of an Environmental Division paragraph in which data files for a given source program are declared.

file name—A word, containing at least one alphabetic character, that names a file described in the Data Division.

footing, control—A report group that is produced at the end of the control group to which it belongs.

footing, page—A report group that is produced at or near the end of a report page upon encountering a page break.

footing, report—A report group that is produced at the end of a report; it is produced only when the report is terminated.

format—The predetermined arrangement of characters, fields, lines, page numbers, and punctuation marks, usually on a single sheet or in a file. This refers to input, output and files.

format, reference—A format that provides a standard method for describing COBOL source programs.

format, report—The format of a report defined in the Report Section and produced by the Report Writer.

format, standard data—The concept used to describe data in the Data Division. The characteristics of the data are expressed as they would appear on a printed page of infinite size.

group, control—A set of report groups produced for a given value of a control identifier. Each control group may begin with a control heading, end with a control footing, and contain detail report groups as well as control heading and control footing report groups.

group, footing—A report group defined as control footing, page footing, or report footing.

group, heading—A report group defined as control heading, report heading, or page heading.

group, print—*See* group, report.

group, report—The set of related data described by a report group description.

group item—*See* item, group.

header, division—COBOL words that indicate the beginning of a particular division. Division Headers are:
  IDENTIFICATION DIVISION.
  ENVIRONMENT DIVISION.
  DATA DIVISION.
  PROCEDURE DIVISION.

header, paragraph—A reserved word, immediately followed by a period, that identifiers and precedes each entry in the Identification and Environment Divisions. Permissible paragraph headers are:
  In the Identification Division:
    PROGRAM-ID.
    AUTHOR.
    INSTALLATION.
    DATE-WRITTEN.
    DATE-COMPILED.
    SECURITY.
    REMARKS.
  In the Environmental Division:
    SOURCE-COMPUTER.
    OBJECT-COMPUTER.
    SPECIAL-NAMES.
    FILE-CONTROL.
    I-O-CONTROL.

header, section—A combination of reserved words that identifies and precedes each section in the Environment, Data, and Procedure Divisions. Permissible section headers are:

In the Environment Division:
 CONFIGURATION SECTION
 INPUT-OUTPUT SECTION.
In the Data Division.
 FILE SECTION.
 WORKING-STORAGE SECTION
 REPORT SECTION
In the Procedure Division:
 DECLARATIVES.

The section header is composed of a section name, followed by the reserved word SECTION, followed by a priority number (optional), followed by a period.

heading, control—A report group that is produced at the beginning of a control group, if required, it is produced each time the control group is produced.

heading, page—A report group that is produced at the beginning of a report page, it is produced during page break execution.

heading, report—A report group that is produced at the beginning of a report, it is produced only once when the report is initiated.

high order end—The leftmost character of a string of characters.

identifier—A data name followed by a combination of qualifiers, subscripts, and indexes necessary to make unique reference to a data item.

imperative statement—*See* statement, imperative.

implementor name—A word, specified by the implementor, that refers to a particular feature available on that implementor's computing system.

index—A symbol or a number used to identify a particular quantity in an array of similar quantities; e.g., X5 is the fifth item in an array of X's.

index data item—*See* data item, index.

index name—A word with at least one alphabetic character, that names an index associated with a table.

indexed data name—*See* data name, indexed.

inline procedure—*See* procedure, inline.

input procedure—*See* procedure, input.

INPUT-OUTPUT SECTION—*See* section, input-output.

integer—A numeric literal or a numeric data item with no character positions to the right of the assumed decimal point. Where the term integer appears in general formats (options), integer must not be defined elsewhere in the program as a numeric data item, and must be unsigned.

invalid key condition—*See* condition, invalid key.

I-O-CONTROL—The name of an Environment Division paragraph in which object program requirements for rerun points, sharing of same

I-O-CONTROL—literal

areas by several data files, and multiple files storage on a single input-output device are specified.

item, elementary—A data item that is not further logically subdivided.

item, group—A named contiguous set of elementary or group items.

item, noncontiguous—A data item, in the Working-Storage Section, that bears no hierarchic relationship to other noncontiguous items.

item, nonnumeric—A data item whose description permits its contents to be composed of any combination of characters from the computer's character set. Certain categories of nonnumeric items may be formed from more restricted character sets.

item, numeric—A data item whose description restricts its contents to a value represented by characters chosen from the digits 0 through 9, with or without an operational sign.

items, contiguous—Data items that are described by consecutive entries in the Data Division, and that bear a definite hierarchic relationship to each other.

key—(1) A group of characters which identifies or is part of a record or item, thus any entry in a record or item can be used as a key for collating or sorting purposes. (2) A marked lever manually operated for copying a character; e.g., a typewriter, paper tape perforator, card punch, manual keyboard, digitizer or manual word generator. (3) A lever or switch on a computer console for the purpose of manually altering computer action.

key, actual—A key that directly expresses the physical location of a logical record on a mass storage medium.

key ascending—A key on which data is ordered starting with the lowest value of key up to the highest value of key.

key, descending—A key on which data is ordered starting with the highest value of key down to the lowest value of key.

key word—*See* word, key.

level indicator—Two alphabetic characters that identify a specific type of file or a position in a hierarchy.

level number—A number from the set 1 (or 01) to 49 used to indicate the hierarchical structure of a logical record, or one of the numbers 66, 77, or 88, used to identify special properties of a data description entry.

library name—A word that identifies a library entry which consists of a set of COBOL entries and/or procedures. The library name must conform to the rules for formation of a procedure name. The portion of the library name actually used to interact with the COBOL library is specified by the implementor.

line, report—A division of a page representing one row of characters.

literal—A string of characters whose value is that of the characters comprising the string.

literal, nonnumeric—A string of characters bounded by quotation marks. The string of characters may include any character in the computer's character set; with the exception of the quotation mark.

literal, numeric—A literal composed of one or more numeric characters that may contain either a decimal point (except as the rightmost character) or an algebraic sign (as the leftmost character), or both.

literal constant—*See* literal.

logical operator—*See* operator, logical.

logical record—*See* record, logical.

low order end—The rightmost character of a string of characters.

mass storage—A storage medium on which data may be organized and maintained for either sequential or random access modes.

mass storage control system—*See* control system, mass storage.

mass storage file—*See* file, mass storage.

mass storage file segment—A part of a mass storage file whose beginning and end are defined by the FILE-LIMITS clause in the Environment Division.

mnemonic name—A word, supplied by the programmer, that is associated in the Environment Division with a specific implementor name.

noncontiguous item—*See* item, noncontiguous.

nonnumeric item—*See* item, nonnumeric.

nonnumeric literal—*See* literal, nonnumeric.

numeric character—*See* character, numeric.

numeric item—*See* item, numeric.

numeric literal—*See* literal, numeric.

object of entry—*See* entry, object of.

object program—The program which is the output of an automatic coding system. Often the object program is a machine language program ready for execution, but it may well be in an intermediate language. Synonymous with (target program); (object routine) and contrasted with (program, source).

object time—*See* time, object. Also called run time.

OBJECT-COMPUTER—The name of an Environment Division paragraph in which the computer environment for object program execution is described.

operand—A quantity entering or arising in an instruction. An operand may be an argument, a result, a parameter, or an indication of the location of the next instruction, as opposed to the operation code or symbol itself. It may even be the address portion of an instruction.

operational sign—*See* sign, operational.

operator, arithmetic—A single character, or a fixed two character combination, that belongs to the set;

Binary Arithmetic Operators	Meaning
+	addition
−	subtraction
×	multiplication
/	division
**	exponentiation

Unary Arithmetic Operator	Meaning
−	same effect as if multiplied by numeric literal −1

operator, logical—One of the reserved words AND, OR, or NOT. In the formation of a condition, AND and OR are logical connectives. NOT is used for logical negation.

operator, relational—A reserved word, a relation character, a group of consecutive reserved words, or a group of consecutive reserved words and relation characters used in the construction of a relation condition. The permissible operators and their meaning are:

Relational Operator	Meaning
Is (Not) Greater Than	greater than or not
Is (Not)	greater than
Is (Not) Less Than	less than or not
Is Not	less than
Is (Not) Equal to	equal to or not
Is (Not) =	equal to

operator, unary—*See* operator, arithmetic.
optional word—*See* word, optional.
out-of-line procedure—*See* procedure, out-of-line.
output procedure—*See* procedure, output.

page—A vertical division of a report representing a physical separation of report data, the separation being based on internal reporting requirements and/or external characteristics of the reporting medium.
page footing—*See* footing, page.
page heading—*See* heading, page.

paragraph—A paragraph name (in the Procedure Division) followed by one or more sentences, or a paragraph header (in the Identification or Environment Divisions) followed by one or more entries.

paragraph header—*See* header, paragraph.

paragraph-name—A word that identifies and begins a paragraph in the Procedure Division.

physical record—*See* block.

print group—*See* group, report.

priority number—A number, ranging in value from 0 to 99, that classifies a source program section in the Procedure Division, to guide object program segmentation.

procedure—A precise step-by-step method for effecting a solution to a problem.

procedure, inline—The set of statements that constitutes the main or controlling flow of the program, excluding statements executed under control of the asynchronous control system.

procedure, output—A set of statements executed each time a sorted record is returned from the sort file.

procedure name—A word used to refer to a paragraph or section in the source program in which it occurs. It may be a paragraph name (which may be qualified) or a section name.

processing, asynchronous—The processing of logical records within inline procedures in the order in which the records are made available.

processing cycle—A single execution of a defined out-of-line procedure.

program name—A word that identifies a COBOL source program.

punctuation character—*See* character, punctuation.

qualified data name—*See* data name, qualified.

qualifier—A data name appended to a nonunique data name or a section name appended to a nonunique paragraph name, for the purpose of making the nonunique data-name or paragraph name unique.

random access—*See* access, random.

record—(1) A group of related facts or fields of information treated as a unit, thus a listing of information, usually in printed or printable form: (2) to put data into a storage device.

record, logical—A group of related information, uniquely identifiable, and treated as a unit.

record, physical—*See* block.

record description—The total set of data description entries associated with a particular record.

record name—A data name that names a record.

reference format—*See* format, reference.

registers, special—Compiler generated storage areas, the primary use of which is to store information produced in conjunction with the use of specific COBOL features.
relation—*See* operator, relational.
relation character—*See* character, relation.
relation condition—*See* condition, relation.
relational operator—*See* operator, relational.
report—A presentation of a set of data described in a report file.
report description entry—*See* entry, report description.
report file—*See* file, report.
report footing—*See* footing, report.
report format—*See* format, report.
report group—*See* group, report.
report heading—*See* heading, report.
report line—*See* section, report.
report name—A data name that names a report.
REPORT SECTION—*See* section, report.
reserved word—*See* word, reserved.

saved area—*See* area, saved.
saved area description entry—*See* entry, saved area description.
section—A set of one or more paragraphs or entries, the first of which is preceded by a section header.
section, configuration—A section of the Environment Division that describes overall specifications of source and object computers.
section, file—A section of the Data Division that contains file description entries.
section, input-output—The section of the Environment Division that names the files and external media required by an object program, and provides information required for transmission and handling of data during execution of the object program.
section, report—The section of the Data Division that contains one or more report description entries.
section, working storage—The section of the Data Division that describes working storage data items, composed either of noncontiguous items or of working-storage records or of both.
section header—*See* header, section.
section name—A word that identifies a section written in the Procedure Division.
sentence—A sequence of one or more statements, the last of which is terminated by a period followed by a space.
separator—An optional character that enhances readability.
sequence, collating—The implementor defined sequence in which the characters acceptable to a computer are ordered for purposes of comparison.

sequential access—*See* access sequential.

sign, operational—An algebraic sign in a numeric literal or data item that indicates whether the number is positive or negative.

sign condition—*See* condition sign.

simple condition—*See* condition, simple.

sort file—*See* file, sort.

sort file description entry—*See* entry, sort file description.

SOURCE-COMPUTER—The name of an Environment Division paragraph in which the computer environment for compiling the source program is described.

source program, COBOL—A representation of the solution of a processing problem that uses the language, format and syntax of COBOL.

SPECIAL CHARACTER—*See* character, special.

SPECIAL-NAMES—The name of an Environment Division paragraph that relates implementor names to user specified mnemonic names.

special registers—*See* registers, special.

standard characters—*See* characters, standard.

standard data format—*See* format, standard data.

statement—A syntactically valid combination of words and symbols beginning with a verb in the Procedure Division.

statement, compiler directing—A statement, beginning with a compiler directing verb, that causes the compiler to take a specific action during compilation.

statement, conditional—A statement that tests the truth value of a condition and directs the object program accordingly.

statement, imperative—A statement that begins with an imperative verb and specifies an unconditional action to be taken. An imperative statement may consist of a sequence of imperative statements.

subject of entry—*See* entry, subject of.

subscript—An integer whose value identifies a particular element in a table.

subscripted data name—*See* data name, subscripted.

switch status condition—*See* condition, switch status.

synchronous processing—*See* processing synchronous.

table—A collection of data in a form suitable for ready reference, frequently as stored in sequenced machine locations or written in the form of an array of rows and columns for easy entry and in which an intersection of labeled rows and columns serves to locate a specific piece of data or information.

table element—*See* element, table.

time, compile—The time at which a COBOL source program is translated by a COBOL computer into a COBOL object program.

time, execution—The portion of an instruction cycle during which the actual work is performed or operation executed; i.e., the time required to decode and perform an instruction.

time, object—The time at which an object program is executed. Also called run time.

truth value—The representation of the result of the evaluation of a condition in terms of one of two values; true or false.

unary operator—*See* operator, arithmetic.

unit—A portion or subassembly of a computer which constitutes the means of accomplishing some inclusive operation or function.

variable—(1) A quantity which can assume any of the numbers of some set of numbers, (2) a condition, transaction or event which changes or may be changed as a result of processing additional data thru the system.

variable, condition—A data item which has a condition name assigned to it.

verb—A word that expresses an action to be taken by a COBOL compiler or object program.

word—An ordered set of characters which occupies one storage location and is treated by the computer circuits as a unit and transferred as such. Ordinarily a word is treated by the control unit as an instruction, and by the arithmetic unit as a quantity. Word lengths may be fixed or variable depending on the particular computer.

word, key—A reserved word that is required when the format option in which the word appears is used in a source program.

word, optional—A reserved word included in a format only to improve readability of the language. Its use is optional when the format in which the word appears is used in a source program.

word, reserved—One of a specified list of words which may be used in a COBOL source program, but which must not appear in a program as a user defined word.

WORKING-STORAGE SECTION—*See* section, working storage.

Glossary

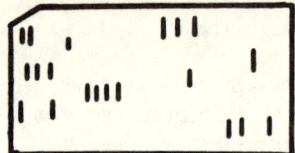

Data Processing

absolute address—An address which indicates the exact storage location where the referenced operand is to be found or stored in the actual machine code address numbering system. *Synonymous with* specific address. *Related to* absolute code.

absolute code—A code using absolute addresses and absolute operation codes; i.e., a code which indicates the exact location where the referenced operand is to be found or stored. *Synonymous with* one level code *and* specific code. *Related to* absolute address.

absolute error—The magnitude of the error disregarding the algebraic sign or if a vectorial error, disregarding its direction.

absolute value computer—A computer which processes all data expressed in full values of all variables at all times. *Contrasted with* computer, incremental.

ac dump—The removal of all alternating current power intentionally, accidentally or conditionally from a system or component. An ac dump usually results in the removal of all power, since direct current is usually supplied through a rectifier or converter.

acceleration time—The time between the interpretation of instructions to read or write on tape and the transfer of information to or from the tape into storage, or from storage into tape, as the case may be. *Synonymous with start time.*

access, immediate—*See* immediate access.
access, parallel—*See* parallel access.
access, random—*See* random access.
access, serial—*See* serial access.
access, simultaneous—*Same as* parallel access.
access, time—*See* time, access.
accounting machine—*See* tabulator.

154

accumulator—(1) The register and associated equipment in the arithmetic unit of the computer in which arithmetical and logical operations are performed. (2) A unit in a digital computer where numbers are totaled; i.e., accumulated. Often the accumulator stores one operand and upon receipt of any second operand, it forms and stores the result of performing the indicated operation on the first and second operands. *Related to* adder.

accuracy—The degree of exactness of an approximation or measurement. High accuracy thus implies low error. Accuracy normally denotes absolute quality of computed results; precision usually refers to the amount of detail used in representing those results. Thus, four place results are less precise than six place results; nevertheless a four place table might be more accurate than an erroneously computed six place table.

acoustic delay line—A delay line using a medium providing acoustic delay; such as, mercury or quartz delay lines. *Synonymous with* sonic delay line. *Related to* line, mercury delay.

action, rate—*See* rate action.

add subtract time—The time required to perform an addition or subtraction, exclusive of the time required to obtain the quantities from storage and put the sum or difference back into storage.

adder—A device which forms, as output, the sum of two, or more numbers presented as inputs. Often no data retention feature is included; i.e., the output signal remains only as long as the input signals are present. *Related to* accumulator, 2.

address—(1) An identification, represented by a name, label or number, for a register or location in storage. Addresses are also a part of an instruction word along with commands, tags, and other symbols. (2) The part of an instruction which specifies an operand for the instruction.

address, absolute—*See* absolute address.

address, base—*See* base address.

address, direct—*See* direct address.

address, effective—*See* effective address.

address, first level—*Same as* address, direct.

address, floating—*See* floating address.

address, four—*See* four address.

address, immediate—*See* immediate address.

address, indexed—*See* indexed address.

address, indirect—*See* indirect address.

address, machine—*See* machine address.

address, multi—*Same as* address, multiple.

address, multiple—*See* multiple address.

address, one—*See* one address.

address, one plus one—*See* one plus one address.

address part—The part of an instruction word that defines the address of a register or location.

address, presumptive—*Same as* address, base, 1.
address, reference—*Same as* address, base, 1.
address, relative—*See* relative address.
address, second level—*Same as* address, indirect.
address, single—*Same as* address, one.
address, specific—*Same as* address, absolute.
address, symbolic—*See* symbolic address.
address, three—*See* three address.
address, three plus one—*See* three plus one address.
address, variable—*Same as* address, indexed.
address, zero level—*Same as* address, immediate.
addressing system—The procedure used to label storage locations in a computer; e.g., on a magnetic storage drum, storage locations might be identified by four digit addresses which are numbered consecutively in each band as follows:

First band	0000-0199
Second band	0200-0399
Third band	0400-0599

* * * * * * * * *

| Twenty-fourth band | 4600-4799 |
| Twenty-fifth band | 4800-4999 |

The consecutively numbered band addresses begin with 0000, to which increments of 200 are added until the address of the last band, 4800 is reached. Within each band, particular locations might be consecutively numbered from 0 to 199 to give each location an address indicative of a position on the drum or drum level. This level is added to the band address to produce the address of a particular storage location. In a magnetic core storage unit, the locations might be addressed consecutively from 0000 to 4095.

ADP—(*A*utomatic *D*ata *P*rocessing), Data processing performed by a system of electronic or electrical machines so interconnected and interacting as to reduce to a minimum the need for human assistance or intervention.

advance, item—*See* item advance.

algebra, boolean—*See* boolean algebra.

ALGOL (*ALGO*rithmic *L*anguage)—An arithmetic language by which numerical procedures may be precisely presented to a computer in a standard form. The language is intended not only as a means of directly presenting any numerical procedure to any suitable computer for which a compiler exists, but also as a means of communicating numerical procedures among individuals. The language itself is the result of international cooperation to obtain a standardized algorithmic language. The International Algebraic Language is the forerunner of ALGOL.

algorithm translation—A specific, effective, essentially computational method for obtaining a translation from one language to another.

algorithmic—analog representation

algorithmic—Pertaining to a constructive calculating process usually assumed to lead to the solution of a problem in a finite number of steps.

algorithmic language—*Same as* ALGOL.

allocation storage—*See* storage allocation.

alphabet—A specific kind of character set excluding numerals; i.e., the character set most frequently used in a natural language. *Clarified by* set, character.

alphabetic code—A system of alphabetic abbreviations used in preparing information for input into a machine; e.g., Boston, New York, Philadelphia, and Washington may in alphabetical coding be reported as BS, NY, PH, WA. *Contrasted with* numeric code.

alphabetic-numeric—The characters which include letters of the alphabet, numerals, and other symbols such as punctuation or mathematical symbols.

alphameric—A contraction of alphanumeric.

alphanumeric instruction—The name given to instructions which can be used equally well with alphabetic or numeric kinds of fields of data.

ALU—(*A*rithmetic and *L*ogical *U*nit) The portion of the hardware of a computer in which arithmetic and logical operations are performed. The arithmetic unit generally consists of an accumulator, some special registers for the storage of operands and results supplemented by shifting and sequencing circuitry for implementing multiplication, division, and other desired operations.

analog—The representation of numerical quantities by means of physical variable; e.g., translation, rotation, voltage, or resistance. *Contrasted with* digital.

analog computer—A computer which represents variables by physical analogies. Thus any computer which solves problems by translating physical conditions such as flow, temperature, pressure, angular position, or voltage into related mechanical or electrical quantities and uses mechanical or electrical equivalent circuits as an analog for the physical phenomenon being investigated. In general it is a computer which uses an analog for each variable and produces analogs as output. Thus an analog computer measures continuously whereas a digital computer counts discretely. *Related to* machine, data processing.

analog device—A mechanism which represents numbers by physical quantites; e.g., by lengths, as in a slide rule, or by voltage currents as in a differential analyzer or a computer of the analog type.

analog network—A circuit or circuits which represent(s) physical variables in such a manner as to permit the expression and solution of mathematical relationships between the variables or permits the solution directly by electric or electronic means.

analog representation—A representation which does not have discrete values but is continuously variable.

analysis, numerical—*See* numerical analysis.

analysis, systems—*See* systems analysis.

analyst—A person skilled in the definition of and the development of techniques for the solving of a problem; especially those techniques for solutions on a computer.

analytic relationship—The relationship which exists between concepts, and corresponding terms, by virtue of their definition and inherent scope of meaning.

analyzer—A computer routine whose purpose is to analyze a program written for the same or a different computer. This analysis may consist of summarizing instruction references to storage and tracing sequences of jumps.

analyzer, differential—*See* differential analyzer.

analyzer, digital differential—*See* digital differential analyzer.

analyzer, electronic differential—*See* electronic differential analyzer.

analyzer, mechanical differential—*See* mechanical differential analyzer.

analyzer, network—*See* network analyzer.

AND—*Same as* and operator.

AND circuit—*Same as* and gate.

AND gate—A signal circuit with two or more input wires in which the output wire gives a signal, if and only if, all input wires receive coincident signals. *Synonymous with* and circuit. *Clarified by* conjunction.

AND operator—(1) A logical operator which has the property that if P is a statement and Q is a statement, then P and Q is true if both statements are true, false if either is false or both are false. Truth is normally expressed by the value 1, falsity by 0. The AND operator is often represented by a centered dot (P•Q), by no sign (PQ), by an inverted "u" or logical product symbol (P∩Q), or by the letter "X" or multiplication symbol (P×Q). Note that the letters AND are capitalized to differentiate between the logical operator AND the word "and" in common usage. (2) The logical operation which makes use of the AND operator or logical product. *Synonymous with* and; logical multiply. *Clarified by* conjunction.

application—The system or problem to which a computer is applied. Reference is often made to an application as being either of the computational type, wherein arithmetic computations predominate, or of the data processing type, wherein data handling operations predominate.

application, standby—*See* standby application.

application study—The detailed process of determining a system or set of procedures for using a computer for definite functions or operations, and establishing specifications to be used as a base for the selection of equipment suitable to the specific needs.

area, constant—*See* constant area.

area, input—*Same as* input block (1).

argument—(1) An independent variable, e.g., in looking up quantity in a table, the number or any of the numbers which identifies the location of the desired value; or in a mathematical function the variable which when a certain value is substituted for it the value of the function is determined. (2) An operand in an operation on one or more variables.

arithmetic check—A check which uses mathematical identities or other properties, occassionally with some degree of discrepancy being acceptable, e.g., checking multiplication by verifying that $A \times B = B \times A$.

arithmetic, fixed point—*See* fixed point arithmetic.

arithmetic, floating decimal—*Same as* arithmetic, floating point.

arithmetic, floating point—*See* floating point arithmetic.

arithmetic, internal—*See* internal arithmetic.

arithmetic, multi precision—*See* multi precision arithmetic.

arithmetic section—*Same as* unit, arithmetic.

arithmetic shift—To multiply or divide a quantity by a power of the number base; e.g., if binary 1101, which represents decimal 13, is arithmetically shifted twice to the left, the result is 110100, which represents 52, which is also obtained by multiplying 13 by 2 twice; on the other hand, if the decimal 13 were to be shifted to the left twice, the result would be the same as multiplying by 10 twice, or 1300. *Related to* shift *and* shift, cyclic.

arithmetic unit—*Same as* ALU.

arithmetic operation—A computer operation in which the ordinary elementary arithmetic operations are performed on numerical quantities. *Contrasted with* operation, logical.

artificial intelligence—The study of computer and related techniques to supplement the intellectual capabilities of man. As man has invented and used tools to increase his physical powers, he now is beginning to use artificial intelligence to increase his mental powers. In a more restricted sense, the study of techniques for more effective use of digital computers by improved programming techniques.

array—A series of items arranged in a meaningful pattern.

artificial language—A language specifically designed for ease of communication in a particular area of endeavor, but one that is not yet natural to that area. This is contrasted with a natural language which has evolved through long usage.

aspect card—A card on which is entered the accession numbers of documents in an information retrieval system. The documents are judged to be related in an important fashion to the concept for which the card is established. *Related to* system, peek-a-boo; system, uniterm; docuterm; and uniterm.

assemble—(1) To integrate subroutines that are supplied, selected, or generated into the main routine, by means of preset parameters, by adapting, or changing relative and symbolic addresses to absolute form,

assemble—automatic code

or by placing them in storage; (2) to operate, or perform the functions of an assembler.

assembler—A computer program which operates on symbolic input data to produce from such data machine instructions by carrying out such functions as: translation of symbolic operation codes into computer operating instructions; assigning locations in storage for successive instructions; or computation of absolute addresses from symbolic addresses. An assembler generally translates input symbolic codes into machine instructions time for item, and produces as output the same number of instructions or constants which were defined in the input symbolic codes. *Synonymous with* assembly routine; assembly program. *Related to* compiler.

assembly list—A printed list which is the by-product of an assembly procedure. It lists in logical instruction sequence all details of a routine showing the coded and symbolic notation next to the actual notations established by the assembly procedure. This listing is highly useful in the debugging of a routine.

assembly program—*Same as* assembler.

assembly routine—*Same as* assembler.

assembly unit—(1) A device which performs the function of associating and joining several parts or piecing together a program, (2) a portion of a program which is capable of being assembled into a larger whole program.

asynchronous—Pertaining to a lack of time coincidence in a set of repeated events where this term is applied to a computer to indicate that the execution of one operation is dependent on a signal that the previous operation is completed.

asynchronous computer—A computer in which the performance of each operation starts as a result of a signal either that the previous operation has been completed; or that the parts of the computer required for the next operation are now available. *Contrasted with* computer, synchronous.

attenuation, signal—*See* signal attenuation.

audit, trail—*See* trail audit.

auto-abstract—(1) A collection of words selected from a document, arranged in a meaningful order, commonly by an automatic or machine method; (2) to select an assemblage of key words from a document, commonly by an automatic or machine method.

automatic check—A provision constructed in hardware for verifying the accuracy of information transmitted, manipulated, or stored by any unit or device in a computer. *Synonymous with* built in check; built in automatic check; hardware check. *Related to* check program, 2.

automatic code—A code which allows a machine to translate or convert a symbolic language into a machine language for automatic machine or computer operations.

automatic computer—A computer which performs long sequences of operations without human intervention.

automatic data processing—*See* ADP.

automatic data processing equipment—(1) A machine, or group of interconnected machines, consisting of input, storage, computing, control, and output devices, which uses electronic circuitry in the main computing element to perform arithmetic and/or logical operations automatically by means of internally stored or externally controlled programmed instructions. Synonymous with (equipment, electronic data processing). (2) The data processing equipment which directly supports or services the central computer operation. *Clarified by* equipment, peripheral.

automatic data processing system—The term descriptive of an interacting assembly of procedure, processes, methods, personnel and automatic data processing equipment to perform a complex series of data processing operations.

automatic dictionary—The component of a language translating machine which will provide a word for word substitution from one language to another. In automatic searching systems, the automatic dictionary is the component which substitutes codes for words or phrases during the encoding operation. *Related to* translation, machine.

automatic error correction—A technique, usually requiring the use of special codes and or automatic retransmission, which detects and corrects errors occurring in transmission. The degree of correction depends upon coding and equipment configuration.

automatic feed punch—A card punch having a hopper, a card track and a stacker. The movement of cards through the punch is automatic.

automatic programming—The method or technique whereby the computer itself is used to transform or translate programming from a language or form that is easy for a human being to produce, into a language that is efficient for the computer to carry out. Examples of automatic programming are compiling, assembling, and interpretive routines.

automatic routine—A routine that is executed independently of manual operations, but only if certain conditions occur within a program or record, or during some other process.

automatic stop—An automatic halting of a computer processing operation as the result of an error detected by built in checking devices.

automation—(1) The implementation of processes by automatic means; (2) the theory, art, or technique of making a process more automatic; (3) the investigation, design, development, and application of methods of rendering processes automatic, self-moving, or self controlling.

automation, source data—*See* source data automation.

automonitor—To make an electronic computer prepare a record of its own data processing operations, or a program or routine for this purpose.

auxiliary equipment—*Same as* equipment, off line.

auxiliary routine—A routine designed to assist in the operation of the computer and in debugging other routines.

auxiliary storage—A storage device in addition to the main storage of a computer; e.g., magnetic tape, disk or magnetic drum. Auxiliary storage usually holds much larger amounts of information than the main storage, and the information is accessible less rapidly. *Contrasted with* storage, main.

available machine time—*Same as* available time.

available time—(1) The number of hours a computer is available for use. (2) The time during which a computer has the power turned on, is not under maintenance, and is known or believed to be operating correctly. *Synonymous with* available machine time.

average effectiveness level—A percentage figure determined by subtracting the total computer down time from the total performance period hours, and dividing the difference by the total performance period hours. For this computation, equipment down time can be measured by those intervals during the performance period between the time that the contractor or other person having maintenance responsibility is notified of equipment failure, and the time the equipment is returned to the user in proper operating condition.

balanced error (range of)—(1) A range of error in which the maximum and minimum possible errors are opposite in sign and equal in magnitude, (2) a range of error in which the average value is zero.

band—(1) The gamut or range of frequencies; (2) the frequency spectrum between two defined limits; (3) the frequencies which are within two definite limits and are used for a different purpose; (4) a group of channels. *Same as* channel, 3.

band, dead— *See* dead band.

band, proportional—*See* proportional band.

bandwidth— (1) A group of consecutive frequencies constituting a band which exists between limits of stated frequency attenuation. A band is normally defined as more than 3.0 decibels greater than the mean attenuation across the band. (2) A group of consecutive frequencies constituting a band exists between limits of stated frequency delay.

base—*Same as* radix.

base address—(1) A number which appears as an address in a computer instruction, but which serves as the base, index, initial or starting point for subsequent addresses to be modified. *Synonymous with* presumptive address; reference address. (2) A number used in symbolic coding in conjunction with a relative address.

base notation—*Same as* notation, radix.

base number—*Same as* radix.

batch processing—A technique by which items to be processed must be coded and collected into groups prior to processing.

batch total—binary coded decimal notation

batch total—The sum of certain quantities, pertaining to batches of unit records, used to verify accuracy of operations on a particular batch of records; e.g., in a payroll calculation, the batches might be departments and batch totals would be number of employees in the department, total hours worded in the department, total pay for the department. Batches, however, may be arbitrary, such as orders received from 9 a.m. to 11 a.m. on a certain day.

batten system—*Same as* system, peek-a-boo.

baud—(1) A unit of signalling speed equal to the number of code elements per second; (2) the unit of signalling speed equal to twice the number of Morse code dots continuously sent per second. *Clarified by* rate, bit; capacity, channel.

B-box—*Same as* index register.

benchmark problem—A routine used to determine the speed performance of a computer. One method is to use one tenth of the time required to perform nine complete additions and one complete multiplication. A complete addition or a complete multiplication time includes the time required to procure two operands from storage, perform the operation and store the result, and the time required to select and execute the required number of instructions to do this.

bias—(1) An unbalanced range of error; i.e., having an average error that is not zero. (2) The average dc voltage maintained between certain elements of a circuit, such as between the cathode and the control grid of a vacuum tube.

binary—A characteristic, property, or condition in which there are but two possible alternatives; e.g., the binary number system using 2 as its base and using only the digits zero (0) and one (1). *Related to* decimal, binary coded. *Clarified by* systems, number.

binary cell—(1) A cell of one binary digit capacity, (2) a one bit register or bit position.

binary code—(1) A coding system in which the encoding of any data is done through the use of bits; i.e., 0 or 1. (2) A code for the ten decimal digits, 0, 1, ..., 9 in which each is represented by its binary, radix 2, equivalent; i.e., straight binary.

binary coded character—One element of a notation system representing alphameric character such as decimal digits, alphabetic letters, and punctuation marks by a predetermined configuration of consecutive binary digits.

binary coded decimal—Describing a decimal notation in which the individual decimal digits are represented by a pattern of ones and zeros; e.g., in the 8-4-2-1 coded decimal notation, the number twelve is represented as 0001 0010 for 1 and 2, respectively, whereas in pure or straight binary notation it is represented as 1100. *Related to* binary.

binary coded decimal notation—A method of representing each figure in a decimal number by a four figured binary number.

binary coded decimal number—A number usually consisting of successive groups of figures, in which each group of four figures is a binary number that represents but does not necessarily equal arithmetically, a particular figure in an associated decimal number; e.g., if the three rightmost figures of a decimal number are 262, the three rightmost figure groups of the binary coded decimal number might be 0010, 0110, and 0010.

binary counter—(1) A counter which counts according to the binary number system, (2) a counter capable of assuming one of two stable states.

binary digit—A numeral in the binary scale of notation. This digit may be zero (0), or one (1). It may be equivalent to an on or off condition, a yes, or a no. Often *abbreviated to* bit.

binary notation—A number system written to the base two notation.

binary number—A number, usually consisting of more than one figure, representing a sum, in which the individual quantity represented by each figure is based on a radix of two. The figures used 0 and 1.

binary number system—*Same as* system, number, 2.

binary point—The radix point in a binary number system; i.e., the dot that marks the position between the integral and fractional, or units and halves in a binary number.

binary search—A search in which the series of items is divided into two parts, one of which is rejected, and the process repeated on the unrejected part until the item with the desired property is found. This process usually depends upon the presence of a known sequence in the series. *Synonymous with* dichotomizing search.

binary signalling—A communications mode in which information is passed by the presence and absence or plus and minus variations of one parameter of the signalling medium only.

binary to decimal conversion—The process of converting a number written to the base of two to the equivalent number written to the base of ten.

binary variable—*Same as* two valued variable.

bionics—The application of knowledge gained from the analysis of living systems to the creation of hardware that will perform functions in a manner analogous to the more sophisticated functions of the living system.

biquinary code—A two part code in which each decimal digit is represented by the sum of the two parts, one of which has the value of decimal zero or five and the other the values zero through four. The abacus and soroban both use biquinary codes. An example follows:

Decimal	Biquinary	Interpretation
0	0 000	0+0
1	0 001	0+1
2	0 010	0+2

biquinary coded decimal number, biquinary notation—block

Decimal	Biquinary	Interpretation
3	0 011	0+3
4	0 100	0+4
5	1 000	5+0
6	1 001	5+1
7	1 010	5+2
8	1 011	5+3
9	1 100	5+4

biquinary coded decimal number, biquinary notation—A method for expressing a quantity less than ten, using two figures, wherein the first (left) figure is of radix two and the second (right) figure is of radix five.

biquinary number—(1) A number, consisting of a pair of figures representing a sum, in which the quantity represented by the left figure is based on the radix two, and the quantity represented by the right figure is based on the radix five. The figures 0 and 1 are used for the left figure, and 0, 1, 2, 3, and 4 are used for the right figure. (2) A number consisting of successive pairs of figures, representing a sum, in which the quantity represented by each pair of figures is based on a radix of ten.

bi-stable—The capability of assuming either of two stable states, hence of storing one bit of information.

bit—(1) An abbreviation of *bi*nary digi*t*. (2) A single character in a binary number. (3) A single pulse in a group of pulses. (4) A unit of information capacity of a storage device. The capacity in bits is the logarithm to the base two of the number of possible states of the device. *Related to* capacity, storage.

bit check—A binary check digit; often a parity bit. *Related to* check, parity number, self checking.

bit location—A storage position on a record capable of storing one bit.

bit, parity—*See* parity bit.

bit rate—The rate at which binary digits, or pulses representing them pass a given point on a communications line or channel. Clarified by (baud) and (capacity, channel).

bit, sign—*See* sign bit.

bit, zone—*See* zone bit.

blank—(1) A regimented place of storage where data may be stored; e.g., a location in a storage medium. *Synonymous with* space. (2) A character used to indicate an output space on a printer in which nothing is printed.

blank, switching—*Same as* dead band.

block—(1) A group of computer words considered as a unit of virtue of their being stored in successive storage locations. (2) The set of locations or tape positions in which a block of words, as defined above, is stored or recorded. (3) A circuit assemblage which functions as a unit; e.g., a

block—box, decision

circuit building block of standard design, and the logic block in a sequential circuit.

block diagram—(1) A graphical representation of the hardware in a computer system. The primary purpose of a block diagram is to indicate the paths along with information and/or control flows between the various parts of a computer system. It should not be confused with the term flowchart. (2) A coarser and less symbolic representation than a flowchart.

block, input— *See* input block.

block length—The total number of records, words or characters contained in one block.

block, output—*See* output block.

block sort—A sort of one or more of the most significant characters of a key to serve as a means of making workable sized groups from a large volume of records to be sorted.

block, standby—*See* standby block.

block transfer—The conveyance of a group of consecutive words from one place to another.

blockette—A subdivision of a group of consecutive machine words transferred as a unit, particularly with reference to input and output.

blocking—The combining of two or more records into one block.

bookkeeping operation—A computer operation which does not directly contribute to the result; i.e., arithmetical, logical, and transfer operations used in modifying the address section of other instructions, in counting cycles and in rearranging data. *Synonymous with* red tape operation.

Boolean algebra—A process of reasoning, or a deductive system of theorems using a symbolic logic, and dealing with classes, propositions, or on-off circuit elements. It employs symbols to represent operators such as AND, OR, NOT, EXCEPT, IF . . . THEN, etc., to permit mathematical calculation. Named after George Boole, famous English mathematician (1815-1864).

bootstrap—A technique for loading the first few instructions of a routine into storage; then using these instructions to bring in the rest of the routine. This usually involves either the entering of a few instructions manually or the use of a special key on the console.

borrow—An arithmetically negative carry. It occurs in direct subtraction by raising the low order digit of the minuend by one unit of the next higher order digit; e.g., when subtracting 67 from 92, a tens digit is borrowed from the 9, to raise the 2 to a factor of 12; the 7 of 67 is then subtracted from the 12 to yield 5 as the units digit of the difference; the 6 is then subtracted from 8, or 9 − 1, yielding 2 as the tens digit of the difference. *Related to* carry (3).

box, B—*Same as* index register.

box, decision—*See* decision box.

branch—The selection of one or two or more possible paths in the flow of control based on some criterion. The instructions which mechanize this concept are sometimes called branch instructions; however, the terms transfer of control and jump are more widely used. *Related to* transfer, conditional.

branch instruction—An instruction to a computer that enables the programmer to instruct the computer to choose between alternative subprograms depending upon the conditions determined by the computer during the execution of the program. *Synonymous with* transfer instruction.

branch, conditional—*See* transfer conditional.

branch, unconditional—*Same as* transfer, unconditional.

branchpoint—A point in a routine where one of two or more choices is selected under control of the routine.

breakpoint—A point in a computer program at which conditional interruption, to permit visual check, printing out, or other analyzing, may occur. Breakpoints are usually used in debugging operations.

breakpoint instruction—(1) An instruction which will cause a computer to stop or to transfer control in some standard fashion to a supervisory routine which can monitor the progress of the interrupted program; (2) an instruction which, if some specified switch is set, will cause the computer to stop or take other special action.

breakpoint switch—A manually operated switch which controls conditional operation at breakpoints, used primarily in debugging.

breakpoint symbol—A symbol which may be optionally included in an instruction, as an indication, tag, or flag, to designate it as a breakpoint.

B-register—(1) *Same as* index register; (2) a register used as an extension of the accumulator during multiply and divide processes.

broadband noise—The thermal noise which is uniformally distributed across the frequency spectrum at a wide range of energy levels.

brush—An electrical conductor for reading data from a punch card.

bucket—A slang expression used to indicate some portion of storage specifically reserved for accumulating data, or totals; e.g., "throw it in bucket #1." is a possible expression. Commonly used in initial planning.

buffer—(1) An internal portion of a data processing system serving as intermediary storage between two storage or data handling systems with different access times or formats; usually to connect an input or output device with the main or internal highspeed storage. *Clarified by* storage, buffer (4). (2) A logical OR circuit. (3) An isolating component designed to eliminate the reaction of a driven circuit on the circuits driving it; e.g., a buffer amplifier. (4) A diode.

buffer storage—(1) A synchronizing element between two different forms of storage, usually between internal and external. (2) An input device in which information is assembled from external or secondary storage and stored ready for transfer to internal storage. (3) An output device into

buffer storage—card, edge notched

which information is copied from internal storage and held for transfer to secondary or external storage. Computation continues while transfers between buffer storage and secondary or internal storage or vice versa take place. (4) Any device which stores information temporarily during data transfers. *Clarified by* buffer.

buffer computer—A computing system with a storage device which permits input and output data to be stored temporarily in order to match the slow speed of input-output devices with the higher speeds of the computer. Thus, simultaneous input-output computer operations are possible. A data transmission trap is essential for effective use of buffering since it obviates frequency testing for the availability of a data channel.

bug—A mistake in the design of a routine or a computer, or a malfunction.

built in check—*Same as* check, automatic.

built in automatic check—*Same as* check, automatic.

bus—(1) A circuit over which data or power is transmitted. Often one which acts as a common connection among a number of locations. *Synonymous with* trunk. (2) A communications path between two switching points.

byte—(1) A generic term to indicate a measurable portion of consecutive binary digits; e.g., an 8 bit or 6 bit byte. (2) A group of binary digits usually operated upon as a unit.

calculation, fixed point—*See* fixed point calculation.

calculation, floating point—*See* floating point calculation.

calculator—(1) A device that performs primarily arithmetic operations based upon data and instructions inserted manually or contained on punch cards. It is sometimes used interchangeably with computer. (2) A computer.

calculator, network—*Same as* network analyzer.

call in—To transfer control of a digital computer temporarily from a main routine to a subroutine, which is inserted in the sequence of calculating operations to fulfill a subsidiary purpose.

call number—(1) A group of characters identifying a subroutine and containing (a) information concerning parameters to be inserted in the subroutine, (b) information to be used in generating the subroutine, or (c) information related to the operands. (2) A call word, if the quantity of characters in the call number is equal to the length of a computer word.

calling sequence—The instructions used for linking a closed subroutine with a main routine; i.e., standard linkage and a list of the parameters.

capacity, channel—*See* channel capacity.

capacity, circuit—*See* circuit capacity.

capacity, memory—*Same as* storage capacity.

capacity, storage—*See* storage capacity.

card, aspect—*See* aspect card.

card, control—*See* control card.

card, edge notched—*See* edge notched card.

card, edge punched—*See* edge punched card.

card, eighty (80) column—*See* eighty (80) column card.

card feed—A mechanism which moves cards serially into a machine.

card field—A set of card columns, either fixed as to number and position or, if variable, then identifiable by position relative to other fields. Corresponding fields on successive cards are normally used to store similar information.

card image—A representation in storage of the holes punched in a card, in such a manner that the holes are represented by one binary digit and the unpunched spaces are represented by the other binary digit.

card jam—A pile up of cards in a machine.

card, master—*See* master card.

card, ninety (90) column—*See* ninety (90) column card.

card programmed—(1) The capability of being programmed by punch cards, (2) The capability of performing sequences of calculating operations according to instructions contained in a stack of punch cards.

card, punch—*See* punch card.

card punch unit—*Same as* punch card.

card reader—(1) A mechanism that senses information punched into cards. (2) An input device consisting of a mechanical punch card reader and related electronic circuitry which transcribes data from punch cards to working storage or magnetic tape. *Synonymous with* card reader unit.

card reader unit—*Same as* card reader, 2.

card reproducer—A device that reproduces a punch card by punching another similar card.

card stacker—(1) A receptacle that accumulates cards after they have passed through a machine. (2) A hopper. *Synonymous with* hopper.

card to tape converter—A device which converts information directly from punched cards to punched or magnetic tape.

card, transfer—*Same as* card, transistion.

card, transfer of control—*Same as* card, transistion.

card, transistion—*See* transistion card.

carrier wave—The basic frequency or pulse repetition rate of a signal, bearing no intrinsic intelligence until it is modulated by another signal which does bear intelligence. A carrier may be amplitude, phase, or frequency modulated; e.g., in a typical mercury delay line storage of a digital computer, the 8 megacycle/second sound wave carrier is amplitude or pulse modulated by a 1 megacycle/second pulse code signal, the presence or absence of a pulse determining whether or not a one or a zero is present in the binary number being represented.

carry—(1) A signal, or expression, produced as a result of an arithmetic operation on one digit place of two or more numbers expressed in positional notation and transferred to the next higher place for processing there. (2) A signal or expression as defined in (1) above which arises in adding, when the sum of two digits in the same digit place

carry—center, data processing

equals or exceeds the base of the number system in use. If a carry into a digit place will result in a carry out of the same digit place, and if the normal adding circuit is by-passed when generating this new carry, it is called a high speed carry, or standing on nines carry. If the normal adding circuit is used in such a case, the carry is called a cascaded carry. If a carry resulting from the addition of carries is not allowed to propagage; e.g., when forming the partial product in one step of a multiplication process, the process is called a partial carry. If it is allowed to propagage, the process is called a complete carry. If a carry generated in the most significant digit place is sent directly to the least significant place; e.g., when adding two negative numbers using nine complements, that carry is called an end around carry. *Synonymous with* cascaded carry; complete carry; end around carry; high-speed carry; and partial carry. (3) A signal or expression in direct subtraction, as defined in (1) above which arises when the difference between the digits is less than zero. Such a carry is frequently called a borrow. *Relate* to borrow. (4) The action of forwarding a carry. (5) The command directing a carry to be forwarded.

carry, cascaded—*Same as* carry, 2.

carry, complete—*Same as* carry, 2.

carry complete signal—A signal generated by a digital parallel adder, indicating that all carries from an adding operation have been generated and propagated and the addition operation is completed.

carry, end around—*Same as* carry, 2.

carry, high speed—*Same as* carry, 2.

carry, partial—*Same as* carry, 2.

carry, standing on nines—*See* standing-on-nines carry.

carry time—(1) The time required for transferring a carry digit to the higher column and there add it, (2) the time required for transferring all the carry digits to higher columns and adding them for all digits in the number.

cascade control—An automatic control system in which various control units are linked in sequence, each control unit regulating the operation of the next control unit in line.

cascaded carry—*Same as* carry, 2.

cathode follower—A vacuum tube circuit in which the input signal is applied to the control grid and the output is taken from the cathode. Electrically, such a circuit possesses high input impedance and low output impedance characteristics. The equivalent circuit using a transistor is called an emitter follower.

cell—(1) The storage for one unit of information, usually one character or one word. (2) A location specified by whole or part of the address and possessed of the faculty of store. Specific terms such as column, field, location, and block, are preferable when appropriate.

cell, binary—*See* binary cell.

center, data processing—*See* data processing center.

central processing unit—*Same as* main frame, 2.

centralized data processing—Data processing performed at a single, central location on data obtained from several geographical locations or managerial levels. Decentralized data processing involves processing at various managerial levels or geographical points throughout the organization.

chad—A small piece of paper tape or punch card removed when punching a hole to represent information.

chaded paper tape—A paper tape with the holes fully punched.

chadless—A type of punching of paper tape in which each chad is left fastened by about a quarter of the circumference of the hole, at the leading edge. This mode of punching is useful where it is undesirable to destroy information written or printed on the punched tape or it is undesirable to produce chads. Chadless punched paper tape must be sensed by mechanical fingers, for the presence of chad in the tape would interfere with reliable electrical or photoelectric reading of the paper tape.

chadless paper tape—A paper tape with the holes partially punched. It is commonly used in teletype operations.

chain—(1) Any series of items linked together; (2) pertaining to a routine consisting of segments which are run through the computer in tandem, only one being within the computer at any one time and each using the output from the previous program as its input.

change dump—A print out or output recording of the contents of all storage locations in which a change has been made since the previous change dump.

change tape—A paper tape or magnetic tape carrying information that is to be used to update filed information. This filed information is often on a master tape. *Synonymous with* transaction tape.

change, step—*See* step change.

channel—(1) A path along with information, particularly a series of digits or characters, may flow. (2) One or more parallel tracks treated as a unit. (3) In a circulating storage, a channel is one recirculating path containing a fixed number of words stored serially by word. *Synonymous with* band. (4) A path for electrical communication. (5) A band of frequencies used for communication.

channel capacity—(1) The maximum number of binary digits or elementary digits to other bases which can be handled in a particular channel per unit time. (2) The maximum possible information transmission rate through a channel at a specified error rate. The channel capacity may be measured in bits per second or bauds. *Clarified by* bit rate; baud.

channel reliability—The percentage of time the channels meet the arbitrary standards established by the user.

character—(1) One symbol of a set of elementary symbols such as those corresponding to the keys on a typewriter. The symbols usually include

character—check code

the decimal digits 0 through 9, the letters A through Z, punctuation marks, operation symbols, and any other single symbols which a computer may read, store, or write. (2) The electrical, magnetic, or mechanical profile used to represent a character in a computer, and its various storage and peripheral devices. A character may be represented by a group of other elementary marks, such as bits or pulses.

character, binary coded—*See* binary coded character.

character density—The number of characters that can be stored per unit of length; e.g., on some makes of magnetic tape drives, 200 or 556 bits can be stored serially, linearly, and axially to the inch.

character, illegal—*See* illegal character.

character reader—A specialized device which can convert data represented in one of the type fonts or scripts read by human beings directly into machine language. Such a reader may operate optically; or if the characters are printed in magnetic ink, the device may operate magnetically or optically.

character recognition—The technology of using a machine to sense and encode into a machine language characters which are written or printed to be read by human beings.

character, redundant—*See* redundant character.

character set—An agreed set of representations, called characters from which selections are made to denote and distinguish data. Each character differs from all others, and the total number of characters in a given set is fixed; e.g., a set may include the numerals 0 to 9, the letters A to Z, punctuation marks and a blank or space. *Clarified by* alphabet.

characteristic impedance—(1) The ratio of voltage to current at every point along a transmission line on which there are no standing waves. (2) The square root of the product of the open and short circuit impedance of the line. When a transmission line is terminated in its characteristic impedance, energy is not reflected, but is fully absorbed in the terminating impedance.

chart, logical flow—*See* logical flowchart.

chart, process—*Same as* flowchart.

check—A process of partial or complete testing of the correctness of machine operations, the existence of certain prescribed conditions within the computer, or the correctness of the results produced by a program. A check of any of these conditions may be made automatically by the equipment or may be programmed. *Related to* marginal check.

check, arithmetic—*Same as* mathematical check.

check, automatic—*See* automatic check.

check bit—A binary check digit; often a parity bit. *Related to* parity check; self-checking number.

check, built in—*Same as* automatic check.

check, built in automatic—*Same as* automatic check.

check code—To isolate and remove mistakes from a routine.

check digit—check, system

check digit—One or more redundant digits carried along with a machine word and used in relation to the other digits in the word as a self checking or error detecting code to detect malfunctions of equipment in data transfer operations. *Related to* forbidden combination check; parity check.

check, dump—*See* dump check.

check, duplication—*See* duplication check.

check, echo—*See* echo check.

check, forbidden combination—*See* forbidden combination check.

check, hardware—*Same as* automatic check.

check indicator—A device which displays or announces that an error has been made or that a checking operation has determined that a failure has occurred.

check indicator instruction—An instruction which directs that a signal device which is turned on to call operators' attention to the fact that there is some discrepancy in the instruction now in use.

check, marginal—*See* marginal check.

check, mathematical—*See* arithmetic check.

check, modulo N—*See* modulo N check.

check number—A number composed of one or more digits and used to detect equipment malfunctions in data transfer operations. If a check number consists of only one digit, it is synonymous with check digit. *Related to* check digit.

check, odd-even—*Same as* parity check.

check, parity—*See* parity check.

checkpoint—A point in time in a machine run at which processing is momentarily halted to make a magnetic tape record of the condition of all the variables of the machine run such as the position of input and output tapes and a copy of working storage. Checkpoints are used in conjunction with a restart routine to minimize reprocessing time occasioned by functional failures.

check problem—A problem chosen to determine whether the computer or a program is operating correctly.

check, program—*See* program check.

check, redundant—*See* redundant check.

check register—A register used to store information temporarily where it may be checked with the result of a succeeding transfer of this information.

check, residue—*See* residue check.

check, routine—*Same as* program check, 2.

check, selection—*See* selection check.

check, sequence—*See* sequence check.

check sum—The sum used in a summation check.

check, summation—*See* summation check.

check, system—*See* system check.

check, transfer—*See* transfer check.
check, twin—*See* twin check.
check, validity—*See* validity check.
chinese binary—*Same as* column binary code.
circuit—(1) A system of conductors and related electrical elements through which electrical current flows, (2) a communications link between two or more points.
circuit capacity—The number of communications channels which can be handled by a given circuit at the same time.
circuit, AND—*Same as* and gate.
circuit dropout—The momentary interruption of a transmission because of the complete failure of a circuit.
circuit, Eccles-Jordan—*Same as* flip-flop.
circuit, four wire—*See* four wire circuit.
circuit, OR—*Same as* or gate.
circuit reliability—The percentage of time the circuit meets arbitrary standards by the user.
circular shift—*Same as* cyclic shift.
circulating register—(1) A shift register in which the stored information is moved right or left, and the information from one end is reinserted at the other end. In the case of a one character right shift, the rightmost character reappears as the new leftmost character, and every other character is shifted one position to the right. (2) A register in which the process, as in 1, is continuously occurring. This can be used as a delaying mechanism.
circulating storage—A device or unit which stores information in a train or pattern of pulses, where the pattern of pulses issuing at the final end are sensed, amplified, reshaped and reinserted into the device at the beginning end.
clear—To erase the contents of a storage device by replacing the contents with blanks, or zeros. *Contrasted with* hold. *Clarified by* erase.
clock—(1) A master timing device used to provide the basic sequencing pulses for the operation of a synchronous computer; (2) a register which automatically records the progress of real time, or perhaps some approximation to it, records the number of operations performed, and whose contents are available to a computer program.
clock frequency—The master frequency of periodic pulses which schedules the operation of the computer. *Clarified by* computer, synchronous.
clock rate—The time rate at which pulses are emitted from the clock. The clock rate determines the rate at which logical or arithmetic gating is performed with a synchronous computer.
clock, real time—*See* real time clock.
closed loop—Pertaining to a system with feedback type of control, such that the output is used to modify the input.

closed routine—A routine which is not inserted as a block of instructions within a main routine but is entered by basic linkage from the main routine.

closed shop—The operation of a computer facility where programming service to the user is the responsibility of a group of specialists, thereby effectively separating the phase of task formulation from that of computer implementation. The programmers are not allowed in the computer room to run or oversee the running of their programs. *Contrasted with* open shop.

closed subroutine—A subroutine not stored in the main path of the routine. Such a subroutine is entered by a jump operation and provision is made to return control to the main routine at the end of the operation. The instructions related to the entry and re-entry function constitute a linkage. *Synonymous with* linked subroutine.

COBOL—*CO*mmon *B*usiness *O*riented *L*anguage. *See* language; common business oriented.

code—(1) A system of symbols for meaningful communications. *Related to* instruction, (1). (2) A system of symbols for representing data or instructions in a computer or a tabulating machine. (3) To translate the program for the solution of a problem on a given computer into a sequence of machine language or psuedo instructions and addresses acceptable to that computer. *Related to* encode. (4) A machine language program.

code, absolute—*See* absolute code.

code, alphabetic—*See* alphabetic code.

code, automatic—*See* automatic code.

code, binary—*See* binary code.

code, biquinary—*See* biquinary code.

code, check—*See* check code.

code checking time—The time spent checking out a problem on the machine making sure that the problem is set up correctly, and that the code is correct.

code, column binary—*Same as* column binary code.

code, computer—*See* computer code.

code, cyclic—*Same as* gray code.

code, dictionary—*See* dictionary code.

code, direct—*See* direct code.

code element—The elemental unit from which a code is constructed; e.g., Baudot code is a binary representation of the alphabet and numerals in which a grouping, presence or absence, of five elements expresses the code information.

code, error correcting—*See* error correcting code.

code, error detecting—*See* error detecting code.

code, excess three—*See* excess three code.

code, gray—*See* gray code.

code, instruction—*See* instruction code.

code, interpretive—*Same as* interpretive routine.
code, line—*See* line code.
code, machine—*Same as* computer code (1).
code, machine language—*Same as* computer code, (1). *Contrasted with* symbolic code.
code, micro—*See* micro code.
code, minimum access—*See* minimum access code.
code, minimum latency—*Same as* minimum access code. *Related to* minimum access coding.
code, mnemonic operation—*See* mnemonic operation code.
code, modulation—*See* modulation code.
code, multiple address—*See* multiple address code.
code, numeric—*See* numeric code.
code, one level—*Same as* absolute code.
code, operation—*See* operation code.
code, optimum—*See* optimum code.
code, pseudo—*Same as* symbolic code.
code, pulse—*See* pulse code.
code, punch tape—*See* punch tape code.
code, quibinary—*See* quibinary code.
code, relative—*See* relative code.
code, self checking—*Same as* error detecting code.
code, self demarcating—*See* self demarcating code.
code, skeletal—*See* skeletal code.
code, specific—*See* absolute code.
code, straight line—*See* straight line code.
code, symbolic—*See* symbolic code.
code, two-out-of-five—*See* two-out-of-five code.
coded decimal—Describing a form of notation by which each decimal digit separately is expressed in some other number system; e.g., in the 8-4-2-1 coded decimal notation, the number twelve is represented as 1100. Other coded decimal notations used are the 5-4-2-1, the excess three, and the 2-3-2-1 codes.
coded decimal number—A number consisting of successive characters or a group of characters in which each character or group of characters usually represents a specific figure in an associated decimal number; e.g., if the figures of a decimal number are 45, the coded decimal number might be represented as GQ, or LLZZ, or 1101 0110.
coded program—A program which has been expressed in the code or language of a specific machine or programming system.
coded stop—A stop instruction built into the routine.
coder—A person who prepares instruction sequences from detailed flow charts and other algorithmic procedures prepared by others, as *contrasted with* a programmer who prepares the procedures and flowcharts.
coding—The ordered list in computer code or pseudo code, of the succes-

sive computer instructions representing successive computer operations for solving a specific problem.

coding, minimum access—*See* minimum access coding.

coincidence gate—A circuit with the ability to produce an output which is dependent upon a specified type of or the coincident nature of the input; e.g., an AND gate has an output pulse when there are pulses in time coincidence at all inputs; an OR gate has an output when any one or any combination of input pulses occur in time coincidence. Any gate may contain a number of inhibits, in which there is no output under any condition of input if there is time coincidence of an inhibit or except signal.

collate—To merge two or more ordered sets of data, or cards in order to produce one or more ordered sets which still reflect the original ordering relations. The collation process is the merging of two sequences of cards, each ordered on some mutual key, into a single sequence ordered on the mutual key.

collation sequence—The sequence in which the characters acceptable to a computer are ordered.

collator—A device used to collate or merge sets or decks of cards or other units into a sequence. A typical example of a card collator has two input feeds, so that two ordered sets may enter into the process, and four output stackers, so that four ordered sets can be generated by the process. Three comparison stations are used to route the cards to one stacker or the other on the basis of comparison of criteria as specified by plugboard wiring.

column—(1) A character or digit position in a positional information format, particularly one in which characters appear in rows, and the rows are placed one above another; e.g., the rightmost column in a five decimal place table, or in a list of data. (2) A character or digit position in a physical device, such as punch card or a register, corresponding to a position in a written table or list; e.g., the rightmost place in a register; or the third column in an eighty column punch card.

column-binary code—A code used with punch cards in which successive bits are represented by the presence or absence of punches on contiguous positions in successive columns as opposed to rows. Column binary code is widely used in connnection with 36 bit word computers where each group of 3 columns is used to represent a single word. *Synonymous with* chinese binary code.

command—(1) An electronic pulse, signal or set of signals to start, stop or continue some operation. It is incorrect to use command as a synonym for instruction. (2) The portion of an instruction word which specifies the operation to be performed.

comment—An expression which explains or identifies a particular step in a routine, but which has no effect on the operation of the computer in performing the instructions for the routine.

Common Business Oriented Language—A specific language by which business data processing procedures may be precisely described in a standard form. The language is intended not only as a means for directly presenting any business program to any suitable computer, for which a compiler exists, but also as a means of communicating such procedures among individuals. *Synonymous with* COBOL.

common machine language—A machine sensible information representation which is common to a related group of data processing machines.

comparator—(1) A device for comparing two different transcriptions of the same information to verify the accuracy of transcription, storage, arithmetic operation, or other processes, in which a signal is given dependent upon some relation between two items; i.e., one item is larger than, smaller than, or equal to the other. (2) A form of verifier.

compare—To examine the representation of a quantity to discover its relationship to zero, or to examine two quantities usually for the purposes of discovering identity or relative magnitude.

comparison—The act of comparing and, usually, acting on the result of the comparison. The common forms are comparison of two numbers for identity, comparison of two numbers for relative magnitude, and comparison of two signs plus or minus.

compatibility, equipment—*See* equipment compatibility.

compile—To produce a machine language routine from a routine written in source language by selecting appropriate subroutines from a subroutine library, as directed by the instructions or other symbols of the original routine, supplying the linkage which combines the subroutines into a workable routine and translating the subroutines and linkage into machine language. The compiled routine is then ready to be loaded into storage and run; i.e., the compiler does not usually run the routine it produces.

compiler—A computer program more powerful than an assembler. In addition to its translating function which is generally the same process as that used in an assembler it is able to replace certain items of input with series of instructions, usually called subroutines. Thus, where an assembler translates item for item, and produces as output the same number of instructions or constants which were put into it, a compiler will do more than this. The program which results from compiling is a translated and expanded version of the original. *Synonymous with* compiling routine. *Related to* assembler.

compiling routine—*Same as* compiler.

complement—(1) A quantity expressed to the base N, which is derived from a given quantity by a particular rule; frequently used to represent the negative of the given quantity. (2) A complement on N, obtained by subtracting each digit of the given quantity from N−1, adding unity to the least significant digit, and performing all resultant carrys; e.g., the twos complement of binary 11010 is 00110; the tens complement of decimal

456 is 554. (3) A complement on N−1, obtained by subtracting each digit of the given quantity from N−1; e.g., the ones complement of binary 11010 is 00101; the nines complement of decimal 456 is 543. *Synonymous with* radix minus 1 complement; radix complement.

complement, radix—*Same as* complement, 3.

complement, radix, minus 1—*Same as* complement, 2.

complete carry—*Same as* carry, 2.

complete operation—An operation which includes obtaining the instruction, obtaining all the operands from storage, performing the operation, and returning the results to storage.

computer—A device capable of accepting information, applying prescribed processes to the information, and supplying the results of these processes. It usually consists of input and output devices, storage, arithmetic, and logical units, and a control unit.

computer, absolute value—*See* absolute value computer.

computer, analog—*See* analog computer.

computer, asynchronous—*See* asynchronous computer.

computer, automatic—*See* automatic computer.

computer, buffered—*See* buffered computer.

computer code—(1) A system of combinations of binary digits used by a given computer. *Synonymous with* machine code. (2) A repertoire of instructions.

computer, digital—*See* digital computer.

computer efficiency—*Same as* operating ratio.

computer, fixed program—*See* fixed program computer.

computer, general purpose—*See* general purpose computer.

computer, incremental—*See* incremental computer.

computer limited—Pertaining to a situation in which the time required for computation exceeds the time required to read inputs and write outputs.

computer operation—The electronic action resulting from an instruction. In general it is a computer manipulation required to secure results.

computer parallel—*See* parallel computer.

computer, serial—*See* serial computer.

computer, solid state—*See* solid state computer.

computer, special purpose—*See* special purpose computer.

computer, stored program—*See* stored program computer.

computer, synchronous—*See* synchronous computer.

computer, wired program—*See* wired program computer.

concept coordination—A term used to describe the basic principles of various punched card and mechanized information retrieval systems which involve the multidimensional analysis of information and coordination retrieval. In concept coordination, independently assigned concepts are used to characterize the subject contents of documents and the latter are identified during searching by means of either such assigned concepts or a combination of the same.

condensed instruction deck—The card output from an assembly program in which several instructions per card are punched in machine language. Input to the assembly program may consist of one instruction per card, thus, the name condensed is used for output.

conditional branch—*Same as* conditional transfer.

conditional breakpoint instruction—A conditional jump instruction which, if some specified switch is set or situation exists, will cause the computer to stop; after which either the routine may be continued as coded, or a jump may be forced.

conditional jump—*Same as* conditional transfer.

conditional transfer of control—A computer instruction which when reached in the course of a program will cause the computer either to continue with the next instruction in the original sequence or to transfer control to another stated instruction, depending on a condition regarding some property of a number or numbers which has then been determined.

conditional transfer—An instruction which, if a specified condition or set of conditions is satisfied, is interpreted as an unconditional transfer. If the condition is not satisfied, the instruction causes the computer to proceed in its normal sequence of control. A conditional transfer also includes the testing of the condition. Synonymous *with* conditional jump *and* conditional branch. *Related to* branch.

conditional, signal—*See* signal conditioning.

configuration—A group of machines which are interconnected and are programmed to operate as a system.

conjunction—The logical operation which makes use of the AND operator or logical product. The conjunction of two variables, or expressions, may be written as $A.B$, $A \wedge B$, $A \cap B$, or just plain AB. These may also be described as an intersection when using Venn diagrams. *Clarified by* Operator, and; gate, and *Contrasted with* disjunction.

conjunctive search—A search defined in terms of a logical product; i.e., conjunctive form, in contrast to a disjunctive form, or logical sum.

connectives, logical—*See* logical connectives.

connector, variable—*See* variable connector.

console—A portion of the computer which may be used to control the machine manually, correct errors, determine the status of machine circuits, registers, and counters, determine the contents of storage, and manually revise the contents of storage.

constant area—A part of storage designated to store the invariable quantities required for processing.

constant instruction—An instruction not intended to be executed as an instruction, written in the form of a constant. *Related to* instruction, dummy.

constant(s)—The quantities or messages, which will be present in the machine and available as data for the program and which, usually, are not subject to change with time.

content(s)—The data contained in any storage medium. Quite prevalently, the symbol ( ) is used to indicate the contents of; e.g., (M) indicates the contents of the storage location whose address is M; or (T2) may indicate the contents of the tape on input-output unit two.

control—(1) The part of a digital computer or processor which determines the execution and interpretation of instructions in proper sequence, including the decoding of each instruction and the application of the proper signals to the arithmetic unit and other registers in accordance with the decoded information. (2) Frequently, it is one or more of the components in any mechanism responsible for interpreting and carrying out manually initiated directions. Sometimes it is called manual control. (3) In some business applications, a mathematical check. (4) In programming, instructions which determine conditional jumps are often referred to as control instructions, and the time sequence of execution of instructions is called the flow of control.

control card—A card which contains input data or parameters for a specific application of a general routine.

control, cascade—*See* cascade control.

control counter—A device which records the storage location of the instruction word, which is to be operated upon following the instruction word in current use. The control counter may select storage locations in sequence, thus obtaining the next instruction word from the subsequent storage location, unless a transfer or special instruction is encountered.

control data—The items of data, one or more of which is used to identify, select, execute or modify another routine, record, file, operation or data value.

control, feedback—*See* feedback control.

control field—A constant location where information for control purposes is placed; e.g., in a set of punch cards, if columns 79 and 80 contain various codes which control whether or not certain operations will be performed on any particular card, then columns 79 and 80 constitute a control field.

control grid—The electrode of a vacuum tube other than a diode upon which a signal voltage is impressed in order to regulate the plate current, usually electrode or grid number 1.

control, manual—*See* manual control.

control, master—*See* master control.

control, numerical—*See* numerical control.

control panel—(1) An interconnection device, usually removable, which employs removable wires to control the operation of computing equipment. It is used on punch card machines, to carry out functions which are under control of the user. On computers it is used primarily to control input and output functions. (2) A device or component of some data processing machines, which permits the expression of instructions in a semi-fixed computer program by the insertion of pins, plugs, or wires into sockets, or humbs in the device, in a pattern to represent instructions, and thus making electrical interconnections which may be sensed by the data processing machine. *Synonymous with* plugboard. *Related to* pinboard.

control, process—*See* process control.

control, program—*See* program control.

control, proportional—*See* proportional control.

control register—A register which holds the identification of the instruction word to be executed next in time sequence, following the current operation. The register is often a counter which is incremented to the address of the next sequential storage location, unless a transfer or other special instruction is specified by the program. *Synonymous with* program counter. *Contrasted with* register, program (1).

control sequence—The normal order of selection of instructions for execution. In some computers one of the addresses in each instruction specifies the control sequence. In most other computers, the sequence is consecutive except where a transfer occurs.

control, sequential—*See* sequential control.

control, supervisory—*See* supervisory control.

control total—A sum of numbers in a specified record field of a batch of records, determined repetitiously, during the processing operation so that any discrepancy from the control indicates an error. A control total often has some significance in itself, but may not, as for example, when a control total is determined as the sum of identification numbers of records. *Related to* total, hash.

control, transfer—*Same as* transfer, 4.

control, unconditional transfer of—*Same as* unconditional transfer.

control unit—The portion of a computer which directs the sequence of operations, interprets the coded instructions, and initiates the proper commands to the computer circuits preparatory to execution.

control word—A word, usually the first or last of a record, or first or last word of a block which carries indicative information for the following words, records, or blocks.

conversion—(1) The process of changing information from one form of representation to another; such as, from the language of one type of machine to that of another or from magnetic tape to the printed page. *Synonymous with* conversion, data. (2) The process of changing from one data processing method to another, or from one type of equipment to another; e.g., conversion from punch card equipment to magnetic tape equipment.

conversion, binary to decimal—*See* binary to decimal conversion.

conversion, data—*Same as* conversion, 1.

conversion, decimal to binary—*See* decimal to binary conversion.

conversion equipment—The equipment that is capable of transposing or transcribing the information from one type of data processing medium to render it acceptable as input to another type of processing medium.

convert—(1) To change numerical information from one number base to another (2) to transfer information from one recorded medium to another.

converter—A device which converts the representation of information, or which permits the changing of the method for data processing from one form to another; e.g., a unit which accepts information from punch cards and records the information on magnetic tape, and possibly including editing facilities.

converter, card to tape—*See* card to tape converter.

converter, tape to card—*See* tape to card converter.

coordinate indexing—An indexing scheme by which descriptors may be correlated or combined to show any interrelationships desired to purposes of more precise information retrieval.

coordinate paper—Marginally punched, continuous form graph paper normally used for printout on an XY plotter.

copy—To reproduce information in a new location, replacing whatever was previously stored there, and usually leaving the information unchanged at the original location.

copy, hard—*See* hard copy.

cordonnier system—*Same as* peek-a-boo system.

core dump—*Same as* storage dump.

core storage—*Same as* magnetic core storage.

correction, automatic error—*See* automatic error correction.

counter—A device, register, or location in storage for storing numbers or number representations in a manner which permits these numbers to be increased or decreased by the value of another number, or to be changed or reset to zero or to an arbitrary value.

counter, binary—*See* binary counter.

counter, control—*See* control counter.

counter, instruction—*Same as* location counter, 2.

counter, location—*See* location counter.

counter program—*Same as* control register.

counter, program address—*Same as* location counter, 2.

counter, ring—*See* ring counter.

CPU—*C*entral *P*rocessing *U*nit. *Same as* main frame, 1.

crippled leap frog test—A variation of the leapfrog test, modified so that it repeats its tests from a single set of storage locations rather than a changing set of locations. *Related to* leapfrog test.

cross bar—An automatic telephone switching system using movable switches mounted on bars. The dialed information is received and stored by common circuits which select and test the switching paths and control

the operation of the switching mechanisms.
crosstalk—(1) The unwanted signals in a channel which originate from one or more other channels in the same communications system; (2) signals electrically coupled from another circuit, usually undesirably, but sometimes for useful purposes.
cryogenics—The field of technology in which the use of devices utilizing properties assumed by metals at absolute zero. At these temperatures large current changes can be obtained by relatively small magnetic field changes.
cybernetics—The field of technology involved in the comparative study of the control and intracommunication of information handling machines and nervous systems of animals and man in order to understand and improve communication.
cycle—(1) The *same as* loop, 1. (2) A nonarithmetic shift in which digits dropped off at one end of a word are returned at the other end in circular fashion; e.g., cycle left and cycle right. (3) To repeat a set of operations, indefinitely or until a stated condition is met. The set of operations may be subject to variation on each repetition, as by address changes obtained by programmed computation or by use of devices such as an index register. (4) An occurrence, phenomena, or interval of space or time that recurs regularly and in the same sequence; e.g., the interval required for completion of one operation in a repetitive sequence of operations.
cycle, grandfather—*See* grandfather cycle.
cycle-index—The number of times a cycle has been executed or the difference, or the negative of the difference, between the number that has been executed and the number of repetitions desired.
cycle, major—*See* major cycle.
cycle, minor—*See* minor cycle.
cycle-reset—To return a cycle index to its initial value.
cycle, storage—*See* storage cycle.
cyclic code—*See* gray code.
cyclic shift—A shift in which the digits dropped off at one end of a word are returned at the other in a circular fashion; e.g., if, register holds eight digits, 23456789, the result of a cyclic shift two columns to the left would be to change the contents of the register to 45678923. *Synonymous with* circular shift; end around shift; logical shift; nonarithmetic shift; and ring shift.

damping—A characteristic built into electrical circuits and mechanical systems to prevent rapid or excessive corrections which may lead to instability or oscillatory conditions; e.g., connecting a register on the terminals of a pulse transformer to remove natural oscillations or placing a moving element in oil or sluggish grease to prevent mechanical overshoot of the moving parts.

data—A general term used to denote any or all facts, numbers, letters and symbols, or facts that refer to or describe an object, ideal, condition, situation, or other factors. It connotes basic elements of information which can be processed or produced by a computer. Sometimes data is considered to be expressible only in numerical form, but information is not so limited. *Related to* information.

data, control—*See* control data.

data conversion—*Same as* conversion, 1.

data element—A specific item of information appearing in a set of data; e.g., in the following set of data, each item is a data element: the quantity of a supply item issued, a unit rate, an amount, and the balance of stock items on hand.

data error—A deviation from correctness in data, usually an error, which occurred prior to processing the data.

data handling—*Same as* processing, data 2.

data, master—*See* master data.

data origination—The act of creating a record in a machine sensible form, directly or as a by-product of a human readable document.

data phone—A generic term to describe a family of devices available to facilitate data communication.

data processing—(1) The preparation of source media which contain data or basic elements of information, and the handling of such data according to precise rules of procedure to accomplish such operations as classifying, sorting, calculating, summarizing, and recording. (2) The production of records and reports. *Synonymous with* data handling.

data processing center—A computer installation providing data processing service for others, sometimes called customers, on a reimbursable or non-reimbursable basis.

data processing machine—A general name for a machine which can store and process numeric and alphabetic information. *Related to* analog computer; digital computer; automatic data processing equipment.

data purification—The reduction of the number of errors as much as possible prior to using data in an automatic data processing system.

data, raw—*See* raw data.

data reduction—The process of transforming masses of raw test or experimentally obtained data, usually gathered by automatic recording equipment, into useful, condensed, or simplified intelligence.

data reduction, on-line—*See* on-line data reduction.

data, test—*See* test data.

data, transaction—*See* transaction data.

data transmission equipment—The communications equipment used in direct support of data processing equipment.

data word—A word which may be primarily regarded as part of the information manipulated by a given program. A data word may be used to modify a program instruction, or to be arithmetically combined with other data words.

datamation—A shortened term for automatic data processing; taken from data and automation.

date, delivery—*See* delivery date.

date, installation—*See* installation date.

dc coupled—The connection by a device which passes the steady state characteristics of a signal and which largely eliminates the transient or oscillating characteristics of the signal.

dc dump—The removal of all direct current power, intentionally, accidentally or conditionally, from a system or component.

DDA—*Digital Differential Analyzer.* An incremental differential analyzer, usually electronic.

dead band—A specific range of values in which the incoming signal can be altered without also changing the outgoing response. *Synonymous with* dead space; dead zone; switching blank. *Similar to* zone, neutral.

dead halt—*Same as* drop dead halt.

dead space—*Same as* dead band.

dead time—Any definite delay deliberately placed between two related actions in order to avoid overlap that might cause confusion or to permit a particular different event such as a control decision, switching event or similar action to take place.

dead zone—*Same as* dead band.

debug—(1) To locate and correct any errors in a computer program. (2) To detect and correct malfunctions in the computer itself. *Related to* diagnostic routine.

debugging aid routine—A routine to aid programmers in the debugging of their routines. Some typical routines are: storage, print out, tape print out and drum print out routines.

decade—A group of assembly of ten units, e.g., a counter which counts to ten in one column or a resistor box which inserts resistance quantities in multiples of powers of 10.

decay time—The time in which a voltage or current pulse will decrease to one tenth of its maximum value. Decay time is proportional to the time constant of the circuit.

deceleration time—The time which elapses between completion of reading or writing of a tape record and the time when the tape stops moving. *Synonymous with* stop time.

decimal, binary coded—*See* binary coded decimal.

decimal, coded—*See* coded decimal.

decimal coded digit—A digit or character defined by a set of decimal digits, such as a pair of decimal digits specifying a letter or special character in a system of notation.

decimal number—A number, usually of more than one figure, representing a sum, in which the quantity represented by each figure is based on

decimal number—definition, problem

the radix of ten. The figures used are 0, 1, 2, 3, 4, 5, 6, 7, 8, and 9.

decimal numbering system—A system of reckoning by 10 or the powers of 10 using the digits 0-9 to express numerical quantities.

decimal to binary conversion—The process of converting a number written in the base of two from the equivalent number written in the base of ten.

decision—The computer operation of determining if a certain relationship exists between words in storage or registers, and taking alternative courses of action. This is effected by conditional jumps or equivalent techniques. Use of this term has given rise to the misnomer "magic brain;" actually the process consists of making comparisons by use of arithmetic to determine the relationship of two terms (numeric, alphabetic or a combination of both); e.g., equal, greater than, or less than.

decision box—The symbol used in flow charting to indicate a choice or branching in the information processing path.

decision, logical—*See* logical decision.

deck—A collection of cards, commonly a complete set of cards which have been punched for a definite service or purpose.

deck, condensed instruction—*See* condensed instruction deck.

decode—(1) To apply a code so as to reverse some previous encoding; (2) to determine the meaning of individual characters or groups of characters in a message; (3) to determine the meaning of an instruction from the set of pulses which describes the instruction, command, or operation to be performed.

decoder—(1) A device which determines the meaning of a set of signals and initiates a computer operation based thereon. (2) A matrix of switching elements which selects one or more output channels according to the combination of input signals present. *Contrasted with* encoder. *Clarified by* matrix.

decoding—(1) Performing the internal operations by which a computer determines the meaning of the operation code of an instruction; also sometimes applied to addresses. In interpretive routines and some subroutines, an operation by which a computer determines the meaning of parameters in the routine. (2) Translating a secretive language into the clear.

decrement—(1) The quantity by which a variable is decreased. (2) A specific part of an instruction word in some binary computers, thus a set of digits.

decrement field—A portion of an instruction word set aside specifically for modifying the contents of a register or storage location.

definition—(1) The resolution and sharpness of an image, or the extent to which an image is brought into sharp relief; (2) The degree with which a communication system reproduces sound images or messages.

definition, problem—*See* problem definition.

deflection sensitivity—Used in connection with cathode ray tubes, the quotient of the change in displacement of the electron beam at the place of impact, divided by the change in the deflecting field. It is usually expressed in millimeters per volt applied between the deflection electrode plates for electrostatic field deflection, or in millimeters per gauss for magnetic field deflection.

delay—(1) The length of time after the close of a reporting period before information pertaining to that period becomes available. Delay may also cover the time to process data, and prepare and distribute reports. (2) The retardation of the flow of information in a channel for a finite period of time.

delay, differential—*See* differential delay.

delay line—A device capable of retarding a pulse of energy between input and output, based on the properties of materials, or circuit parameters or mechanical devices. Examples of delay lines are material media such as mercury, in which sonic patterns may be propagated in item; lumped constant electrical lines; coaxial cables, transmission lines and recirculating magnetic drum loops. *Related to* magnetic delay line.

delimiter—A character which limits a string of characters, and therefore cannot be a member of the string.

delivery date—The data of physical delivery on site of the components of the computer configuration without regard to whether or not they have been unpacked, placed in final position, or interconnected. Delivery of equipment carries no connotation of operational status.

demodulator—(1) A device which receives tones from a transmission circuit and converts them to electrical pulses, or bits, which may be accepted by a business machine. (2) A device which detects the modulating signals, thus removes the carrier signal and reconstitutes the intelligence. *Clarified by* modulation code. *Contrasted with* modulator.

density, character—*See* character density.

density, packing—*See* packing density.

descriptor—An elementary term, word, or simple phrase used to identify a subject, concept, or idea.

design, item—*See* item design.

design, logical—*See* logical design.

detail file—A file of information which is relatively transient. This is contrasted with a master file which contains relatively more permanent information; e.g., in the case of weekly payroll for hourly employees, the detail file will contain employee number, regular time, and overtime, the hours such employee has worked in a given week, and other information changing weekly. The master file will contain the employee's name, number, department, rate of pay, deduction specifications, and other information which regularly stays the same from week to week.

device, analog—*See* analog device.

device, film optical sensing—*See* film optical sensing device.

device, input—*See* input device.

device, output—*See* output device.

diagnostic routine—A routine used to locate a malfunction in a computer, or to aid in locating mistakes in a computer program. Thus, in general any routine specifically designed to aid in debugging or troubleshooting. *Synonymous with* malfunction routine. *Related to* debugging (2).

diagnostic test—The running of a machine program or routine for the purpose of discovering a failure or a potential failure of a machine element, and to determine its location or its potential location.

diagnotor—A combination diagnostic and edit routine which questions unusual situations and notes the implied results.

diagram—(1) A schematic representation of a sequence of subroutines designed to solve a problem. (2) A coarser and less symbolic representation than a flowchart, frequently including descriptions in English words. (3) A schematic or logical drawing showing the electrical circuit or logical arrangements within a component.

diagram, block—*See* block diagram.

diagram, flow—*Same as* flow chart.

diagram, logical—*See* logical diagram.

diagram, Venn—*See* Venn, diagram.

di-cap storage—A device capable of holding data in the form of an array of charged capacitors, or condensers, and using diodes for controlling information flow.

dichotomizing search—*Same as* binary search.

dictionary—A list of code names used in a routine or system and their intended meaning in that routine or system.

dictionary, automatic—*See* automatic dictionary.

dictionary code—An alphabetic arrangement of English words and terms, associated with their code representations. *Related to* reverse code dictionary.

difference, logical—*See* logical difference.

differential analyzer—A computer (usually analog) designed and used primarily for solving many types of differential equations.

differential delay—The difference between the maximum and the minimum frequency delays occurring across a band.

differentiator—A device whose output function is proportional to a derivative; i.e., the rate of change, of its input function with respect to one or more variables.

digit—A sign or symbol used to convey a specific quantity of information either by itself or with other numbers of its set; e.g., 2, 3, 4, and 5 are digits. The base or radix must be specified and each digit's value assigned.

digit, binary—*See* binary digit.

digit, check—*See* check digit.

digit, decimal coded—*See* decimal coded digit.

digit, octal—*See* octal digit.

digit, sign—*See* sign digit.

digital—Pertaining to the utilization of discrete integral numbers in a given base to represent all the quantities that occur in a problem or a calculation. It is possible to express in digital form all information stored, transferred, or processed by a dual state condition, e.g., on-off, open-closed, and true-false.

digital computer—A computer which processes information represented by combinations of discrete or discontinuous data as compared with an analog computer for continuous data. More specifically, it is a device for performing sequences of arithmetic and logical operations, not only on data but its own program. Still more specifically it is a stored program digital computer capable of performing sequences of internally stored instructions, as opposed to calculators, such as card programmed calculators, on which the sequence is impressed manually. *Related to* machine, data processing.

digital differential analyzer—An incremental differential analyzer, usually electronic.

digitize—To convert an analog measurement of a physical variable into a numerical value, thereby expressing the quantity in digital form. *Synonymous with* quantize.

digitizer—A device which converts an analog measurement into digital form. *Synonymous with* quantizer.

digit(s), equivalent binary—*See* equivalent binary digit.

digit(s), significant—*See* significant digit.

diode—A device used to permit current flow in one direction in a circuit and to inhibit current flow in the other. In computers, these are primarily germanium or silicon crystals.

direct address—An address which indicates the location where the referenced operand is to be found or stored with no reference to an index register or B-Box. Synonymous with first level address.

direct code—A code which specifies the use of actual computer command and address configurations.

direct insert subroutine—*Same as* open subroutine.

directory—A file with the layout for each field of the record which it describes; thus a directory describes the layout of a record within a file.

disjunction—The logical operation which makes use of the OR operator or the logical sum. The disjunction of two variables, or expressions, may be written as A+B, A∨B, or A∩B. These may also be described as a union when using Venn diagrams. *Clarified by* or operator; gate, or. *Contrasted with* conjunction.

disjunctive search—A search defined in terms of a logical sum; i.e., disjunctive form, *in contrast to* a conjunctive form or logical product.

disk, magnetic—*See* magnetic disk.

disk storage—The storage of data on the surface of magnetic disks.

disk storage—dummy

Related to magnetic disk; magnetic disk storage.

disperse—A data processing operation in which input items or fields are distributed or duplicated in more than one output item or field.

display tube—A cathode ray tube used to display information.

distributor—The electronic circuitry which acts as an intermediate link between the accumulator and drum storage.

distributor, time pulse—*See* time pulse distributor.

document—(1) A form, voucher, or written evidence of a transaction; (2) to instruct, as by citation of references; (3) to substantiate, as by listing of authorities.

document, source—*See* source document.

documentation—The group of techniques necessary for the orderly presentation, organization and communication of recorded specialized knowledge, in order to maintain a complete record of reasons for changes in variables. Documentation is necessary not so much to give maximum utility as to give an unquestionable historical reference record.

docuterm—A word or phrase descriptive of the subject matter or concept of an item of information and considered important for later retrieval of information. *Related to* aspect card.

double length number—A number having twice as many figures as are normally handled in a particular device. *Synonymous with* double precision number.

double precision—The retention of twice as many digits of a quantity as the computer normally handles; e.g., if a computer, whose basic word consists of 10 decimal digits is called upon to handle 20 decimal digit quantities, then double precision arithmetic must be resorted to.

double precision number—*Same as* double length number.

double precision quantity—A quantity having twice as many digits as are normally carried in a word of a fixed word length computer.

down time—The period during which a computer is malfunctioning or not operating correctly due to mechanical or electronic failure, as opposed to available time, idle time, or stand-by time, during which the computer is functional. *Contrasted with* up time.

drive, tape—*Same as* tape transport. *Synonymous with* tape unit. and *Clarified by* magnetic tape unit; paper tape unit.

drop dead halt—A machine halt from which there is no recovery. Such a halt may be deliberately programmed. A drop dead halt may occur through a logical error in programming. Examples in which a drop dead halt could occur are division by zero and transfer to a nonexistent instruction word. *Synonymous with* dead halt.

drops, false—*See* false drops.

drum, magnetic—*See* magnetic drum.

drum mark—A character used to signify the end of a record on a drum.

dummy—An artificial address, instruction, or record of information inserted solely to fulfill prescribed conditions, such as to achieve a fixed word length or block length, but without itself affecting machine operations except to permit the machine to perform desired operations.

dummy instruction—An artificial instruction or address inserted in a list to serve a purpose other than the execution as an instruction. *Related to* constant instruction.

dump, ac—*See* ac dump.

dump, change—*See* change dump.

dump check—A check which usually consists of adding all the digits during dumping, and verifying the sum when retransferring.

dump, core—*Same as* storage dump.

dump, dc—*See* dc dump.

dump, memory—*Same as* memory dump.

dump, post mortem—*See* post mortem dump.

dump, power—*See* power dump.

dump, snapshot—*See* snapshot dump.

dump, storage—*See* storage dump.

duodecimal number—A number, consisting of successive characters, representing a sum, in which the individual quantity represented by each character is based on a radix of twelve. The characters used are 0, 1, 2, 3, 4, 5, 6, 7, 8, 9, T (for ten), and E (for eleven). *Related to* number systems.

duoprimed word—A computer word containing a representation of the 6, 7, 8, and 9 rows of information from an 80-column card.

duplex—Pertaining to a twin, a pair or a two-in-one situation; e.g., a channel providing simultaneous transmission in both directions or a second set of equipment to be used in event of the failure of the primary or either device.

duplication check—A check which requires that the results of two independent performances, either concurrently on duplicate equipment or at different times on the same equipment, of the same operation, be identical.

dynamic memory—*Same as* dynamic storage.

dynamic storage—The storage of data on a device or in a manner that permits the data to move or vary with time, and thus the data is not always available instantly for recovery; e.g., acoustic delay line, magnetic drum, or circulating or recirculating of information in a medium.

dynamic subroutine—A subroutine which involves parameters, such as decimal point position or item size, from which a relatively coded subroutine is derived. The computer itself is expected to adjust or generate the subroutine according to the parametric values chosen.

EAM—*E*lectrical *A*ccounting *M*achine. The set of conventional punch card equipment including sorters, collators and tabulators. *Synonymous with* EAM. *Clarified by* tabulating equipment.

Eccles-Jordan circuit—*Same as* flip-flop.

Eccles-Jordan Trigger—*Same as* flip-flop.

echo check—A check of accuracy of transmission in which the information which was transmitted to an output device is returned to the information source and compared with the original information to insure accuracy of output.

edge notched card—A card of any size provided with a series of holes on one or more edges for use in coding information for a simple mechanical search technique. Each hole position may be coded to represent an item of information by notching away the edge of the card into the hole. Cards containing desired information may then be mechanically selected from a deck by inserting a long needle in a hole position and lifting the deck to allow the notched cards to fall from the needle. Unwanted cards remain in the deck.

edge punched card—A card of fixed size into which information may be recorded or stored by punching holes along one edge in a pattern similar to that used for punch tape. Hole positions are arranged to form coded patterns in 5, 6, 7, or 8 channels and usually represent data by a binary coded decimal system.

edit—To rearrange data or information. Editing may involve the deletion of unwanted data, the selection of pertinent data, the application of format techniques, the insertion of symbols such as page numbers and typewriter characters, the application of standard processes such as zero suppression, and the testing of data for reasonableness and proper range. Editing may sometimes be distinguished between input edit (rearrangement of source data) and output edit (preparation of table formats).

edit, post—*See* post edit.

editor—A routine which performs editing operations.

EDP—*E*lectronic*D*ata*P*rocessing. Data processing performed largely by electronic equipment.

effective address—(1) A modified address. (2) The address actually considered to be used in a particular execution of a computer instruction.

eighty (80) column card—A punch card with 80 vertical columns representing 80 characters. Each column is divided into two sections, one with character positions labeled zero through nine, and the other labeled eleven (11) and (12) twelve. The 11 and 12 positions are also referred to as the X and Y zone punches, respectively. *Related to* punch card; ninety column card.

electric delay line—A delay line using properties of lumped or distributed capacitive and inductive elements.

electrical accounting machine—*Same as* EAM.

electronic—Pertaining to that branch of science which deals with the motion, emission and behavior of currents of free electrons, especially in vacuum, gas or phototubes and special conductors or semi-conductors. This is *contrasted with* electric which pertains to the flow of large currents in metal conductors.

electronic calculating punch—A card punch machine which reads a punch card, performs arithmetic and other operations sequentially and punches the result in a card.

electronic data processing—*Same as* EDP.

electronic data processing equipment—*Same as* automatic data processing equipment, (1).

electronic data processing machine—*Same as* automatic data processing equipment.

electronic data processing system—The general term used to define a system for data processing by means of machines utilizing electronic circuitry at electronic speed, as opposed to electromechanical equipment.

electronic differential analyzer—A form of analog computer using interconnected electronic integrators to solve differential equations.

electronic switch—A circuit element causing a start and stop action or a switching action electronically, usually at high speeds.

electrostatic printer—*Same as* xerographic printer.

electrostatic storage—(1) The storage of data on a dielectric surface such as the screen of a cathode ray tube, in the form of the presence or absence of spots bearing electrostatic charges, that can persist for a short time after the electrostatic charging force is removed. (2) A storage device so used.

element, data—*See* data element.

element, logical—*See* logical element.

eleven punch (11-punch)—*Same as* punch, ×, (2).

encipher—*Same as* encode, (1) and (2).

encode—(1) To apply a code, frequently one consisting of binary numbers, to represent individual characters or groups of characters in a message. *Synonymous with* encipher. *Inverse of* decode. (2) To substitute letters, numbers, or characters for other numbers, letters, or characters, usually to intentionally hide the meaning of the message except to certain individuals who know the enciphering scheme. *Synonymous with* encipher.

encoded question—A question set up and encoded in a form appropriate for operating, programming or conditioning a searching device.

encoder—A device capable of translating from one method of expression to another method of expression, e.g., translating a message, "add the contents of A to the contents of B", into a series of binary digits. *Contrasted with* decoder. *Clarified by* matrix.

end around carry—*Same as* carry, (2).

end around shift—*Same as* cyclic shift.

end of file—Termination or point of completion of a quantity of data. End of the file marks are used to indicate this point. *Synonymous with* EOF.

end of file indicator—A device associated with each input and output unit that makes an end of file condition known to the routine and operator

end of file indicator—erasable storage

controlling the computer.

end mark—An indicator to signal the end of a word or the end of a unit of data.

engineering time—The total machine down time necessary for routine testing, good or bad, for machine servicing due to breakdowns, or for preventive servicing measures; e.g., block tube changes. This includes all test time, good or bad, following breakdown and subsequent repair or preventive servicing. *Synonymous with* servicing time.

English, ruly—*See* ruly English.

entry—(1) A statement in a programming system. In general each entry is written on one line of a coding form and punched on one card, although some systems permit a single entry to overflow several cards. (2) A member of a list.

entry, keyboard—*See* keyboard entry.

EOF—*E*nd *Of File*. *See* end of file.

equation solver—A calculating device, usually analog, which solves systems of linear simultaneous non-differential equations or determines the roots of polynomials or both.

equipment, automatic data processing—*See* automatic data processing equipment.

equipment, auxiliary—*See* auxiliary equipment.

equipment compatibility—The characteristic of computers by which one computer may accept and process data prepared by another computer without conversion or code modification.

equipment, conversion—*See* conversion equipment.

equipment, data transmission—*See* data transmission equipment.

equipment, electronic data processing—*Same as* automatic data processing equipment, (1).

equipment failure—A fault in the equipment, excluding all external factors, which prevents the accomplishment of a scheduled job.

equipment, input—*See* input equipment.

equipment, off line—*See* off line equipment.

equipment, on-line—*See* on-line equipment.

equipment, output—*See* output equipment.

equipment, peripheral—*See* peripheral equipment.

equipment, tabulating—*See* tabulating equipment.

equivalent binary digits—The number of binary digits required to express a number in another base with the same precision; e.g., approximately 3-1/3 binary digits are required to express in binary form each digit of a decimal number. For the case of coded decimal notation, the number of binary digits required is usually 4 times the number of decimal digits.

erasable storage—(1) A storage device whose data can be altered during the course of a computation; e.g., magnetic tape, drum and cores. (2) An area of storage used for temporary storage.

195

erase—To replace all the binary digits in a storage device by binary zeros. In a binary computer, erasing is equivalent to clearing, while in a coded decimal computer where the pulse code for decimal zero may contain binary ones, clearing leaves decimal zero while erasing leaves all zero pulse codes in all storage locations. *Clarified by* clear.

error—(1) The general term referring to any deviation of a computed or a measured quantity from the theoretically correct or true value. (2) The part of the error due to a particular identifiable cause; e.g., a truncation error, or a rounding error. In a restricted sense, that deviation due to unavoidable random disturbances, or to the use of finite approximations to what is defined by an infinite series. Contrasted with mistake. (3) The amount by which the computed or measured quantity differs from the theoretically correct or true value.

error, absolute—*See* absolute error.

error, balanced (range of)—*See* balanced error, range of.

error correcting code—An error detecting code in which the forbidden pulse combination produced by gain or loss of a bit indicates which bit is wrong.

error, data—*See* data error.

error detecting code—A code in which errors produce forbidden combinations. A single error detecting code produces a forbidden combination if a digit gains or loses a single bit. A double error detecting code produces a forbidden combination if a digit gains or loses either one or two bits and so forth. *Synonymous with* self checking code. *Related to* self checking number.

error detection routine—A routine used to detect whether or not an error has occurred, usually without special provision to find or indicate its location.

error, inherent—*Same as* inherited error.

error, inherited—*See* inherited error.

error, machine—*See* machine error.

error, propagated—*See* propagated error.

error range—(1) The range of all possible values of the error of a particular quantity, (2) The difference between the highest and the lowest of these values.

error rate—The total amount of information in error, due to the transmission media, divided by the total amount of information received.

error, residual—*See* residual error.

error, rounding—*See* rounding error.

error, round-off—*Same as* rounding error.

error, truncation—*See* truncation error.

evaluation, performance—*See* performance evaluation.

except gate—A gate in which the specified combination of pulses producing an output pulse is the presence of a pulse on one or more input lines and the absence of a pulse on one or more other input lines.

exception principle system—An information system or data processing system which reports on situations only when actual results differ from planned results. When results occur within a normal range they are not reported.

excess fifty—A binary representation in which the decimal number 'n' is represented by the binary equivalent of (n+50).

excess three code—A binary coded decimal code in which each digit is represented by the binary equivalent of that number plus three, for example:

Decimal Digit	XS 3 Code	Binary Value
0	0011	3
1	0100	4
2	0101	5
3	0110	6
4	0111	7
5	1000	8
6	1001	9
7	1010	10
8	1011	11
9	1100	12

exchange—To interchange the contents of two storage devices or locations.

exchange message—*See* message exchange.

Exclusive OR operator—A logical operator which has the property that if P and Q are two statements, then the statement P*Q, where the * is the Exclusive OR operator, is true if either P or Q, but not both are true, and false if P and Q are both false or both true, according to the following table, wherein the figure 1 signifies a binary digit or truth.

P	Q	P*Q	
0	0	0	(Even)
0	1	1	(odd)
1	0	1	(odd)
1	1	0	(even)

Note that the Exclusive OR is the same as the Inclusive OR, except that the case with both inputs true yields no output; i.e., P*Q is true if P or Q are true, but not both. Primarily used in compare operations.

execute—To interpret a machine instruction and perform the indicated operation(s) on the operand(s) specified.

execution of an instruction—The set of elementary steps carried out by the computer to produce the result specified by the operation code of the instruction.

execution time—The portion of an instruction cycle during which the actual work is performed or operation executed; i.e., the time required

execution time—feedback control

to decode and perform an instruction. *Synonymous with* instruction time, (2).

executive routine—A routine which controls loading and relocation of routines and in some cases makes use of instructions which are unknown to the general programmer. Effectively, an executive routine is part of the machine itself. *Synonymous with* monitor routine; supervisory routine; supervisory program; and operating system.

executive system—*Same as* operating system.

exit—A way of momentarily interrupting or leaving a repeated cycle of operations in a program.

expression—Any symbol representing a variable or a group of symbols representing a group of variables possibly combined by symbols representing operators in accordance with a set of definitions and rules.

external memory—*Same as* external storage.

external storage—(1) The storage of data on a device which is not an integral part of a computer, but in a form prescribed for use by the computer. (2) A facility or device, not an integral part of a computer, on which data usable by a computer is stored such as, off line magnetic tape units, or punch card devices. *Synonymous with* external memory. *Contrasted with* internal storage.

extract—(1) To copy from a set of items all those items which meet a specified criterion. (2) To remove only a given set of digits or characters occupying certain specified locations in a computer word, such as extract the 8, 9, and 10 binary digits of a 44-bit word, as specified by the filter. *Clarified by* filter. (3) To derive a new computer word from part of another word, usually by masking. *Related to* unpack.

extractor—*Same as* filter.

factor, scale—*See* scale factor.

false drops—The documents spuriously identified as pertinent by an information retrieval system, but which do not satisfy the search requirements, due to cause such as improper coding, punching spurious or wrong combinations of holes, or improper use of terminology. *Related to* noise.

false retrievals—The library references which are not pertinent to but are vaguely related to the subject of the library search and are sometimes obtained by automatic search methods.

fast access storage—The section of the entire storage from which data may be obtained most rapidly.

feed—(1) To supply the material to be operated upon to a machine. (2) A device capable of feeding as in definition #1.

feed, card—*See* card feed.

feed, tape—*See* tape feed.

feedback—The part of a closed loop system which automatically brings back information about the condition under control.

feedback control—A type of system control obtained when a portion of the output signal is operated upon and fed back to the input in order to obtain a desired effect.

feedback control signal—That portion of the output signal which is returned to the input in order to achieve a desired effect, such as fast response.

ferroelectric—Pertaining to a phenomenon exhibited by certain materials in which the material is polarized in one direction or the other, or reversed in direction by the application of a positive or negative electric field of magnitude greater than a certain amount. The material retains the electric polarization unless it is disturbed. The polarization can be sensed by the fact that a change in the field induces an electromotive force which can cause a current.

ferromagnetic—Pertaining to a phenomenon exhibited by certain materials in which the material is polarized in one direction or the other, or reversed in direction by the application of a positive or negative magnetic field of magnitude greater than a certain amount. The material retains the magnetic polarization unless it is disturbed. The polarization can be sensed by the fact that a change in the field induces an electromotive force, which can cause a current.

fetch—To obtain a quantity of data from a place of storage.

field—An assigned area in a record to be marked with information.

field, card—*See* card field.

field, control—*See* control field.

field, decrement—*See* decrement field.

field, fixed—*See* fixed field.

field, free—*See* free field.

field length—The physical extent of a field. On a punch card it refers to the number of columns. On a tape it refers to bit positions.

field, signed—*See* signed field.

file—An organized collection of information directed toward some purpose. The records in a file may or may not be sequenced according to a key contained in each record.

file, detail—*See* detail file.

file gap—An interval of space or time associated with a file to indicate or signal the end of the file. *Related to* gap (2).

file identification—The coding required to identify each physical unit of the outputs of electronic data processing machine runs.

file maintenance—The periodic modification of a file to incorporate changes which occurred during a given period.

file, master—*See* master file.

file protection—A device or method which prevents accidental erasure of operative data on magnetic tape reels.

film optical sensing device—A piece of equipment capable of reading the contents of a film by optical methods; i.e., a system consisting of a light source, lenses, photo cells and a film moving mechanism. The output of the device is digitized and transferred directly to an electronic computer.

An example of such a device is the FOSDIC system developed jointly by the Bureau of Census and the National Bureau of Standards.

filmorex system—A system for the electronic selection of microfilm cards devised by Jacques Samain. Each card has a micro reproduction of the document or abstract and a field of twenty 5 digit code numbers giving the bibliographic references and the subjects treated.

filter—A machine word that specifies which parts of another machine word are to be operated upon, thus the criterion for an external command. *Synonymous with* extractor mask. *Clarified by* extract (2).

first level address—*Same as* direct address.

fixed cycle operation—(1) A type of computer performance whereby a fixed amount of time is allocated to an operation. (2) A synchronous or clock type arrangement within a computer in which events occur as a function of measured time. *Contrasted with* variable cycle operation.

fixed field—A given field on punch cards or a given number of holes along the edge of an edge punched card, set aside for the recording of a given type or classification of information.

fixed length record—A record whose number of characters is fixed. The restriction may be deliberate-to simplify and speed processing or may be caused by the characteristics of the equipment used.

fixed point arithmetic—(1) A method of calculation in which operations take place in an invariant manner, and in which the computer does not consider the location of the radix point. This is illustrated by desk calculators or slide rules, with which the operator must keep track of the decimal point. Similarly with many automatic computers, in which the location of the radix point is the programmer's responsibility. *Contrasted with* arithmetic, floating point. (2) A type of arithmetic in which the operands and results of all arithmetic operations must be properly scaled so as to have a magnitude between certain fixed values.

fixed point calculation—A calculation made with fixed point arithmetic.

fixed program computer—A computer in which the sequence of instructions are permanently stored or wired in, and perform automatically and are not subject to change either by the computer or the programmer except by rewiring or changing the storage input. *Related to* wired program computer.

fixed word length—Having the property that a machine word always contains the same number of characters or digits.

flag—(1) A bit of information attached to a character or word to indicate the boundary of a field. (2) An indicator used frequently to tell some later part of a program that some condition occurred earlier. (3) An indicator used to identify the members of several sets which are intermixed. *Synonymous with* sentinel.

flip-flop—(1) A bi-stable device; i.e., a device capable of assuming two stable states. (2) A bi-stable device which may assume a given stable state depending upon the pulse of history of one or more input points and

flip-flop—forbidden combination check

having one or more output points. The device is capable of storing a bit of information. (3) A control device for opening or closing gates; i.e., a toggle. *Synonymous with* Eccles-Jordan circuit Eccles-Jordan trigger.

floating address—Formerly, an address written in such a way that it can easily be converted to a machine address by indexing, assembly, or by some other means.

floating decimal arithmetic—A method of calculation which automatically accounts for the location of the radix point. This is usually accomplished by handling the number as a signed mantissa times the radix raised to an integral exponent; e.g. the decimal number +88.3 might be written as $+.883 \times 10^2$; the binary number $-.0011$ as $-.11 \times 2^{-2}$. *Synonymous with* floating decimal arithmetic. *Contrasted with* fixed point arithmetic (1).

floating point arithmetic—*Same as* floating decimal arithmetic.

floating point calculation—A calculation made with floating point arithmetic.

floating point routine—A set of subroutines which cause a computer to execute floating point arithmetic. These routines may be used to simulate floating point operations on a computer with no built in floating point hardware.

flowchart—A graphic representation of the major steps of work in process. The illustrative symbols may represent documents, machines, or actions taken during the process. The area of concentration is on where or who does what rather than how it is to be done. *Synonymous with* process chart; flow diagram.

flow diagram—*Same as* flowchart.

flying spot—A small, rapidly moving, spot of light, usually generated by a cathode ray tube and used to illuminate successive spots of a surface containing dark and light areas. The varying amount of light reflected is detected by a phototube and used to produce a time succession of electronic signals which effectively describe the surface.

forbidden combination check—A check, usually an automatic check, which tests for the occurrence of a nonpermissible code expression. A self checking code, or error detecting code, uses code expressions such that one or more errors in a code expression produces a forbidden combination. A parity check makes use of a self-checking code employing binary digits in which the total number of 1's, or 0's in each permissible code expression is always even or always odd. A check may be made either for even parity or odd parity. A redundancy check employs a self checking code which makes use of redundant digits called check digits. Some of the various names that have been applied to this type of check are: forbidden pulse combination, unused order, improper instruction, unallowable digits, improper command, false code, forbidden digit, nonexistent code, and unused code.

force—frequency response

force—To intervene manually in a routine and cause the computer to execute a jump instruction.

form stop—The automatic device on a printer which stops the machine when paper has run out.

formal logic—A branch of logic that deals with the study of the structure and forms of valid argument without regard to content.

format—The predetermined arrangement of characters, fields, lines, page numbers, and punctuation marks, usually on a single sheet or in a file. This refers to input, output and files.

FORTRAN—A programming language designed for problems which can be expressed in algebraic notation, allowing for exponentation and up to three subscripts. The FORTRAN compiler is a routine for a given machine which accepts a program written in FORTRAN source language and produces a machine language routine object program. FORTRAN II added considerably to the power of the original language by giving it the ability to define and use almost unlimited hierarchies of subroutines, all sharing a common storage region if desired. Later improvements have added the ability to use Boolean expressions, and some capabilities for inserting symbolic machine language sequences within a source program.

FOSDIC—*F*ilm *O*ptical *S*ensing *D*evice for *I*nput to *C*omputers. *Same as* film optical sensing device.

four address—A method of specifying the location of operands and instructions in which the storage location of the two operands and the storage location of the results of the operation are cited, and the storage location of the next instruction to be executed are cited.

four address instruction—A machine instruction usually consisting of the addresses of two operands, the address for storing the result, the address of the next instruction, the command to be executed, and miscellaneous indices. *Synonymous with* three plus one address instruction.

four wire circuit—A two way circuit using two paths so arranged that communication currents are transmitted in one direction only on one path, and in the opposite direction on the other path. The transmission path may or may not employ four wires.

frame, main—*See* main frame.

free field—A property of information processing recording media which permit recording of information without regard to a preassigned or fixed field; i.e., in information retrieval devices information may be dispersed in the record in any sequence or location.

frequency, clock—*See* clock frequency.

frequency response—A measure of the ability of a device to take into account, follow or act upon a varying condition; e.g., as applied to amplifiers, the frequencies at which the gain has fallen to the one-half power point or to 0.707 of the voltage gain, either at the high or low end of the frequency spectrum. When applied to a mechanical controller, the maximum rate at which changes in condition can be followed and acted upon, since it is implied that the controller can follow slow changes.

function switch—A circuit having a fixed number of inputs and outputs designed such that the output information is a function of the input information, each expresses in a certain code, signal configuration, or pattern.

function table—(1) The two or more sets of information so arranged that an entry in one set selects one or more entries in the remaining sets; (2) a dictionary; (3) a device constructed of hardware, or a subroutine, which can either decode multiple inputs into a single output or encode a single input into multiple outputs; (4) a tabulation of the values of a function for a set of values of the variable.

function, transfer—*See* transfer function.

functor—An improper term to be avoided. This term is sometimes used to designate a logic element which performs a specific function or provides a linkage between variables.

gain—The ratio between the output signal and the input signal of a device.

game theory—A mathematical process developed by Von Neumann of selecting an optimum strategy in the face of an opponent who has a strategy of his own.

gang punch—To punch identical or constant information into all of a group of punch cards.

gap—(1) An interval of space or time used as an automatic sentinel to indicate the end of a word, record, or file of data on a tape; e.g., a word gap at the end of a word, a record or item gap at the end of a group of words, and a file gap at the end of a group of records or items. (2) The absence of information for a specified length of time or space on a recording medium, as contrasted with marks and sentinels which are the presence of specific information to achieve a similar purpose. Marks are used primarily internally in variable word length machines. Sentinels achieve similar purposes either internally or externally; however, sentinels are programmed rather than inherent in the hardware. *Related to* file gap; symbol, terminating. (3) The space between the reading or recording head and the recording medium, such as tape, drum, or disk. *Related to* head gap.

gap, head—*See* head gap.

gap, inter-record—*See* inter-record gap.

gap, record—*See* record gap.

gate—A circuit which yields an output signal that is dependent on some function of its present or past input signals.

gate, AND—*See* AND gate.

gate, coincidence—*See* coincidence gate.

gate, except—*See* except gate.

gate, or—*See* or gate.

gate pulse—A pulse which enables a gate circuit to pass a signal; usually, the gate pulse is of longer duration than the signal, to make sure that coincidence in time occurs.

general program—A program expressed in computer code designed to solve a class of problems, or specializing on a specific problem when appropriate parametric values are supplied. *Synonymous with* general routine.

general purpose computer—A computer designed to solve a large variety of problems, e.g., a stored program computer which may be adapted to any of a very large class of applications.

general routine—*Same as* general program.

generate—To produce or prepare a specific item in accordance with a specific and defined rule or program over a period of time.

generating routine—A form of compiling routine, capable of handling less fully defined situations.

generator, program—*See* program generator.

generator, random number—*See* random number generator.

generator, report—*See* report generator.

gigacycle—A kilomegacycle per second, 10^9 cycles per second. *Synonymous with* kilomegacycle.

grandfather cycle—The period during which magnetic tape records are retained before reusing so that records can be reconstructed in the event of loss of information stored on a magnetic tape.

graphic panel—A master control panel which, pictorially and usually colorfully, traces the relationship of control equipment and the process operation. It permits an operator at a glance, to check on the operation of a far flung control system by noting dials, valves, scales, and lights.

gray code—A binary code in which sequential numbers are represented by expressions which are the same except in one place and in that place differ by one unit; e.g.,

Decimal	Binary	Gray
0	000	000
1	001	001
2	010	011
3	011	010
4	100	110
5	001	111

thus in going from one decimal digit to the next sequential digit, only one binary digit changes its value. *Synonymous with* cyclic code.

grid, control—*See* control grid.

group mark—A special character used to designate the end of a record in storage for a write instruction.

grouping of records—The combining of two or more records into one block of information on tape, to decrease the wasted time due to tape acceleration and deceleration and to conserve tape space. This is also called blocking of records.

gulp—Several bytes, thus a part of a word.

half adder—A circuit having two output points, S and C, representing sum and carry; and two input points, A and B, representing addend and augend, such that the output is related to the input according to the following table:

Input	Output
A B	S C
0 0	0 0
0 1	1 0
1 0	1 0
1 1	0 1

A and B are arbitrary input pulses, and S and C are sum without carry and carry, respectively. Two half-adders, properly connected, may be used for performing binary addition and form a full serial adder.

half adjust—A kind of rounding in which the value of the least significant digit of a number determines whether or not a one shall be added to the next higher significant digit, or, in which the two least significant digits determine whether or not a one is to be added to the next higher significant digit. If the least significant digits represent less than one-half, nothing is added to the next higher significant digit, if the least significant digits represent one-half or more than a one is added to the next higher significant digit.

half duplex service—A type of communication channel which is capable of transmitting and receiving signals, but is not capable for simultaneous and independent transmission and reception.

halt, dead—*Same as* drop dead halt.

halt, drop dead—*See* drop dead halt.

handling, data—*Same as* data processing (2).

hang up—A nonprogrammed stop in a routine. It is usually an unforeseen or unwanted halt in a machine pass. It is most often caused by improper coding of a machine instruction or by the attempted use of a non-existent or improper operation code.

hard copy—A printed copy of machine output; e.g., printed reports, listings, documents, and summaries.

hardware—The physical equipment or devices forming a computer and peripheral equipment. *Contrasted with* software.

hardware check—*Same as* automatic check.

hash total—A sum of numbers in a specified field of a record or of a batch of records used for checking purposes. No attention is paid to the significance of the total. Examples of such numbers are customer numbers or part numbers. If alphabetic characters have a numerical interpretation to a computer, they also could be added. *Related to* control total.

head—homostasis

head—A device which reads, records or erases information in a storage medium, usually a small electromagnet used to read, write or erase information on a magnetic drum or tape or the set of perforating or reading fingers and block assembly for punching or reading holes in paper tape or cards.

head gap—(1) The space between the reading or recording head and the recording medium, such as tape, drum or disk; (2) the space or gap intentionally inserted into the magnetic circuit of the head in order to force or direct the recording flux into the recording medium.

head, read write—*See* read write head.

heuristic—Pertaining to trial and error methods of obtaining solutions to problems.

heuristic program—*Same as* heuristic routine.

heuristic routine—A routine by which the computer attacks a problem not by a direct algorithmic procedure, but by a trial and error approach frequently involving the act of learning. *Synonymous with* heuristic program.

hexadecimal number—*Same as* sexadecimal number.

hi-erarchy—A specified rank or order of items, thus, a series of items classified by rank or order.

high-low bias test—*Same as* marginal check.

high order—Pertaining to the weight or significance assigned to the digits of a number; e.g., in the number 123456, the highest order digit is one; the lowest order digit is six. One may refer to the three high order bits of a binary word, as another example. *Clarified by* order (3).

high speed carry— *Same as* carry (2).

high speed printer— A printer which operates at a speed more compatible with the speed of computation and data processing so that it may operate on-line. At the present time a printer operating at a speed of 250 lines per minute, 100 characters per line is considered high-speed. *Synonymous with* HSP.

high speed reader—A reading device capable of being connected to a computer so as to operate on-line without seriously holding up the computer. A card reader reading more than 250 cards per minute would be called a high speed reader. A reader which reads punched paper tape at a rate greater than 50 characters per second could also be called a high speed reader. *Synonymous with* HSR.

hold—The function of retaining information in one storage device after also transferring it to another device. *Contrasted with* clear.

hollerith—A widely used system of encoding alphanumeric information onto cards, hence Hollerith cards is synonymous with punch cards. Such cards were first used in 1890 for the U.S. Census and were named after Herman Hollerith, their originator.

homostasis—The dynamic condition of a system wherein the input and output are balanced precisely, thus presenting an appearance of no

change, hence a steady state.
hopper—*Same as* card stacker.
horizontal system—A programming system in which instructions are written horizontally; i.e., across the page.
housekeeping—Pertaining to administrative or overhead operations or functions which are necessary in order to maintain control of a situation; e.g., for a computer program, housekeeping involves the setting up of constants and variables to be used in the program. *Synonymous with* red tape.
housekeeping operation—A general term for the operation which must be performed for a machine run usually before actual processing begins. Examples of housekeeping operations are: establishing controlling marks, setting up auxiliary storage units, reading in the first record for processing, initializing, set up verification operations, and file identification.
housekeeping routine—The initial instructions in a program which are executed only one time; e.g., clear storage.
HSP—*H*igh *S*peed *P*rinter.
HST—*H*igh *S*peed *R*eader.
hub—A socket on a control panel or plugboard into which an electrical lead or plug wire may be connected in order to carry signals, particularly to distribute the signals over many other wires.
hunting—A continuous attempt on the part of an automatically controlled system to seek a desired equilibrium condition. The system usually contains a standard, a method of determining deviation from this standard and a method of influencing the system such that the difference between the standard and the state of the system is brought to zero. *Clarified by* servomechanism (2).
hystersis—(1) The lagging in the response of a unit of a system behind an increase or a decrease in the strength of a signal, (2) A phenomenon demonstrated by materials which make their behavior a function of the history of the environment to which they have been subjected.

IAL— *I*nternational *A*lgebraic *L*anguage. *See* language, international algebraic.
identification, file—*See* file identification.
idle time—(1) The period between the end of one programmed computer run and the commencement of a subsequent programmed run; (2) the time normally used to assemble cards, paper, tape reels, and control panels required for the next computer operation; (3) the time between operations when no work is scheduled.
IDP—*I*ntegrated *D*ata *P*rocessing. *See* integrated data processing.
ignore—(1) A typewriter character indicating that no action whatsoever be taken; e.g., in teletype or flexowriter code, a character code consisting of holes punched in every hole position is an ignore character; this

convention makes possible erasing any previously punched character. (2) An instruction requiring nonperformance of what normally might be executed; i.e., not to be executed. This instruction should not be confused with a NO OP or Do Nothing instruction, since these generally refer to an instruction outside themselves.

illegal character—A character or combination of bits which is not accepted as a valid representation by the machine design or by a specific routine. Illegal characters are commonly detected and used as an indication of machine malfunction.

image—An exact duplicate array of information or data stored in, or in transit to, a different medium.

image, card—*See* Card image.

immediate access—Pertaining to the ability to obtain data from or place data in a storage device, or register directly without serial delay due to other units of data, and usually in a relatively short period of time.

immediate address—An instruction address in which the address part of the instruction is the operand. *Synonymous with* zero level address.

impedance, characteristic—*See* characteristic impedance.

Inclusive OR operator—A logical operator which has the property that P or Q is true, if P or Q or both is true; when the term OR is used alone, as in OR gate, the Inclusive OR is usually implied.

impulse noise—A pulse appearing at the output of a circuit which was not transmitted from the originating input to the circuit. These pulses usually are induced from circuit functioning or from sources outside the circuit and its associated input-output equipment.

incremental computer—A computer in which changes in the variables rather than the variables themselves are represented. Those changes correspond to a change in an independent variable as defined by the equations being solved. *Contrasted with* absolute value computer.

index—A symbol or a number used to identify a particular quantity in an array of similar quantities, e.g., X5 is the fifth item in an array of X's.

index register—A register which contains a quantity which may be used to modify addresses. *Synonymous with* B-register (1); B-box.

index, word—*See* word index.

index word—A storage position or register the contents of which may be used to modify automatically the effective address of any given instruction.

indexed address—An address that is to be modified or has been modified by an index register or similar device. *Synonymous with* variable address.

indexing, coordinate—*See* coordinate indexing.

indexing, uniterm—*See* uniterm indexing.

indicator, check—*See* check indicator.

indicator, end of file—*See* end of file indicator.

indicator, machine check—*See* machine check indicator.

indicator, overflow check—*See* overflow check indicator.

indicator, read write check—*See* read write check indicator.

indicator, role—*See* role indicator.

indicator, sign check—*See* sign check indicator.

indicators—The devices which register conditions, such as high or equal conditions resulting from a comparison of plus or minus conditions resulting from a computation. A sequence of operations within a procedure may be varied according to the position of an indicator.

indirect address—An address in a computer instruction which indicates a location where the address of the referenced operand is to be found. In some computers the machine address indicated can itself be indirect. Such multiple levels of addressing are terminated either by prior control or by a termination symbol. *Synonymous with* second level address.

information—A collection of facts or other data especially as derived from the processing of data. *Related to* data.

information processing—A less restrictive term than data processing, encompassing the totality of scientific and business operations performed by a computer.

information requirements—The actual or anticipated questions which may be posed to an information system.

information retrieval—The recovering of desired information or data from a collection of documents or other graphic records.

information retrieval system—A system for locating and selecting, on demand, certain documents, or other graphic records relevant to a given information requirement from a file of such material. Examples of information retrieval systems are classification, indexing, and machine searching systems.

information system—The network of all communication methods within an organization. Information may be derived from many sources other than a data processing unit, such as by telephone, by contact with other people, or by studying an operation.

information theory—The mathematical theory concerned with information rate, channels, channel width, noise and other factors affecting information transmission. Initially developed for electrical communications, it is now applied to business systems, and other phenomena which deal with information units and flow of information in networks.

information word—An ordered set of characters bearing at least one meaning and handled by a computer as a unit, including separating and spacing, which may be contrasted with instruction words. *Related to* machine word.

inherent error—*Same as* inherited error.

inherited error—The error in the initial values. Especially the error inherited from the previous steps in the step-by-step integration. This error could also be the error introduced by the inability to make exact measurements of physical quantities. *Synonymous with* inherent error.

inhibiting input—A gate input which, if in its prescribed state, prevents any output which might otherwise occur.

inhibiting signal—A signal, which when entered into a specific circuit will prevent the circuit from exercising its normal function; e.g., an inhibit signal fed into an AND gate will prevent the gate from yielding an output when all normal input signals are present.

initialize—(1) To set various counters, switches and addresses to zero or other starting values, at the beginning of, or at the prescribed points in a computer routine; (2) Used as an aid to recovery and restart during a long computer run.

in line processing—*Same as* on line (2).

in line subroutine—A subroutine inserted directly into the linear operational sequence. Such a subroutine must be recopied at each point that it is needed in a routine.

input—(1) Information or data transferred or to be transferred from an external storage medium into the internal storage of the computer, (2) describing the routines which direct input as defined in (1) or the devices from which such information is available to the computer. (3) The device or collective set of devices necessary for input as defined in (1).

input area—*Same as* input block (1).

input block—(1) A section of internal storage of a computer reserved for the receiving and processing of input information. *Synonymous with* input area. (2) An input buffer. (3) A block of computer words considered as a unit and intended or destined to be transferred from an external source or storage medium to the internal storage of the computer.

input device—The mechanical unit designed to bring data to be processed into a computer; e.g., a card reader, a tape reader, or a keyboard.

input equipment—(1) The equipment used for transferring data and instructions into an automatic data processing system, (2) the equipment by which an operator transcribes original data and instructions to a medium that may be used in a automatic data processing system.

input, inhibiting—*See* inhibiting input.

input magazine—The card feed magazine in a reader, or read-punch unit. *Synonymous with* input stacker.

input-output—A general term for the equipment used to communicate with a computer and the data involved in the communication. *Synonymous with* I/O.

input-output limited—Pertaining to a system or condition in which the time for input and output operation exceeds other operations.

input routine—A routine, sometimes stored permanently in a computer, to allow reading of programs and data into the machine.

input stacker—*Same as* input magazine.

inquiry—A technique whereby the interrogation of the contents of a computer's storage may be initiated at a keyboard.

inquiry station—The remote terminal device from which an inquiry into computing or data processing equipment is made.

installation date—The date new equipment is ready for use. The commencement of rental normally begins on the day following the date on which the contractor officially notifies the using organization that the equipment is installed and ready for use, subject to the acceptance and standard of performance provisions of the applicable contract.

instruction—(1) A set of characters which defines an operation together with one or more addresses, or no address, and which, as a unit, causes the computer to perform the operation on the indicated quantities. The term instruction is preferable to the terms command and order; command is reserved for a specific portion of the instruction word; i.e., the part which specifies the operation which is to be performed, order is reserved for the ordering of the characters, implying sequence, or the order of the interpolation, or the order of the differential equation. *Related to* code, 1. (2) The operation or command to be executed by a computer, together with associated addresses, tags and indices.

instruction, alphanumeric—*See* alphanumeric instruction.

instruction area—(1) A part of storage allocated to receive and store the group of instructions to be executed; (2) the storage locations used to store the program.

instruction, branch—*See* branch instruction.

instruction, breakpoint—*See* breakpoint instruction.

instruction, check indicator—*See* check indicator instruction.

instruction code—The list of symbols, names and definitions of the instructions which are intelligible to a given computer or computing system.

instruction, conditional breakpoint—*See* conditional breakpoint instruction.

instruction, constant—*See* constant instruction.

instruction counter—*Same as* location counter, 2.

instruction dummy—*See* dummy instruction.

instruction, four address—*See* four address instruction.

instruction, macro—*See* macro instruction.

instruction, micro—*See* micro instruction.

instruction, multiple address—*See* multiple address instruction.

instruction, no address—*See* no address instruction.

instruction, no-op—*See* no-op instruction.

instruction, one address—*See* one address instruction.

instruction, one plus one address—See one plus one address instruction.

instruction, pseudo—*See* pseudo instruction.

instruction, quasi—*Same as* pseudo instruction.

instruction register—*Same as* program register, (2).

instruction repertory—internally stored program

instruction repertory—(1) The set of instructions which a computing or data processing system is capable of performing, (2) the set of instructions which an automatic coding system assembles.

instruction, skip—*See* skip instruction.

instruction, symbolic—*See* symbolic instruction.

instruction time—(1) The portion of an instruction cycle during which the control unit is analyzing the instruction and setting up to perform the indicated operation; (2) *same as* execution time.

instruction, three plus one address—*Same as* four address instruction.

instruction, transfer—*See* transfer instruction.

instruction, two, three or four address—*See* two, three or four address instruction.

instruction, waste—*See* waste instruction.

instruction, zero address—*See* zero address instruction.

integrated data processing—(1) A system that treats as a whole, all data processing requirements to accomplish a sequence of data processing steps, or a number or related data processing sequences, and which strives to reduce or eliminate duplicating data entry or processing steps. (2) The processing of data by such a system. *Synonymous with* IDP.

integrator—A device whose output is proportional to the integral of the input variable with respect to time.

intelligence, artificial—*See* artificial intelligence.

interface—A common boundary between automatic data processing systems or parts of a single system.

interfix—A technique which allows the relationships of key words in an item or document to be described so that very specific inquiries can be answered without false retrievals due to crosstalk.

interlace—To assign successive storage locations; e.g., on a magnetic drum, usually for the purpose of reducing access time.

interlock—To arrange the control of machines or devices so that their operation is interdependent in order to assure their proper coordination.

internal arithmetic—The computations performed by the arithmetic unit of a computer.

internal memory—*Same as* internal storage.

internal storage—(1) The storage of data on a device which is an integral part of a computer. (2) The storage facilities forming an integral physical part of the computer and directly controlled by the computer. In such facilities all data are automatically accessible to the computer; e.g., magnetic core, and magnetic tape on-line. *Synonymous with* internal memory. *Contrasted with* external storage.

internally stored program—A sequence of instructions, stored inside the computer in the same storage facilities as the computer data, as opposed to external storage on punched paper tape and pinboards.

international algebraic language—The forerunner of ALGOL. *Synonymous with* IAL. *Clarified by* algorithmic language.

interpret—(1) To print on a punch card the information punched in that card, (2) to translate non-machine language into machine language instructions.

interpreter—(1) A punch card machine which will take a punch card with no printing on it, read the information in the punched holes, and print a translation in characters in specified rows and columns on the card. (2) An executive routine which, as the computation progresses, translates a stored program expressed in some machine like pseudo code into machine code and performs the indicated operations, by means of subroutines, as they are translated. An interpreter is essentially a closed subroutine which operates successively on an indefinitely long sequence of program parameters, the pseudo instructions and operands. It may usually be entered as a closed subroutine and left by a pseudo code exit instruction.

interpretive code—*Same as* interpretive routine.

interpretive programming—The writing of programs in a pseudo machine language, which is precisely converted by the computer into actual machine language instructions before being performed by the computer.

interpretive routine—A routine which decodes and immediately executes instructions written as pseudo codes. This is contrasted with a compiler which decodes the pseudo codes into a machine language routine to be executed at a later time. The essential characteristic of an interpretive routine is that a particular pseudo code operation must be decoded each time it is executed. *Synonymous with* interpretive code.

inter-record gap—An interval of space or time deliberately left between recording portions of data or records. Such spacing is used to prevent errors through loss of data or overwriting, and permits tape stop-start operations.

interrupt—To temporarily disrupt the normal operation of a routine by a special signal from the computer. Usually the normal operation can be resumed from that point at a later time.

interstage punching—A system of punching in which only odd numbered rows or cards are used. *Contrasted with* normal stage punching.

inverter—A circuit which takes in a positive pulse and puts out a negative one, or takes in a negative pulse and puts out a positive one. The physical meaning of positive and negative depends on the specific circuit and the conventions established for it.

I/O—The abbreviation for input-output.

item—(1) A set of one or more fields containing related information, (2) a unit of correlated information relating to a single person or object, (3) the contents of a single message.

item advance—A technique in the grouping of records for operating

item advance—label

successively on different records in storage.

item design—The specification of what fields make up an item, the order in which the fields are to be recorded, and the number of characters to be allocated to each field.

item size—(1) The magnitude of an item, usually expressed in numbers of words, characters or blocks; (2) the number of characters in an item.

iterative—Describing a procedure or process which repeatedly executes a series of operations until some condition is satisfied. An iterative procedure can be implemented by a loop in a routine.

iterative process—A process for calculating a desired result by means of a repeating cycle of operations, which comes closer and closer to the desired result; e.g., the arithmetical square root of N may be approximated by an iterative process using additions, subtractions, and divisions only.

jam, card—*See* card jam.

jump—*Same as* transfer (4).

jump, conditional—*Same as* conditional transfer.

jump, unconditional—*Same as* unconditional transfer.

key—(1) A group of characters which identifies or is part of a record or item, thus any entry in a record or item can be used as a key for collating or sorting purposes. (2) A marked lever manually operated for copying a character; e.g., a typewriter, paper tape perforator, card punch, manual keyboard, digitizer or manual word generator. (3) A lever or switch on a computer console for the purpose of manually altering computer action.

keyboard entry—(1) An element of information inserted manually, usually via a set of switches or marked punch levers, called keys, into an automatic data processing system; (2) a medium as in (1) above for achieving access to or entrance into an automatic data processing system.

keypunch—(1) A special device to record information in cards or tape by punching holes in the cards or tape to represent letters, digits, and special characters; (2) to operate a device for punching holes in cards or tape.

key verify—To use the punch card machine known as a verifier, which has a keyboard, to make sure that the information supposed to be punched in a punch card has actually been properly punched. The machine signals when the punched hole and the depressed key disagree.

kilocycle—A thousand cycles per second, or 10^3 cycles per second. *Clarified by* megacycle; gigacycle; teracycle.

kilomegacycle—*Same as* gigacycle.

label—A set of symbols used to identify or describe an item, record, message, or file. Occasionally it may be the same as the address in storage.

lacing—Extra multiple punching in a card column to signify the end of a specific card run. The term is derived from the lace work appearance of the card.

lag—A relative measure of the time delay between two events, states, or mechanisms.

language—A system for representing and communicating information or data between people, or between people and machines. Such a system consists of a carefully defined set of characters and rules for combining them into larger units, such as words or expressions, and rules for word arrangement or usage to achieve specific meanings.

language, algorithmic—*See* algorithmic language.

language, artificial—*See* artificial language.

language, common machine—*See* common machine language.

language, common business oriented—*See* Common Business Oriented Language.

language, international algebraic—*See* international algebraic language.

language, machine—*See* machine language.

language, machine oriented—*See* machine oriented language.

language, object—*See* object language.

language, problem oriented—*See* problem oriented language.

language, procedure oriented—*See* procedure oriented language.

language, program—*See* program language.

language, source—*See* source language.

language, target—*See* target language.

latency time—(1) The time lag between completion of instruction staticizing and the initiation of the movement of data from its storage location, (2) the rotational delay time from a disc file or a drum file.

leader—(1) A record which precedes a group of detail records, giving information about the group not present in the detail records; e.g., beginning of batch 17. (2) An unused or blank length of tape at the beginning of a reel of tape preceding the start of the recorded data.

leapfrog test—A program designed to discover computer malfunction, characterized by the property that it performs a series of arithmetical or logical operations on one group of storage locations, transfers itself to another group of storage locations, checks the correctness of the transfer, then begins the series of operations again. Eventually, all storage positions will have been occupied and the test will be repeated. *Related to* crippled leapfrog test.

length, block—*See* block length.

length, field—*See* field length.

length, record—*See* record length.

length, register—*See* register length.

length, word—*See* word length.

level, average effectiveness—*See* average effectiveness level.

library—(1) A collection of information available to a computer, usually on magnetic tapes; (2) a file of magnetic tapes.

library, routine—*See* routine library.

library, subroutine—*See* subroutine library.

line, acoustic delay—*See* acoustic delay line.

line code—A single instruction written usually on one line, in a code for a specific computer to solve a problem. This instruction is usually stored as a whole in the program register of the computer while it is executed, and it may contain one or more addresses of registers or storage locations in the computer where numbers or machine words are to be obtained or sent, and one or more operations to be executed. *Synonymous with* program line.

line, delay—*See* delay line.

line, electric delay—*See* electric delay line.

line, magnetic delay—*See* magnetic delay line.

line, magnetostrictive delay—*See* magnetostrictive delay line.

line, mercury delay—*See* mercury delay line.

line printer—A device capable of printing one line of characters across a page; i.e., 100 or more characters simultaneously as continuous paper advances line by line in one direction past type bars or a type cylinder that contains all characters in all positions.

line, sonic delay—*See* sonic delay line.

linear programming—A technique of mathematics and operations research for solving certain kinds of problems involving many variables where a best value or set of best values is to be found. This technique is not to be confused with computer programming, although problems using the technique may be programmed on a computer. Linear programming is most likely to be feasible when the quantity to be optimized, sometimes called the objective function, can be stated as a mathematical expression in terms of the various activities within the system, and when this expression is simply proportional to the measure of the activities; i.e., is linear, and when all the restrictions are also linear.

linkage—A technique for providing interconnections between program runs or between routines.

linked subroutine—*Same as* closed subroutine.

list, assembly—*See* assembly list.

list, push down—*See* push down list.

list, push up—*See* push up list.

load—(1) To put data into a register or storage; (2) to put a magnetic tape onto a tape drive, or to put cards into a card reader.

load-and-go—Refers to an automatic coding procedure which not only compiles the program, creating machine language, but also proceeds to execute the created program. Load and go procedures are usually part of a monitor.

load point—A preset point at which magnetic tape is initially positioned under the read-write head to start reading or writing.

loading routine—A routine which, once it's itself in storage, is able to bring other information into storage from cards or tape.

location—A storage position in the main internal storage which can store one computer word and which is usually identified by an address.

location, bit—*See* bit location.

location counter—(1) The control section register which contains the address of the instruction currently being executed. (2) A register in which the address of the current instruction is recorded. *Synonymous with* instruction counter; program address counter.

log—A record of everything pertinent to a machine run including: identification of the machine run, record of alteration switch settings, identification of input and output tapes, copy of manual key ins, identification of all stops, and a record of action taken on all stops.

logger—A device which automatically records physical processes and events, usually chronologically.

logic—(1) The science dealing with the criteria or formal principles of reasoning and thought. (2) The systematic scheme which defines the interactions of signals in the design of an automatic data processing system. (3) The basic principles and application of truth tables and interconnection between logical elements required for arithmetic computation in an automatic data processing system. *Related to* symbolic logic.

logic, formal—*See* formal logic.

logic, mathematical—*Same as* symbolic logic (2).

logic, symbolic—*See* symbolic logic.

logical connectives—The operators or words, such as AND, OR, OR ELSE, IF THEN, NEITHER NOR, and EXCEPT, which make new statements from given statements and which have the property that the truth or falseness of the new statements can be calculated from the truth or falsity of the given statements and the logical meaning of the operator.

logical decision—The choice or ability to choose between alternatives. Basically this amounts to an ability to answer yes or no with respect to certain fundamental questions involving equality and relative magnitude; e.g., in an inventory application, it is necessary to determine whether or not there has been an issue of a given stock item.

logical diagram—A diagram which represents the logical elements of a system and their interconnections without necessarily expressing construction, engineering or electrical schematic circuit details.

logical difference—All elements belonging to class A but not to class B, when two classes of elements, class A and class B, are given.

logical element—The smallest building block in a computer or data processing system, which can be represented by logical operators in an appropriate system of symbolic logic. Typical logical elements are the

logical element—low order

AND-gate and the OR-gate, which can be represented as operators in a suitable symbolic logic.

logical flow chart—A detailed solution of the work order in terms of the logic, or built in operations and characteristics, of a specific machine. Concise symbolic notation is used to represent the information and describe the input, output, arithmetic, and logical operations involved. The chart indicates types of operations by use of a standard set of block symbols. A coding process normally follows the logical flow chart.

logical multiply—*Same as* and operator.

logical operation—(1) A logical or boolean operation on N state variables which yields a single N state variable; e.g., a comparison on the 3-state variables A and B, each represented by −,), or +, which yields: − when A is less than B, 0 when A equals B, and + when A is greater than B. Specifically, operations such as AND, OR, and NOT on two-state variables which occur in the algebra of logic; i.e., Boolean algebra. (2) The operations of logical shifting, masking, and other non-arithmetic operations of a computer. *Contrasted with* arithmetic operation.

logical operator—*Same as* operator, 1.

logical shift—*Same as* cyclic shift.

logical sum—A result, similar to an arithmetic sum, obtained in the process of ordinary addition, except that the rules are such that a result of one is obtained when either one or both input variables is a one, and an output of zero is obtained when the input variables are both zero. The logical sum is the name given the result produced by the (inclusive or operator).

logical symbol—A sign used as an operator to denote the particular operation to be performed on the associated variables.

look up table—*Same as* table. Not to be confused with the verb form (table look up).

loop—(1) A self contained series of instructions in which the last instruction can modify and repeat itself until a terminal condition is reached. The productive instructions in the loop generally manipulate the operands, while bookkeeping instructions modify the productive instructions, and keep count of the number of repetitions. A loop may contain any number of conditions for termination. The equivalent of a loop can be achieved by the technique of straight line coding, whereby the repetition of productive and bookkeeping operations is accomplished by explicitly writing the instructions for each repetition. *Synonymous with* cycle (1). (2) A communications circuit between two private subscribers or between a subscriber and the local switching center.

loop, closed—*See* closed loop.

loop, open—*See* open loop.

loop, rapid access—*See* rapid access loop.

low order—Pertaining to the weight or significance assigned to the digits of a number; e.g., in the number 123456, the low order digit is six. One

low order—machine translation

may refer to the three low-order bits of a binary word, as another example. Clarified by (order, 3).

lpm—Lines Per Minute.

machine, accounting—*Same as* tabulator.

machine address—An absolute, direct, unindexed address expressed as such, or resulting after indexing and other processing has been completed.

machine check indicator—A protective device which will be turned on when certain conditions arise within the machine. The machine can be programmed to stop or run a separate correction routine or to ignore the condition.

machine, code—*Same as* code, computer (1).

machine, data processing—*See* data processing machine.

machine, electrical accounting—*See* electrical accounting machine.

machine, electronic data processing—*See* electronic data processing machine.

machine error—A deviation from correctness in data resulting from an equipment failure.

machine language—*Same as* machine oriented language. *Related to* object language.

machine language code—*Same as* computer code (1). *Contrasted with* symbolic code.

machine operator—The person who manipulates the computer controls, places information media into the input devices, removes the output and performs other related functions.

machine oriented language—(1) A language designed for interpretation and use by a machine without translation. (2) A system for expressing information which is intelligible to a specific machine; e.g., a computer or class of computers. Such a language may include instructions which define and direct machine operations, and information to be recorded by or acted upon by these machine operations. (3) The set of instructions expressed in the number system basic to a computer, together with symbolic operation codes with absolute addresses, relative addresses, or symbolic addresses. *Synonymous with* machine language. *Clarified by* language. *Related to* object language. *Contrasted with* problem oriented language.

machine run—The execution of one or several machine routines which are linked to form one operating unit.

machine, self organizing—*See* self organizing machine.

machine sensible—Pertaining to information in a form which can be read by a specific machine.

machine translation—The automatic translation from one representation to another representation. The translation may involve codes, languages, or other systems of representation. *Related to* automatic dictionary.

machine, turing—*See* turing machine.

machine, universal turing—*See* universal turing machine.

machine word—A unit of information of a standard number of characters which a machine regularly handles in each transfer; e.g., a machine may regularly handle numbers or instruction in units of 36 binary digits; this is then the machine word. *Related to* information word.

macro instruction—(1) An instruction consisting of a sequence of micro instructions which are inserted into the object routine for performing a specific operation, (2) the more powerful instructions which combine several operations in one instruction.

magazine, input—*See* input magazine.

magazine, output—*See* output magazine.

magnetic core storage—A storage device in which binary data is represented by the direction of magnetization in each unit of an array of magnetic material, usually in the shape of toroidal rings, but also in other forms such as wraps on bobbins. *Synonymous with* core storage.

magnetic delay line—A delay line using magnetic material; e.g., a drum channel used as a delay line, or combinations of cores and other components used as a delay line. *Related to* delay line.

magnetic disk—A storage device on which information is recorded on the magnetizable surface of a rotating disk. A magnetic disk storage system is an array of such devices, with associated reading and writing heads which are mounted on movable arms. *Related to* disk storage.

magnetic disk storage—A storage device or system consisting of magnetically coated disks, on the surface of which information is stored in the form of magnetic spots arranged in a manner to represent binary data. These data are arranged in circular tracks around the disks and are accessible to reading and writing heads on an arm which can be moved mechanically to the desired disk and then to the desired track on that disk. Data from a given track are read or written sequentially as the disk rotates. *Related to* disk storage.

magnetic drum—A cylinder having a surface coating of magnetic material, which stores binary information by the orientation of magnetic dipoles near or on its surface. Since the drum is rotated at a uniform rate, the information stored is available periodically as a given portion of the surface moves past one or more flux detecting devices called heads located near the surface of the drum.

magnetic drum storage—The storage of data on the surface of magnetic drums. *Related to* magnetic drum.

magnetic shift register—A register which makes use of magnetic cores as binary storage elements, and in which the pattern of binary digital information can be shifted from one position to the next left or right position.

magnetic storage—A device or devices which utilize the magnetic properties of materials to store information.

magnetic tape—A tape or ribbon of any material impregnated or coated with magnetic or other material on which information may be placed in the form of magnetically polarized spots.

magnetic tape reader—A device capable of sensing information recorded on a magnetic tape in the form of a series of magnetized spots.

magnetic tape storage—A storage device in which data is stored in the form of magnetic spots on metal or coated plastic tape. Binary data are stored as small magnetized spots arranged in column form across the width of the tape. A read-write head is usually associated with each row of magnetized spots so that one column can be read or written at a time as the tape traverses the head.

magnetic tape unit—The mechanism, normally used with a computer, which handles magnetic tape and usually consists of a tape transport, reading or sensing and writing or recording heads, and associated electrical and electronic equipments. Most units may provide for tape to be wound and stored on reels; however, some units provide for the tape to be stored loosely in closed bins. *Clarified by* tape transport, paper tape unit.

magnetic wire—A wire made of or coated with a magnetic material and used for magnetic recording.

magnetostriction—A phenomenon wherein certain materials increase in length in the direction of the magnetic field when subjected to such a field, and restore to their original length when demagnetized.

magnetostrictive delay line—A delay line which utilizes the physical principle of magnetostriction. *Clarified by* magnetostriction.

main frame—(1) The central processor of the computer system. It contains the main storage, arithmetic unit and special register groups. *Synonymous* with CPU, central processing unit. (2) All that portion of a computer exclusive of the input, output, peripheral and in some instances, storage units.

main storage—Usually the fastest storage device of a computer and the one from which instructions are executed. *Contrasted with* auxiliary storage.

management information system—A communications process in which data are recorded and processed for operational purposes. The problems are isolated for higher level decision making and information is fed back to top management to reflect the progress or lack of progress made in achieving major objectives.

maintenance file—*See* file maintenance.

maintenance, preventive—*See* preventive maintenance.

maintenance, remedial—*See* remedial maintenance.

major cycle—(1) The maximum access time of a recirculating serial storage element, (2) the time for one rotation of a magnetic drum or of pulses in an acoustic delay line, (3) a number of minor cycles.

malfunction—A failure in the operation of the hardware of a computer.
malfunction routine—*Same as* diagnostic routine.
malfunction, program sensitive—*See* program sensitive malfunction.
manipulated variable—In a process that is desired to regulate some condition, a quantity or a condition that is altered by the computer in order to initiate a change in the value of the regulated condition.
manual control—The direction of a computer by means of manually operated switches.
MAP—To transform information from one form to another.
marginal check—A preventive maintenance procedure in which certain operating conditions are varied about their normal values in order to detect and locate incipient defective units; e.g., supply voltage or frequency may be varied. *Synonymous with* marginal test; high-low bias test. *Related to* check.
marginal test—*Same as* marginal check.
mark—A sign or symbol used to signify or indicate an event in time or space; e.g., end of word or message mark, a file mark, a drum mark, and end of tape mark.
mark, drum—*See* drum mark.
mark, end—*See* end mark.
mark group—*See* group mark.
mark, record—*See* record mark.
mark, record storage—*See* record storage mark.
mark sensing—A technique for detecting special pencil marks entered in special places on a punch card and automatically translating the marks into punched hole.
mark, segment—*See* segment mark.
mark, storage—*See* storage mark.
mark, tape—*See* tape mark.
mask—*Same as* filter.
masking—(1) The process of extracting a nonword group or a field of characters from a word or a string of words, (2) the process of setting internal program controls to prevent transfers which otherwise would occur upon setting of internal machine latches.
master card—A card containing fixed or indicative information for a group of cards. It is usually the first card of that group.
master control—An application oriented routine usually applied to the highest level of a subroutine hierarchy.
master data—A set of data which is altered infrequently and supplies basic data for processing operations. The data content of a Master File. Examples include: names, badge numbers, or pay rates in personnel data; or stock numbers, stock descriptions, or units of measure in stock control data.
master file—A file containing relatively permanent information.

master instruction tape—A tape on which all the programs for a system of runs are recorded. *Synonymous with* MIT.

match—A data processing operation similar to a merge, except that instead of producing a sequence of items made up from the input, sequences are matched against each other on the basis of some key. The following is a schematic of a two-item match:

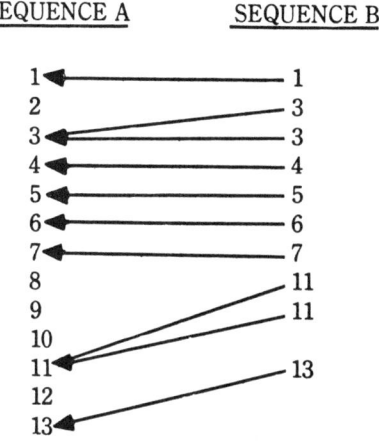

mathematical, logic—*Same as* symbolic logic, 2.

mathematical check—A check which uses mathematical identities or other properties, occasionally with some degree of discrepancy being acceptable: e.g., checking multiplication by verifying that $A \times B = B \times A$. *Synonymous with* (arithmetic check).

mathematical model—The general characterization of a process, object, or concept, in terms of mathmatics, which enables the relatively simple manipulation of variables to be accomplished in order to determine how the process, object, or concept would behave in different situations.

matrix—(1) An array of quantities in a prescribed form; in mathematics, usually capable of being subject to a mathematical operation by means of an operator or another matrix according to prescribed rules. (2) An array of coupled circuit elements; e.g., diodes, wires, magnetic cores, and relays, which are capable of performing a specific function; such as, the conversion from one numerical system to another. The elements are usually arranged in rows and columns. Thus a matrix is the particular type of encoder or decoder. *Clarified by* encoder; decoder.

matrix printer—*Same as* wire printer.

matrix, semantic—*See* semantic matrix.

mechanical differential analyzer—A form of analog computer using interconnected mechanical surfaces to solve differential equations; e.g., the Bush differential analyzer developed by Vannevar Bush at Massachusetts Institute of Technology which used differential gear boxes to perform addition and a combination of wheel disk spherical mechanisms to perform integration.

mechanical replacement—An action originated by the contractor and taken by him to substitute one machine for another that is installed at a customer's site. Such action usually is occasioned by the mechanical condition of the equipment being replaced.

mechanical translation—A generic term for language translation by computers or similar equipment.

medium—The physical substance upon which data is recorded; e.g., magnetic tape, punch cards and paper.

megabit—One million binary bits.

megacycle—A million cycles per second, 10^6 cycles per second.

memory—*Same as* storage.

memory capacity—*Same as* capacity storage.

memory dump—*Same as* storage dump.

memory, dynamic—*Same as* dynamic storage.

memory, external—*Same as* external storage.

memory, internal—*Same as* internal storage.

memory printout—*Same as* storage dump.

memory, random access—*Same as* random access storage.

memory register—*Same as* storage register.

mercury delay line— A sonic or acoustic delay line in which mercury is used as the medium of sound transmission, with transducers on each end to permit conversion to and from electrical energy. Related to (acoustic delay line).

mercury storage—The storage of data in a mercury delay line. *Related to* mercury delay line.

mercury tank—A container used to hold mercury.

merge—To combine items into one sequenced file from two or more similarly sequenced files without changing the order of the items.

message—(1) A group of words, variable in length, transported as a unit; (2) a transported item of information.

Message exchange—A device, placed between a communication line and a computer, in order to take care of certain communication functions and thereby free the computer for other work.

message routing—The function performed at a central message processor of selecting the route, or alternate route if required, by which a message will proceed to the next point in reaching its destination.

method, Monte Carlo—*See* Monte Carlo method.

micro code—(1) A system of coding making use of suboperations not ordinarily accessible in programming; e.g., coding that makes use of parts of multiplication or division operations. (2) A list of small program steps. Combinations of these steps, performed automatically in a prescribed sequence form a macro operation like multiply, divide, and square root.

micro instruction—A small, single, short, add, shift or delete type of command.

micro programming—The technique of using a certain special set of instructions for an automatic computer, that consists only of basic elemental operations which the programmer may combine into higher level instructions, which he may then program using the higher level instructions only; e.g., if a computer has only basic instructions for adding, subtracting, and multiplying, the instruction for dividing would be defined by microprogramming.

microprogram—(1) A program of analytic instructions which the programmer intends to construct from the basic subcommands of a digital computer, (2) a sequence of pseudo commands which will be translated by hardware into machine subcommands, (3) a means of building various analytic instructions as needed from the subcommand structure of a computer, (4) a plan for obtaining maximum utilization of the abilities of a digital computer by efficient use of the subcommands of the machine.

microsecond—One millionth of a second, 10^{-6} seconds, abbreviated microsec.

millimicrosecond—*Same as* nanosecond.

millisecond—One thousandth of a second, 10^{-3} seconds, abbreviated msec. or ms.

minimum access code—A system of coding which minimizes the effect of delays for transfer of data or instructions between storage and other machine components. *Related to* optimum code; minimum latency code; minimum access coding.

minimum access programming—Programming in such a way that minimum waiting time is required to obtain information out of storage. *Synonymous with* minimal latency programming. *Contrasted with* random access programming.

minimum access routine—A routine so coded that by judicious arrangement of data and instructions in storage, the actual access time is less than the expected random access time. Such a routine is used with serial storage systems. *Synonymous with* minimum latency routine.

minimum latency code—*Same as* minimum access code.

minimum latency programming—*Same as* minimum access programming.

minimum latency routine—*Same as* minimum access routine.

minor cycle—The time interval between the appearance of corresponding parts of successive words in a storage device which provides serial access to storage positions.

minuend—The quantity from which another quantity is subtracted or is to be subtracted.

minus zone—The bit positions in a computer code which represent the algebraic minus sign.

mistake—A human failing; e.g., faulty arithmetic, use of incorrect formula, or incorrect instructions. Mistakes are sometimes called gross errors to distinguish from rounding and truncation errors. Thus, computers malfunction and humans make mistakes. Computers do not make mistakes and humans do not malfunction, in the strict sense of the word. *Contrasted with* error (2).

MIT—*M*aster *I*nstruction *T*ape. *Same as* master instruction tape.

mixed base notation—*Same as* mixed radix notation.

mixed base number—*Same as* mixed radix number.

mixed radix notation—A method of expressing a quantity, using two or more characters, where each character is of a different radix.

mixed radix number—A number consisting of two or more characters, representing a sum, in which the quantity represented by each character is based on a different radix. *Synonymous with* mixed base number.

mnemonic—Pertaining to the assisting, or intending to assist, human memory; thus a mnemonic term, usually an abbreviation, that is easy to remember; e.g., mpy for multiply and acc for accumulator.

mnemonic operation code—An operation code in which the names of operations are abbreviated and expressed mnemonically to facilitate remembering the operations they represent. A mnemonic code normally needs to be converted to an actual operation code by an assembler before execution by the computer. Examples of mnemonic codes are ADD for addition, CLR for clear storage and SQR for square root.

mode—(1) A computer system of data representation; e.g., the binary mode. (2) A selected mode of computer operation.

mode, noisy—*See* noisy mode.

model, mathematical—*See* mathematical model.

modifier—A quantity used to alter the normal interpretation and execution of an instruction; e.g., an index tag or indirect address tag.

modify—(1) To alter a portion of an instruction so its interpretation and execution will be other than normal. The modification may permanently change the instruction or leave it unchanged and affect only the current execution. The most frequent modification is that of the effective address through use of index registers. (2) To alter a subroutine according to a defined parameter.

modulation code—A code used to cause variations in a signal in accordance with a predetermined scheme; normally used to alter or modulate a carrier wave to transmit data. *Clarified by* modulator.

modulator—A device which varies a repetitive phenomenon in accordance with some predetermined scheme usually introduced as a signal. *Clarified by* modulation; demodulator code.

module—(1) An interchangeable plug-in item containing components, (2) an incremental block of storage or other building block for expanding the computer capacity.

modulo n check—(1) A check that makes use of a check number that is equal to the remainder of the desired number when divided by N; e.g., in a modulo 4 check, the check number will be 0, 1, 2, or 3 and the remainder of A when divided by 4 must equal the reported check number B; otherwise an equipment malfunction has occurred. (2) A method of verification by congruences; e.g., casting out nines. *Related to* self checking number.

monitor—To supervise and verify the correct operation of a program during its execution, usually by means of a diagnostic routine used from time to time to answer questions about the program.

monitor routine—*Same as* executive routine.

monitor system—*Same as* operating system.

Monte Carlo method—A trial and error method of repeated calculations to discover the best solution of a problem. Often used when a great number of variables are present, with interrelationships so extremely complex as to forestall straightforward analytical handling.

multi-address—*Same as* multiple address.

multi-precision arithmetic—A form of arithmetic similar to double precision arithmetic except that two or more words may be used to represent each number.

multi aspect—Pertaining to searches or systems which permit more than one aspect, or facet, of information to be used in combination, one with the other to effect identifying and selecting operations.

multiple address—A type of instruction which specifies the addresses of two or more items which may be the addresses of locations of inputs or outputs of the calculating unit or the addresses of locations of instructions for the control unit. The term multi-address is also used in characterizing computers; e.g., two, three, or four address machines. *Synonymous with* multi-address.

multiple address code—An instruction code in which an instruction word can specify more than one address to be used during the operation. In a typical instruction of a four address code the addresses specify the location of two operands, the location at which the results are to be stored and the location of the next instruction in the sequence. In a typical three address code, the fourth address specifying the location of the next instructions is dispensed with, the instructions are taken from storage in a preassigned order. In a typical two address code, the addresses may specify the location of the operands. The results may be placed at one of the addresses or the destination of the results may be specified by another instruction.

multiple address instruction—An instruction consisting of an operation code and two or more addresses. Usually specified as a two address, three address, or four address instruction.

multiple length number—A number having two, three, or more times as many figures as are normally handled in a particular device.

multiple programming—The programming of a computer by allowing two or more arithmetical or logical operations to be executed simultaneously. *Contrasted with* serial programming.

multiple punching—(1) The reference to punch cards and more specifically to Hollerith cards; (2) the punching of two or more holes in a column.

multiplex—The process to transferring data from several storage devices operating at relatively low transfer rates to one storage device operating at a high transfer rate in such a manner that the high speed device is not obliged to wait for the low speed devices.

multiplexing—(1) The transmission of a number of different messages simultaneously over a single circuit. (2) Utilizing a single device for several similar purposes or using several devices for the same purpose; e.g., a duplexed communications channel carrying two messages simultaneously.

multiplication time—The time required to perform a multiplication. For a binary number it will be equal to the total of all the addition times and all the shift time involved in the multiplication.

multiply, logical—*Same as* and operator.

multiprocessor—A machine with multiple arithmetic and logic units for simultaneous use.

multiprogramming—A technique for handling numerous routines or programs simultaneously by means of an interweaving process.

nanosecond—One thousandth of a millionth of a second, 10^{-9} seconds. *Synonymous with* millimicrosecond.

nest—(1) To embed a subroutine or block of data into a larger routine or block of data, (2) to evaluate an nth degree polynominal by a particular algorithm which uses (n−1) multiply operations and (n−1) add operations in succession.

network, analog—*See* analog network.

network analyzer—An analog device designed primarily for simulating electrical networks. *Synonymous with* calculator network.

network calculator—*Same as* network analyzer.

neutral zone—An area in space or an interval of time in which a state of being other than the implementing state exists; e.g., a range of values in which no control action occurs or a brief period between words when certain switching action takes place. Similar to (dead band).

ninety (90) column card—A punch card with 90 vertical columns representing 90 characters. The columns are divided in half horizontally, such that the vertical columns in the upper half of the card are numbered 1 through 45, and those in the lower half 46 through 90. Six punching positions may be used in each column; these are designated, from top to bottom, to represent the digits 0, 1, 3, 5, 7 and 9 by a single punch. The digits 2, 4, 6, and 8 and other characters may be represented by a combination of two or more punches. *Related to* punch card; eighty column card.

no address instruction—An instruction specifying an operation which the computer can perform without having to refer to its storage unit.

no charge machine fault time—The unproductive time due to computer fault such as the following: nonduplication, transcribing error, input-output malfunction and machine malfunction resulting in an incomplete run.

noise—The meaningless extra bits or words which must be ignored or removed from the data at the time the data is used. *Related to* false drops.

noise, broadband (white)—*See* broadband noise.

noise, impulse—*See* impulse noise.

noisy mode—A floating point arithmetic procedure associated with normalization in which ".1" bits, rather than "0" bits, are introduced in the low order bit position during the left shift.

non arithmethic shift—*Same as* cyclic shift.

non destructive read—A reading of the information in a register without changing that information.

non erasable storage—A storage device whose information cannot be erased during the course of computation; e.g., punched paper tape, and punched cards, magnetic slug, "missing core," and silvered or aluminized paper.

non scheduled maintenance time—The elapsed time during scheduled working hours between the determination of a machine failure and placement of the equipment back into operation.

non volatile storage—A storage medium which retains information in the absence of power and which may be made available upon restoration of power; e.g., magnetic tapes, cores, drums, and discs. *Contrasted with* volatile storage.

NO-OP instruction—(1) An instruction which specifically instructs the computer to do nothing but process the next instruction in sequence. (2) A blank instruction. (3) A skip instruction. (4) A waste instruction. *Synonymous with* waste instruction and skip.

normal stage punching—A system of punching in which only even numbered rows of the card are used. *Contrasted with* punching, interstage.

normalize—(1) In programming to adjust the exponent and fraction of a floating point quantity so that the fraction lies in the prescribed normal standard, range. (2) In mathematical operations to reduce a set of symbols or numbers to a normal or standard form. *Synonymous with* standardize.

notation—(1) The act, process, or method of representing facts or quantities by a system or set of marks, signs, figures, or characters. (2) A

notation—number, polyvalent

system of such symbols or abbreviations used to express technical facts or quantities; as mathematical notation. (3) An annotation; note.

notation, base—*Same as* radix notation.
notation, binary—*See* binary notation.
notation, binary coded decimal—*See* binary coded decimal notation.
notation, biquinary—*See* biquinary notation.
notation, coded decimal—*See* coded decimal notation.
notation, mixed base—*Same as* notation mixed radix.
notation, mixed radix—*See* mixed radix notation.
notation, polyvalent—*See* polyvalent notation.
notation, positional—*See* positional notation.
notation, radix—*See* radix notation.
notation, symbolic—*See* symbolic notation.
null—(1) An absence of information, as contrasted with zero or blank for the presence of no information; (2) zero; (3) pertaining to no deflection from a center or end position.
number—(1) The, or a total, aggregate, or amount of units. (2) A figure or word, or a group of figures or words, representing graphically an arithmetical sum; a numerical, as the number 45. *Clarified by* number systems. (3) A numeral by which a thing is designated in a series; as a pulse number. (4) A single member of a series designated by consecutive numerals; as, a part number. (5) A character, or a group of characters, uniquely identifying or describing an article, process, condition, document, or class; as, a 6SN7 tube. (6) To count; enumerate. (7) To distinguish by a number.
number, base—*Same as* radix.
number, binary—*See* binary number.
number, binary coded decimal—*See* binary coded decimal number.
number, biquinary—*See* biquinary number.
number, biquinary coded decimal—*See* biquinary coded decimal number.
number, call—*See* call number.
number, check—*see* check number.
number, coded decimal—*See* coded decimal number.
number, decimal—*See* decimal number.
number, double length—*See* double length number.
number, double precision—*Same as* double length number.
number, duodecimal—*See* duodecimal number.
number, hexadecimal—*Same as* sexadecimal number.
number, mixed base—*Same as* mixed radix number.
number, mixed radix—*See* mixed radix number.
number, multiple length—*See* multiple length number.
number, octal—*See* octal number.
number, operation—*See* operation number.
number, polyvalent—*See* polyvalent number.

number, positional—*Same as* positional notation.
number, radix—*Same as* radix.
number, read around—*See* read around number.
number, self checking—*See* self checking number.
number, septinary—*See* septinary number.
number sexadecimal—*See* sexidecimal number.
number, symbolic—*See* symbolic number.
number systems—(1) A systematic method for representing numerical quantities in which any quantity is represented as the sequence of coefficients of the successive powers of a particular base with an appropriate point. Each succeeding coefficient from right to left is associated with and usually multiplies the next higher power of the base. The first coefficient to the left of the point is associated with the zero power of the base. For example, in decimal notation 371.426 represents $(3 \times 10^2) + (7 \times 10^1) + (1 \times 10^0) + (4 \times 10^{-1}) + (2 \times 10^{-2}) + (6 \times 10^{-3})$. (2) The following are names of the number systems with bases 2 through 20: 2, Binary; 3, Ternary; 4, Quaternary; 5, Quinary; 6, Senary; 7, Septenary; 8, Octal, or octonary; 9, Novenary; 10, Decimal; 11, Undecimal; 12, Duodecimal; 13, Terdenary; 14, Quaterdenary; 15, Quindenary; 16, Sexadecimal, or Hexadecimal; 17, Septendecimal; 18, Octodenary; 19, Novemdenary; 20, Vicenary. Also 32, Duosexadecimal, or duotricinary; and 60, Sexagenary. The binary, Octal, Decimal, and Sexadecimal systems are widely used in computers. *Synonymous with* duodecimal number; binary number system. *Related to* positional representation. *Clarified by* octal and binary digit.
numeral—A digit, or digits, normally used to represent a number.
numeric code—A system of numerical abbreviations used in the preparation of information for input into a machine; i.e., all information is reduced to numerical quantities. *Contrasted with* alphabetic code.
numerical analysis—The study of methods of obtaining useful quantitative solutions to mathematical problems, regardless of whether an analytic solution exists or not, and the study of the errors and bounds on errors in obtaining such solutions.
numerical control—Descriptive of systems in which digital computers are used for the control of operations, particularly of automatic machines; e.g., drilling or boring machines, wherein the operation control is applied at discrete points in the operation or process. *Contrasted with* process control.
n way switch—*Same as* variable connector (3).

object language—A language which is the output of an automatic coding routine. Usually object language and machine language are the same; however, a series of steps in an automatic coding system may involve the object language of one step serving as a source language for the next step and so forth.

object program—The program which is the output of an automatic coding system. Often the object program is a machine language program ready for execution, but it may well be in an intermediate language. *Synonymous with* target program; object routine. *Contrasted with* source program.

object routine—*Same as* object program.

octal—Pertaining to eight; usually describing a number system of base or radix eight; e.g., in octal notation, octal 214 is 2 times 64, plus 1 times 8, plus 4 times 1, and equals decimal 140. Octal 214 in binary coded octal is represented as 010, 001, 100; octal 214, as a straight binary number is written 100001100. Note that binary coded octal and straight binary differ only in the use of commas, in the example shown, the initial zero in the straight binary is dropped. *Clarified* by octal number.

octal digit—The symbol 0,1,2,3,4,5,6,7 used as a digit in the system of notation which uses 8 as the base or radix. *Clarified by* number systems.

octal number—A number of one or more figures, representing a sum in which the quantity represented by each figure is based on a radix of eight. The figures used are 0, 1, 2, 3, 4, 5, 6, and 7. *Clarified by* octal.

octonary signalling—A communications mode in which information is passed by the presence and absence or plus and minus variation of eight discrete levels of one parameter of the signalling medium.

odd-even check—*Same as* parity check.

off line—Descriptive of a system and of the peripheral equipment or devices in a system in which the operation of peripheral equipment is not under the control of the central processing unit. *Clarified by* off line equipment.

off line equipment—The peripheral equipment or devices not in direct communication with the central processing unit of a computer. *Synonymous with* auxiliary equipment.

off punch—A punch not properly positioned in a column of a card.

offset—The difference between the value or condition desired and that actually attained.

on-line—Descriptive of a system and of the peripheral equipment or devices in a system in which the operation of such equipment is under control of the central processing unit, and in which information reflecting current activity is introduced into the data processing system as soon as it occurs. Thus, directly in-line with the main flow of transaction processing. *Clarified by* on-line equipment. *Synonymous with* in line processing; on-line processing.

on-line processing—*Same as* on-line.

on-line data-reduction—The processing of information as rapidly as the information is received by the computing system or as rapidly as it is generated by the source.

on the fly printer—A high speed line printer using continuously rotating print wheels and fast acting hammers to print the successive letters contained in one line of text so rapidly that all of the characters in the printed line look as though they were all printed simultaneously.

one address—(1) A single address. (2) A system of machine instruction such that each complete instruction explicitly describes one operation and involves one storage location. *Synonymous with* single address. *Related to* one address instruction.

one address instruction—An instruction consisting of an operation and exactly one address. The instruction code of a signal address computer may include both zero and multi address instructions as special cases. *Related to* one address.

one level code—*Same as* absolute code.

one plus one address—An instruction system having the property that each complete instruction includes an operation and two addresses, one for the location of a register in the storage containing the item to be operated upon, and one for the location containing the next instruction.

one plus one address instruction—An instruction containing two or four addresses one of which specifies explicitly the location of the next instruction to be executed. It is usually used on computers whose storage has a latency factor; e.g., a drum computer.

open ended—The quality by which the addition of new terms, subject headings, or classifications does not disturb the pre-existing system.

open loop—Pertaining to a control system in which there is no self correcting action for misses of the desired operational condition, as there is in a closed loop system.

open routine—A routine which can be inserted directly into a larger routine without a linkage or calling sequence.

open shop—The operation of a computer facility where computer programming, coding and operating can be performed by any qualified employee of the organization, not necessarily by the personnel of the computing center itself and where the programmer may assist in, or oversee the running of his program on the computer. *Contrasted with* closed shop.

open subroutine—A subroutine inserted directly into the linear operational sequence, not entered by a jump. Such a subroutine must be recopied at each point that it is needed in a routine. *Synonymous with* direct insert subroutine.

operand—A quantity entering or arising in an instruction. An operand may be an argument, a result, a parameter, or an indication of the location of the next instruction, as opposed to the operation code or symbol itself. It may even be the address portion of an instruction.

operating ratio—The ratio of the number of hours of correct machine operation to the total hours of scheduled operation; e.g., on a 168 hour week scheduled operation, if 12 hours of preventive maintenance are required and 4.8 hours of unscheduled down time occurs, then the operating ratio is (168-16.8)/168, which is equivalent to a 90% operating ratio. *Synonymous with* computer efficiency.

operating system—An integrated collection of service routines for supervising the sequencing of programs by a computer. Operating systems may perform debugging, input-output, accounting, compilation, and storage assignment tasks. *Synonymous with* monitor system; executive system.

operation—A defined action. The action specified by a single computer instruction or pseudo instruction.

operation, arithmetic—*See* arithmetic operation.

operation, bookkeeping—*See* bookkeeping operation.

operation code—The part of a computer instruction word which specifies, in coded form, the operation to be performed.

operation, complete—*See* complete operation.

operation, computer—*See* computer operation.

operation, fixed cycle—*See* fixed cycle operation.

operation, housekeeping—*See* housekeeping operation.

operation, logical—*See* logical operation.

operation number—(1) A number designating the position of an operation, or its equivalent subroutine in the sequence of operations comprising a routine; (2) A number identifying each step in a program stated in symbolic code.

operation, parallel—*See* parallel operation.

operation, real time—*See* real time operation.

operation, red tape—*Same as* bookkeeping operation.

operation register—A register in which an operation is stored and analyzed in order to set conditions for the execution cycle.

operation, scheduled—*See* scheduled operation.

operation, sequential—*See* sequential operation.

operation, serial—*See* serial operation.

operation, single step—*See* single step operation.

operation, transfer—*See* transfer operation.

operation use time—In Federal Government ADP contracts the time during which the equipment is in operation, exclusive of idle time, standby time, maintenance time, or rerun time due to machine failure. Components not programmed for use in a specified computer run are not considered to be in use even though connected into the computer system.

operation, variable cycle—*See* variable cycle operation.

operations research—The use of analytic methods adopted from mathematics for solving operational problems. The objective is to provide management with a more logical basis for making sound predictions and decisions. Among the common scientific techniques used in operations research are the following: linear programming, probability theory, information theory, game theory, Monte Carlo method, and queuing theory. *Synonymous with* O.R.

operator—(1) A mathematical symbol which represents a mathematical process to be performed on an associated operand, (2) the portion of an instruction which tells the machine what to do, (3) a machine operator.

operator, AND—*See* and operator.

operator, Exclusive OR—*See* exclusive or operator.

operator, inclusive OR—*See* inclusive or operator.

operator, machine—*See* machine operator.

operator, OR—*See* or operator.

optimize—To rearrange the instructions or data in storage so that a minimum number of time consuming jumps or transfers are required in the running of a program.

optimum code—A computer code which is particularly efficient with regard to a particular aspect; e.g., minimum time of execution, minimum or efficient use of storage space, and minimum coding time. *Related to* minimum access code.

optimum programming—Programming in order to maximize efficiency with respect to some criterion; e.g., least storage usage, least time share of peripheral equipment, or least use of time between operations.

O.R.—*O*perations *R*esearch. *Same as* operations research.

OR circuit—*Same as* or gate.

OR gate—An electrical gate or mechanical device which implements the logical OR operator. An output signal occurs whenever there are one or more inputs on a multi-channel input. An OR gate performs the function of the logical "inclusive OR Operator." *Synonymous with* or circuit. *Clarified by* disjunction.

OR operator—A logical operator which has the property such that if P or Q are two statements, then the statement P or Q is true or false varies according to the following table of possible combinations. *Clarified by* disjunction.

P	Q	P or Q
False	True	True
True	False	True
True	True	True
False	False	True

order—(1) A defined successive arrangement of elements or events. This term is losing favor as a synonym for instructions, due to ambiguity. (2) To sequence or arrange in a series. (3) The weight or significance assigned to a digit position in a number. *Clarified by* high order; low order.

origin—The absolute storage address in relative coding to which addresses in a region are referenced.

origination data—*See* data origination.

output—(1) The information transferred from the internal storage of a computer to secondary or external storage, or to any device outside of the computer. (2) The routines which direct 1; (3) the device or collective set of devices necessary for 1; (4) to transfer from internal storage on to external media.

output area—*Same as* output block (2).

output block—(1) A block of computer words considered as a unit and intended or destined to be transferred from an internal storage medium to an external destination. (2) A section of internal storage reserved for storing data which are to be transferred out of the computer. *Synonymous with* output area. (3) A block used as an output buffer.

output device—The part of a machine which translates the electrical impulses representing data processed by the machine into permanent results such as printed forms, punched cards, and magnetic writing on tape.

output equipment—The equipment used for transferring information out of a computer.

output magazine—A mechanism that accumulates cards after they have passed through a machine. *Synonymous with* output stacker.

output stacker—*Same as* output magazine.

overflow—(1) The condition which arises when the result of an arithmetic operation exceeds the capacity of the storage space allotted in a digital computer; (2) the digit arising from this condition if a mechanical or programmed indicator is included, otherwise the digit may be lost.

overflow check indicator—A device which is turned on by incorrect, or unplanned for, operations in the execution of an arithmetic instruction, particularly when an arithmetic operation produces a number too large for the system to handle.

overlay—A technique for bringing routines into high-speed storage from some other form of storage during processing, so that several routines will occupy the same storage locations at different times. Overlay is used when the total storage requirements for instructions exceed the available main storage.

overpunch—To add holes in a card column that already contains one or more holes. *Synonymous with* zone punch. *Related to* zone bits (1).

pack—To include several short items of information into one machine item or word by utilizing different sets of digits to specify each brief item.

packing density—The number of units of useful information contained within a given linear dimension, usually expressed in units per inch; e.g., the number of binary digit magnetic pulses or number of characters stored on tape or drum per linear inch on a single track by a single head.

padding—A technique used to fill out a block of information with dummy records.

panel, control—*See* control panel.

panel, graphic—*See* graphic panel.

paper tape—A strip of paper capable of storing or recording information. Storage may be in the form of punched holes, carbonization or chemical change of impregnated material, or by imprinting. Some paper tapes, such as punched paper tapes, are capable of being ready by the input device of a computer or a transmitting device by sensing the pattern of holes which represent coded information.

paper tape readers—A device capable of sensing information punched on a paper tape in the form of a series of holes.

parallel—(1) To handle simultaneously in separate facilities. (2) To operate on two or more parts of a word or item simultaneously. *Contrasted with* serial.

parallel access—The process of obtaining information from or placing information into storage where the time required for such access is dependent on the simultaneous transfer of all elements of a word from a given storage location. *Synonymous with* simultaneous access.

parallel by character—The handling of all the characters of a machine word simultaneously in separate lines, channels or storage cells.

parallel computer—A computer in which the digits or data lines are handled concurrently by separate units of the computer. The units may be interconnected in different ways as determined by the computation to operate in parallel or serially. Mixed serial and parallel machines are frequently called serial or parallel according to the way arithmetic processes are performed. An example of a parallel computer is one which handles decimal digits in parallel although it might handle the bits which comprise a digit either serially or in parallel. *Contrasted with* serial computer.

parallel operation—The performance of several actions, usually of a similar nature, simultaneously through provision of individual similar or identical devices for each such action. Particularly flow or processing of information. Parallel operation is performed to save time over serial operation. Parallel operation usually requires more equipment. *Contrasted with* serial operation.

parallel processing—The operation of a computer so that programs for more than one run are stored simultaneously in its storage, and executed concurrently.

parallel running—(1) The running of a newly developed system in a data processing area in conjunction with the continued operation of the current system; (2) the final step in the debugging of a system, this step follows a system test.

parallel storage—The storage of data in which all bits, characters, or especially words are essentially equally available in space, without time being one of the factors. When words are in parallel, the storage is said to be parallel by words; when characters within words, or binary digits within words or characters, are dealt with simultaneously, not one after the other, the storage is parallel by characters, or parallel by bit respectively. *Contrasted with* serial storage.

parallel transfer—A method of data transfer in which the characters of an element of information are transferred simultaneously over a set of paths.

parameter—(1) A quantity in a subroutine, whose value specifies or partly specifies the process to be performed. It may be given different values when the subroutine is used in different main routines or in different parts of one main routine, but which remains unchanged throughout any one such use. *Related to* program parameter. (2) A quantity used in a generator to specify machine configuration, designate subroutines to be included, or otherwise to describe the desired routine to be generated. (3) A constant or a variable in mathematics, which remains constant during some calculation. (4) A definable characteristic of an item, device, or system.

parameter, preset—*See* preset parameter.

parameter, program—*See* program parameter.

partial carry—*Same as* carry (2).

parity bit—A check bit that indicates whether the total number of binary "1" digits in a character or word (excluding the parity bit) is odd or even. If a "1" parity bit indicates an odd number of "1" digits, then a "0" bit indicates an even number of them. If the total number of "1" bits, including the parity bit, is always even, the system is called an even parity system. In an odd parity system, the total number of "1" bits, including the parity bit, is always odd.

parity check—A summation check in which the binary digits, in a character or word, are added, modulo 2, and the sum checked against a single, previously computed parity digit; i.e., a check which tests whether the number of ones in a word is odd or even. *Synonymous with* odd-even check. *Related to* redundant check.

part address—The part of an instruction word that defines the address of a register or location.

part operation—The part in an instruction, that specifies the kind of arithmetical or logical operation to be performed, but not the address of the operands.

pass—A completed cycle of reading, processing and writing; i.e., a machine run.

patch—A section of coding inserted into a routine to correct a mistake or alter the routine. It is often not inserted into the actual sequence of the routine being corrected, but placed somewhere else, with an exit to the patch and a return to the routine provided. (2) To insert corrected coding.

pattern recognition—The recognition of shapes or other patterns by a machine system. Patterns may be such as physical shapes or speech patterns.

PCM—*P*unch *C*ard *M*achine. *Same as* electrical accounting machine.

peek-a-boo system—An information retrieval system which uses peek-a-boo cards; i.e., cards into which small holes are drilled at the intersections of coordinates (column and row designations) to represent document numbers. *Synonymous with* batten system; cordonnier system. *Related to* aspect card.

perforated tape—*Same as* punch tape.

perforation rate—The rate at which characters, rows or words are punched in a paper tape.

performance evaluation—The analysis in terms of initial objectives and estimates, and usually made on site, of accomplishments using an automatic data processing system, to provide information on operating experience and to identify corrective actions required if any.

performance period—A period of 30 consecutive calendar days during which a newly installed computer is being tested for acceptance by the U.S. Government. Such a period does not include equipment time used for data purification, file conversion, and similar preparatory operations or those hours of operation rescheduled as a result of equipment failure.

peripheral equipment—The auxiliary machines which may be placed under the control of the central computer. Examples of this are card readers, card punches, magnetic tape feeds and high speed printers. Peripheral equipment may be used on line or off line depending upon computer design, job requirements and economics. *Clarified by* off line equipment.

permanent storage—A method or device used to retain intermediate or final results outside of the machine, usually in the form of punched cards or magnetic tape.

phase shift—The time difference between the input and output signal or between any two synchronized signals, of a control unit, system, or circuit.

phone data—*See* data phone.

photomicrography—The process of making a larger photograph of a much smaller original.

picosecond—One thousandth of a nanosecond, or 10-12 seconds; abbreviated psec.

piezoelectric—A term applied to the phenomenon whereby certain materials, commonly crystalline, develop useful electrical pressures (voltages) when the material is subjected to variable mechanical pressures, strains, or stresses; conversely, the materials develop mechanical strains or stresses when electrical voltages are applied.

pinboard—A type of control panel which uses pins rather than wires to control the operation of a computer. On certain small computers which use pinboards, a program is changed by the operator removing one pinboard and inserting another. *Related to* control panel (2).

ping-pong—The programming technique of using two magnetic tape units for multiple reel files and switching automatically between the two units until the complete file is processed.

plotter—A visual display or board in which a dependent variable is graphed by an automatically controlled pen or pencil as a function of one or more variables.

plotter, XY—*See* XY plotter.

plug, program patching—See program patching plug.

plugboard—*Same as* control panel (2).

plus zone—The bit positions in a computer code which represent the algebraic plus sign.

point—*Same as* radix point.

point, binary—*See* binary point.

point, load—*See* load point.

point, radix—*See* radix point.

polyvalence—The property of being interrelated in several ways.

polyvalent notation—A method for describing salient characteristics, in condensed form, using two or more characters, where each character or group of characters represents one of the characteristics.

polyvalent number—A number, consisting of several figures, used for description, wherein each figure represents one of the characteristics being described.

position, punch—*See* punch position.

positional notation—A method for expressing a quantity, using two or more figures, wherein the successive right to left figures are to be interpreted as coefficients of ascending integer powers of the radix. *Synonymous with* positional number.

positional number—*Same as* positional notation.

positional representation—A number representation or number system in which the significance or value of each digit depends upon its place or position with respect to a radix point.

positions, punching—*See* punching positions.

post—To enter an item on a record.

post edit—To edit the results of a previous computation.

post mortem dump—A listing of the contents of a storage device taken after a routine has been run in order that the final condition of sections of storage may be recorded for debugging purposes.

post mortem routine—A service routine useful in analyzing the cause of a failure, such as a routine that dumps out the content of a store after a failure. *Related to* post mortem.

posting terminal digit—The arranging and recording of serial numbers of documents on the basis of the final digit of each of the numbers.

power dump—The removal of all power accidentally or intentionally.

pre-edit—To edit the input data previous to the computation.

pre-store—To set an initial value for the address of an operand or of a cycle index, (2) to restore, (3) to store a quantity in an available or convenient location before it is required in a routine.

precision—(1) The degree of exactness with which a quantity is stated. (2) The degree of discrimination or amount of detail; e.g., a 3 decimal digit quantity discriminates among 1000 possible quantities. A result may have more precision than it has accuracy; e.g., the true value of pi to 6 significant digits is 3.14159; the value 3.14162 is precise to 6 figures, given to 6 figures, but is accurate only to about 5.

precision, double—*See* double precision.

precision, triple—*See* triple precision.

predicate—To affirm or deny, in mathematical logic, one or more subjects.

preliminary proposal review—An on site review to provide guidance to proponent agencies in the preparation of ADP system proposals.

preselection—A technique for saving time available in buffered computers (by which a block of data is read into computer storage from the next input tape to be called upon before the data are required in the computer. The selection of the next input tape is determined by instructions to the computer.

preset—(1) To set the contents of a storage location to an initial value, (2) to establish the initial control value for a loop.

presumptive address—*Same as* base address (1).

preventive maintenance—The maintenance of a computer system which attempts to keep equipment in top operating condition and to preclude failures during production runs.

primary storage—The main internal storage.

primitive—A primitive usually pertains to the lowest level of a machine instruction or lowest unit of language translation.

printer electrostatic—*Same as* xerographic printer.

printer, high speed—*See* high speed printer.

printer, line—*See* line printer.

printer, matrix—*Same as* wire printer.

printer, on the fly—*See* on the fly printer.

printer, serial—*See* serial printer.

printer, wire—*See* wire printer.

printer, xerographic—*See* xerographic printer.

print out, memory—*Same as* storage dump.

probability theory—A measure of likelihood of occurrence of a chance event, used to predict behavior of a group, not of a single item in the group.

problem, benchmark—*See* benchmark problem.

problem, check—*See* check problem.

problem definition—The art of compiling logic in the form of general flow charts and logic diagrams which clearly explain and present the problem

problem definition—program

to the programmer in such a way that all requirements involved in the run are presented.

problem oriented language—(1) A language designed for convenience of program specification in a general problem area rather than for easy conversion to machine instruction code. The components of such a language may bear little resemblance to machine instructions. (2) A machine independent language where one needs only to state the problem, not the how of solution. *Related to* program generators. *Contrasted with* procedure oriented language.

problem, trouble location—*See* trouble location problem.

procedure—A precise step-by-step method for effecting a solution to a problem.

procedure oriented language—A machine independent language which describes how the process of solving the problem is to be carried out; e.g., FORTRAN.

process—A general term covering such terms as assemble, compile, generate, interpret, and compute.

process chart—*Same as* flow chart.

process control—Descriptive of systems in which computers, most frequently analog computers, are used for the automatic regulation of operations or processes. Typical are operations in the production of chemicals wherein the operation control is applied continuously and adjustments to regulate the operation are directed by the computer to keep the value of a controlled variable constant.

process, iterative—*See* iterative process.

processing, automatic data—*See* automatic data processing.

processing, batch—*See* batch processing.

processing, centralized data—*See* centralized data processing.

processing data—*See* data processing.

processing, electronic data—*See* electronic data processing.

processing, information—*See* information processing.

processing, in line—*Same as* on-line (2).

processing, integrated data—*See* integrated data processing.

processing, on-line—*Same as* on-line (2).

processing, parallel—*See* parallel processing.

processing, real time—*See* real time processing.

processor—(1) A generic term which includes assembly, compiling, and generation; (2) A shorter term for automatic data processor or arithmetic unit.

program—(1) The complete plan for the solution of a problem, more specifically the complete sequence of machine instructions and routines necessary to solve a problem. (2) To plan the procedures for solving a problem. This may involve among other things the analysis of the problem, preparation of a flow diagram, preparing details, testing, and developing subroutines, allocation of storage locations, specification of input and output formats, and the incorporation of a computer run into a complete data processing system.

program address counter—*Same as* location counter (2).

program, assembly—*Same as* assembler.

program check—(1) A system of determining the correct program and machine functioning either by running a sample problem with similar programming and a known answer, or by using mathematical or logic checks such as comparing A times B with B times A. (2) A check system built into the program or computers that do not have automatic checking. This check system is normally concerned with programs run on computers which are not self-checking internally. *Synonymous with* routine check.

program, coded—*See* coded program.

program, control—*See* control program.

program counter—*Same as* control register.

program, general—*See* general program.

program generator—A program which permits a computer to write other programs, automatically. Generators are of two types: (a) the character controlled generator, which operates like a compiler in that it takes entries from a library tape, but unlike a simple compiler in that it examines control characters associated with each entry, and alters instructions found in the library according to the directions contained in the control characters. (b) The pure generator which is a program that writes another program. When associated with an assembler a pure generator is usually a section of program which is called into storage by the assembler from a library tape and which then writes one or more entries in another program. Most assemblers are also compilers and generators. In this case the entire system is usually referred to as an assembly system. *Related to* problem oriented language.

program, heuristic—*Same as* heuristic routine.

program, internally stored—*See* internally stored program.

program language—A language which is used by programmers to write computer routines.

program, object—*See* object program.

program parameter—A parameter incorporated into a subroutine during computation. A program parameter frequently comprises a word stored relative to either the subroutine or the entry point and dealt with by the subroutine during each reference. It may be altered by the routine and/or may vary from one point of entry to another.

program patching plug—A relatively small auxiliary plugboard patched with a specific variation of a portion of a program and designed to be plugged into a relatively larger plugboard patched with the main program.

program register—A register in which the current instruction of the program is stored. *Synonymous with* register instruction. *Contrasted with* register control.

program sensitive malfunction—A malfunction which occurs only when some unusual combination of program steps occur.

program, source—*See* source program.

program, specific—*See* specific program.

program step—A phase of one instruction or command in a sequence of instructions. Thus, a single operation.

program stop—A stop instruction built into the program that will automatically stop the machine under certain conditions, or upon reaching the end of the processing, or completing the solution of a problem.

program storage—A portion of the internal storage reserved for the storage of programs, routines, and subroutines. In many systems protection devices are used to prevent inadvertent alteration of the contents of the program storage.

program, stored—*Same as* stored routine.

program, supervisory—*Same as* executive routine.

program tape—A tape which contains the sequence of instructions required for solving a problem and which is read into a computer prior to running a program.

program, target—*Same as* object program.

program test—A system of checking before running any problem in which a sample problem of the same type with a known answer is run.

program testing time—The machine time expended for program testing, debugging, and volume and compatibility testing.

program, utility—*Same as* utility routine.

programmed switch—*Same as* variable connector (3).

programmer—A person who prepares problem solving procedures and flow charts and who may also write and debug routines.

programming, automatic—*See* automatic programming.

programming, interpretive—*See* interpretive programming.

programming, linear—*See* linear programming.

programming, micro—*See* micro programming.

programming, minimum access—*See* minimum access programming.

programming, minimum latency—*Same as* minimum access programming.

programming, multiple—*See* multiple programming.

programming, optimum—*See* optimum programming.

programming, random access—*See* random access programming.

programming, serial—*See* serial programming.

programming, symbolic—*See* symbolic programming.

propagated error—An error occurring in one operation which spreads through and influences later operations and results

property sort—The selection of items from a group which satisfy a certain criterion.

proportional band—The range of values of a condition being regulated which will cause the controller to operate over its full range. Usually expressed by engineers in terms of percentage of instrument full scale range.

proportional control—A method of control in which the intensity of action varies linearly as the condition being regulated deviates from the condition prescribed.

protection, file—*See* file protection.

pseudo code—*Same as* symbolic code.

pseudo instruction—(1) A symbolic representation in a compiler or interpreter. (2) A group of characters having the same general form as a computer instruction, but never executed by the computer as an actual instruction.

pseudo operation—An operation which is not part of the computer's operation repertoire as realized by hardware; hence an extension of the set of machine operations.

pseudo random—The property of satisfying one or more of the standard criteria for statistical randomness but being produced by a definite calculation process.

pseudo random number sequence—An order of numbers produced by a definite recursive rule but satisfying one or more of the standard tests for randomness. Such numbers may be uniform (any number in the set of possible numbers being equally likely), normal or Gaussian (having the property of normal or Gaussian distribution), or satisfy some other type of statistical distribution.

pulse—A significant, and sudden change of short duration in the level of some electric variable, usually voltage.

pulse code—(1) A code in which sets of pulses have been assigned particular meanings, (2) the binary representation of characters.

pulse, gate—*See* gate pulse.

pulse repetition rate—The number of electric pulses per unit of time experienced by a point in a computer, usually the maximum normal or standard pulse rate.

pulse, sprocket—*See* sprocket pulse.

punch—(1) To shear a hole by forcing a solid or hollow, sharp edged tool through a material into a die; (2) the hole resulting from (1) above.

punch, automatic feed—*See* automatic feed punch.

punch, electronic calculating—*See* electronic calculating punch.

punch card—A heavy stiff paper of constant size and shape, suitable for punching in a pattern that has meaning, and for being handled mechanically. The punched holes are sensed electrically by wire brushes, mechanically by metal finger, or photoelectrically by photocells.

punch, card—*See* card punch.

punch card unit—quaternary signalling

punch card unit—*Same as* card punch.

punch, eleven (11)—*Same as* X punch (2).

punch, gang—*See* gang punch.

punch position—The row position of a punched hole in a specific column of a punch card. In an 80 column punch card the rows are designated 0 to 9, X or Y; in a 90-column card the rows are designated 0, 1, 3, 5, 7, and 9.

punch, spot.—*See* spot punch.

punch, summary—*See* summary punch.

punch tape—A tape, usually paper, upon which data may be stored in the form of punched holes. Hole locations are arranged in columns across the width of the tape. There are usually 5 to 8 positions, channels, per column, with data represented by a binary coded decimal system. All holes in a column are sensed simultaneously in a manner similar to that for punch cards.

punch tape code—A code used to represent data on punch tape.

punch, twelve (12)—*Same as* Y punch (2).

punch, X—*See* X punch.

punch, Y—*See* Y punch.

punch, zone—*Same as* overpunch.

punching, interstage—*See* interstage punching.

punching, multiple—*See* multiple punching.

punching, normal stage—*See* normal stage punching.

punching positions—The specific areas; i.e., row-column intersects, on a punch card where holes may be punched.

punching rate—The number of cards, characters, blocks, fields or words of information placed in the form of holes distributed on cards, or paper tape per unit of time.

purification, data—*See* data purification.

push down list—A list of items where the last item entered is the first item of the list, and the relative position of the other items is pushed back one.

push up list—A list of items where each item is entered at the end of the list, and the other items maintain their same relative position in the list.

quadripuntal—Pertaining to four punches, specifically having four random punches on a punch card. This term is used in determinative documentation.

quantity—A positive or negative real number in the mathematical sense.

quantity, double precision—*See* double precision quantity.

quantize—*Same as* digitize.

quantizer—*Same as* digitizer.

quantum—The subranges resulting from quantization.

quasi instruction—*Same as* pseudo instruction.

quaternary signalling—An electrical communications mode in which information is passed by the presence and absence, or plus and minus

quaternary signalling—random access

variations of four discrete levels of one parameter of the signalling medium.

question, encoded—*See* encoded question.

queuing theory—A form of probability theory useful in studying delays or line-ups at servicing points.

quibinary code—A binary coded decimal code for representing decimal numbers in which each decimal digit is represented by seven binary digits which are coefficients of 8, 6, 4, 2, 0, 1, 0, respectively.

radix—The quantity of characters for use in each of the digital positions of a numbering system. In the more common numbering systems the characters are some or all of the Arabic numerals as follows:

System Name	Characters	Radix
BINARY	(0, 1)	2
OCTAL	(0,1,2,3,4,5,6,7)	8
DECIMAL	(0,1,2,3,4,5,6,7,8,9)	10

Unless otherwise indicated, the radix of any number is assumed to be 10. For positive identification of a radix 10 number, the radix is written in parentheses as a subscript to the expressed number; i.e., $126_{(10)}$. The radix of any nondecimal number is expressed in similar fashion; e.g., $11_{(2)}$ and $5_{(8)}$. *Synonymous with* base; base number; radix number.

radix complement—*Same as* complement (3).

radix minus 1 complement—*Same as* complement (2).

radix notation—(1) An annotation consisting of a decimal number, in parentheses, written as a subscript suffix to a number, its decimal value indicating the radix of the number; e.g., $11_{(2)}$ indicates the number 11 is in the radix of two; $11_{(8)}$ indicates the number 11 is in the radix of eight. (2) A number written without its radix notation is assumed to be in the radix of ten.

radix number—*Same as* radix.

radix point—The dot that delineates the integer digits from the fractional digits of a number; specifically, the dot that delineates the digital position involving the zero exponent of the radix from the digital position involving the minus-one exponent of the radix. The radix point is often identified by the name of the system; e.g., binary point, octal point, or decimal point. In the writing of any number in any system, if no dot is included, the radix point is assumed to follow the rightmost digit.

RAM—*Random Access Memory. Same as* random access storage.

random access—(1) Pertaining to the process of obtaining information from or placing information into storage where the time required for such access is independent of the location of the information most recently obtained or placed in storage; (2) pertaining to a device in which random

247

access, as defined in definition 1, can be achieved without effective penalty in time.

random access memory—*Same as* random access storage.

random access programming—Programming without regard to the time required for access to the storage positions called for in the program.

random access storage—A storage technique in which the time required to obtain information is independent of the location of the information most recently obtained. This strict definition must be qualified by the observation that we usually mean relatively random. Thus, magnetic drums are relatively non random access when compared to magnetic cores for main storage, but are relatively random access when compared to magnetic tapes for file storage.

random number generator—A special machine routine or hardware designed to produce a random number or series of random numbers according to specified limitations.

random number sequence—An unpredictable array of numbers produced by change, and satisfying one or more of the tests for randomness.

range—(1) All the values which a function or word may have, (2) the difference between the highest and lowest of these values.

range, error—*See* error range.

rapid access loop—A small section of storage, particularly in drum, tape or disk storage units, which has much faster access than the remainder of the storage.

rate action—A type of control action in which the rate of correction is made proportional to how fast the condition is going awry. This is also called derivative action.

rate, bit—*See* bit rate

rate, clock—*See* clock rate

rate, error—*See* error rate.

rate, perforation—*See* perforation rate.

rate, pulse repetition—*See* pulse repetition rate.

rate, punching—*See* punching rate.

rate, reading—*See* reading rate.

rate, reset—*See* reset rate.

rate, sampling—*See* sampling rate.

rate, signalling—*See* signalling rate.

ratio, operating—*See* operating ratio.

ratio, signal to noise—*See* signal to noise ratio.

raw data—Data which has not been processed. Such data may or may not be in machine-sensible form.

read—(1) To sense information contained in some source, (2) the sensing of information contained in some source.

read around number—The number of times a specific spot, digit, or location in electrostatic storage may be consulted before spill over will cause a loss of information stored in surrounding spots. The surrounding information must be restored before the loss occurs.

read-in—To sense information contained in some source and transmit this information to an internal storage.

read, non destructive—*See* non destructive read.

read out—To sense information contained in some internal storage and transmit this information to a storage external to the computer.

read punch unit—An input-output unit of a computing system which punches computed results into cards, reads input information into the system, and segregates output cards. The read-punch unit generally consists of a card feed, a read station, a punch station, another read station, and two output card stackers.

read time—*Same as* access time.

read while writing—The reading of a record or group of records into storage from tape at the same time another record or group of records is written from storage to tape.

read write check indicator—A device incorporated in certain computers to indicate upon interrogation whether or not an error was made in reading or writing. The machine can be made to stop, re-try the operation or follow a special subroutine depending upon the result of the interrogation.

read write head—A small electromagnet used for reading, recording, or erasing polarized spots, which represent information, on magnetic tape, disk or drum.

read, card—*See* card read.

reader, character—*See* character reader.

reader, high-speed—*See* high speed reader.

reader, magnetic tape—*See* magnetic tape reader.

reader, paper tape—*See* paper tape reader.

readiness review—An on site examination of the adequacy of preparations for effective utilization upon installation of a computer, and to identify any necessary corrective actions.

reading rate—The number of characters, words, fields, blocks or cards sensed by a sensing device per unit of time.

real time—*Same as* access time.

real time clock—A clock which indicates the passage of actual time, in contrast to a fictitious time set up by the computer program; such as elapsed time in the flight of a missile, wherein a 60 second trajectory is computed in 200 actual milliseconds, or a 0.1 second interval is integrated in 100 actual microseconds.

real time operation—The use of the computer as an element of a processing system in which the times of occurrence of data transmission are controlled by other portions of the system, or by physical events outside the system, and cannot be modified for convenience in computer pro-

real time operation—gramming. Such an operation either proceeds at the same speed as the events being simulated or at a sufficient speed to analyze or control external events happening concurrently.

real time processing—The processing of information or data in a sufficiently rapid manner so that the results of the processing are available in time to influence the process being monitored or controlled.

recognition, character—*See* character recognition.

recognition, pattern—*See* pattern recognition.

record—(1) A group of related facts or fields of information treated as a unit, thus a listing of information, usually in printed or printable form; (2) to put data into a storage device.

record, fixed length—*See* fixed length record.

record gap—An interval of space or time associated with a record to indicate or signal the end of the record.

record length—The number of characters necessary to contain all the information in a record.

record mark—A special character used in some computers either to limit the number of characters in a data transfer, or to separate blocked or grouped records in tape.

record, reference—*See* reference record.

record storage mark—A special character which appears only in the record storage unit of the card reader to limit the length of the record read into storage.

record, trailer—*See* trailer record.

record, unit—*See* unit record.

records, grouping of—*See* grouping of records

recursive—Pertaining to a process which is inherently repetitive. The result of each repetition is usually dependent upon the result of the previous repetition.

red tape—*Same as* housekeeping.

red tape operation—*Same as* bookkeeping operation.

redundant character—A character specifically added to a group of characters to insure conformity with certain rules which can be used to detect computer malfunction.

redundant check—A check which makes use of redundant characters.

reel—A spool of tape, generally magnetic tape.

reference address—*Same as* base address (1).

reference record—An output of a compiler that lists the operations and their positions in the final specific routine, and contains information describing the segmentation and storage allocation of the routine.

reference time—An instant near the beginning of switching chosen as an origin of time measurements. It is variously taken as the first instant at which the instantaneous value of the drive pulse, the voltage response of the magnetic cell, or the integrated voltage response reaches a specified fraction of its peak pulse amplitude.

regeneration—(1) The process of returning a part of the output signal of an amplifier to its input circuit in such a manner that it reinforces the excitation and thereby increases the total amplification, (2) periodic restoration of stored information.

register—A hardware device used to store a certain amount of bits or characters. A register is usually constructed of elements such as transistors or tubes and usually contains approximately one word of information. Common programming usage demands that a register have the ability to operate upon information and not merely store it; hardware usage does not make the distinction.

register, B—(1) *Same as* index register, (2) a register used as an extension of the accumulator during multiply and divide processes.

register, check—*See* check register.

register, circulating—*See* circulating register.

register, control—*See* control register.

register, index—*See* index register.

register, instruction—*Same as* instruction register.

register length—The number of characters in a machine word. In a given computer, the number may be constant or variable.

register, magnetic shift—*See* magnetic shift register.

register, memory—*Same as* program register (2).

register, operation—*See* operation register.

register, program—*See* program register.

register, shift—*See* shift register.

register, standby—*See* standby register.

register, storage—*See* storage register.

registration—The accuracy of the positioning of punched holes in a card.

reimbursed time—The machine time which is loaned or rented to another office, agency or organization either on a reimbursable or reciprocal basis.

relationship, analytic—*See* analytic relationship.

relationship, synthetic—*See* synthetic relationship.

relative address—An address to which the base address must be added in order to find the machine address.

relative code—A code in which all addresses are specified or written with respect to an arbitrarily selected position, or in which all addresses are represented symbolically in a computable form.

reliability—(1) A measure of the ability to function without failure; (2) the amount of credence placed in a result.

reliability, channel—*See* channel reliability.

reliability, circuit—*See* circuit reliability.

relocate—To move a routine to another location.

remedial maintenance—The maintenance performed by the contractor following equipment failure; therefore, is performed as required, on an unscheduled basis.

reperforator—(1) The contraction of the words receiving perforator; (2) any tape punch which automatically converts coded electrical signals into perforations in tape.

repertory instruction—*See* instruction repertory.

replacement, mechanical—*See* mechanical replacement.

report generator—A technique for producing complete data processing reports giving only a description of the desired content and format of the output reports, and certain information concerning the input file.

representation, analog—*See* analog representation.

representation, positional—*See* positional representation.

representative calculating time—A method of evaluating the speed performance of a computer. One method is to use one-tenth of the time required to perform nine complete additions and one complete multiplication. A complete addition or a complete multiplication time includes the time required to procure two operands from high speed storage, perform the operation, and store the result and the time required to select and execute the required number of instructions to do this.

reproducer, card—*See* card reproducer.

requirements, information—*See* information requirements.

rerun—To repeat all or part of a program on a computer.

rerun point—The stage of a computer run at which all information pertinent to the running of the routine is available either to the routine itself, or to a rerun routine in order that a run may be rerun.

rerun routine—A routine designed to be used after a computer malfunction or a coding or operating mistake to reconstitute a routine from the last previous rerun point.

reset—To return a device to zero or to an initial or arbitrarily selected condition.

reset cycle—To return a cycle index to its initial value.

reset rate—The number of corrections per unit of time made by the control system.

residual error—The difference between an optimum result derived from experience or experiment and a supposedly exact result derived from theory.

residue check—(1) Any modulo N check, (2) A check of numerical data or arithmetic operations in which the number A is divided by N and the remainder B accompanies A as a check digit.

resolver—A device which separates or breaks up a quantity, particularly a vector, into constituent parts or elements; e.g., the mutually perpendicular components of a plane vector.

restart—To go back to a specific planned point in a routine, usually in the case of machine malfunction, for the purpose of rerunning the portion of the routine in which the error occurred. The length of time between restart points in a given routine should be a function of the mean free error time of the machine itself.

restore—To return an index register, a variable address, or other computer word to its initial or preselected value.

retrieval, information—*See* information retrieval.

retrievals, false—*See* false retrievals.

return—The mechanism providing for a return in the usual sense. In particular a set of instructions at the end of a subroutine which permit control to return to the proper point in the main routine.

reverse code dictionary—An alphabetic or numeric alphabetic arrangement of codes, associated with their corresponding English words or terms.

review, preliminary proposal—*See* preliminary proposal review.

review, readiness—*See* readiness review.

revolver—*Same as* rapid access loop.

rewind—To return a film or magnetic tape to its beginning or passed location.

rewrite—The process in a storage device of restoring the information in the device to its state prior to reading.

ring counter—A loop of interconnected bistable elements such that one and only one is in a specified state at any given time and such that, as input signals are counted, the position of the element in the specified state moves in an ordered sequence around the loop.

ring shift—*Same as* cyclic shift.

rise time—The time required for the leading edge of a pulse to rise from one-tenth of its final value to nine-tenths of its final value. Rise time is proportional to the time constant of the circuit.

role indicator—A code assigned to a keyword to indicate the role of the keyword; e.g., a keyword may be a noun, verb, adjective, or adverb; therefore, an indicator is used to identify the specified role of the keyword.

rollback routine—*Same as* rerun routine.

roll-out—A process, often used in diagnostic routines, in which a register or counter is read out by the following process: Add 1 to the digits in each column simultaneously; do this n times, where n is the radix of the number in the register; when the result in each column changes from n−1 to 0, issue a signal.

round—Deletion of the least significant digit(s) with or without modifications to reduce bias.

rounding error—The error resulting from rounding off a quantity by deleting the less significant digits and applying some rule of correction to the part retained; e.g., 0.2751 can be rounded to 0.275 with a rounding error of .0001.

round off—*Same as* round.

round off error—*Same as* rounding error.

routine—A set of coded instructions arranged in proper sequence to direct the computer to perform a desired operation or sequence of operations.

A subdivision of a program consisting of two or more instructions that are functionally related; therefore, a program.

routine, assembly—*Same as* assembler.
routine, automatic—*See* automatic routine.
routine, auxiliary—*See* auxiliary routine.
routine check—*Same as* program check (2).
routine, compiling—*Same as* compiler.
routine, diagnostic—*See* diagnostic routine.
routine, executive—*See* executive routine.
routine, general—*Same as* general program.
routine, input—*See* input routine.
routine library—A collection of standard, proven routines and subroutines by which problems and parts of problems may be solved.
routine, malfunction—*Same as* diagnostic routine.
routine, minimum latency—*Same as* minimum access routine.
routine, monitor—*Same as* executive routine.
routine, object—*Same as* object program.
routine, rollback—*Same as* rerun routine.
routine, sequence checking—*See* sequence checking routine.
routine, service—*See* service routine.
routine, specific—*See* specific routine.
routine, stored—*See* stored routine.
routine, supervisory—*Same as* executive routine.
routine, test—*See* test routine.
routine, tracing—*See* tracing routine.
routine, translating—*Same as* translator (1).
routine, utility—*Same as* utility routine.
row binary—A method of representing binary numbers on a card where successive bits are represented by the presence or absence of punches in a successive position in a row as opposed to a series of columns. Row binary is especially convenient in 40 bit word, or less, computers; wherein the card frequently is used to store 12 binary words on each half of the card.
row pitch—The distance measured along paper tape between the centers of the adjacent holes.
ruly English—A form of English in which every word has one and only one conceptual meaning and each concept has one and only one word to describe it. This is a hypothetical language based on English which compiles uniformly to a definite set of rules, without exceptions.
run—The performance of one program on a computer, thus the performance of one routine, or several routines linked so that they form an automatic operating unit, during which manual manipulations by the computer operator are zero, or at least minimal.

sampling rate—The rate at which measurements of physical quantities are made; e.g., if it is desired to calculate the velocity of a missile and its position is measured each millisecond, then the sampling rate is 1,000 measurements per second.

scale—A range of values frequently dictated by the computer word length or routine at hand.

scale factor—The coefficients used to multiply or divide quantities in a problem in order to convert them so as to have them lie in a given range of magnitude; plus one to minus one.

scan—To examine every reference or every entry in a file routinely as a part of a retrieval scheme; occasionally, to collate.

scanner—An instrument which automatically samples or interrogates the state of various processes, files, conditions, or physical states and initiates action in accordance with the information obtained.

scheduled operation—The periods of time during which the user plans to use specified equipment. Such a designation must be made a given number of hours in advance, provided however, that such scheduled hours of the operation may be modified after that time in the event of an emergency, or in the event that equipment failure creates a need for such rescheduling. Usually the foregoing is further modified in that during the performance period the hours rescheduled as a result of equipment failure usually are not considered as scheduled hours of operation in computing equipment effectiveness.

screen—(1) The surface in an electrostatic cathode ray storage tube where electrostatic charges are stored, and by means of which information is displayed or stored temporarily; (2) to make a preliminary selection from a set of entities, selection criteria being based on a given set of rules or conditions.

SDA—*S*ource *D*ata *A*utomation. The many methods of recording information in coded forms on paper tapes, punched cards, or tags that can be used over and over again to produce many other records without rewriting.

search—To examine a series of items for any that have a desired property or properties.

search time—The time required to locate a particular field of data in storage. Searching requires a comparison of each field with a predetermined standard until an identity is obtained. This is contrasted with access time which is based upon locating data by means of the address of its storage location.

second level address—*Same as* indirect address.

secondary storage—The storage facilities not an integral part of the computer but directly connected to and controlled by the computer; e.g., magnetic drum and magnetic tapes.

section, arithmetic—*Same as* arithmetic unit.

seek—semantic matrix

seek—To look for data according to information given regarding that data; occasionally used interchangeably and erroneously for (search), (scan) and (screen).

segment—(1) To divide a routine in parts, each consisting of an integral number of subroutines, and each part capable of being completed stored in the internal storage and containing the necessary instructions to jump to other segments. (2) That portion of a routine too long to fit into internal storage which is short enough to be stored entirely in the internal storage; such a segment contains the coding necessary to call in other segments automatically. Routines which exceed internal storage capacity may be automatically divided into segments by a compiler.

segment mark—A special character written on tape to separate one section of a tape file from another.

select—(1) To take the alternative A if the report on a condition is of one state, and alternative B if the report on the condition is of another state; (2) to choose a needed subroutine from a file of subroutines.

selection check—A check, usually automatic, to verify that the correct register or other device has been selected in the performance of an instructor.

selective trace—A tracing routine wherein only instructions satisfying certain specified criteria are subject to tracing. Typical criteria are: (a) Instruction type; e.g., arithmetic jump. (b) Instruction location; e.g., specific region. (c) Data location; e.g., specific region. For Case a, where tracing is performed on transfer, jump, instructions the term logical trace is sometimes used.

selector—A device which interrogates a condition and initiates one of several alternate operations.

self checking code—*Same as* error detecting code.

self checking number—A number with a suffix figure related to the figure(s) of the number, used to check the number after it has been transferred from one medium or device to another.

self demarking code—A code A code in which the symbols are so arranged and selected that the generation of false combinations by interaction of segments from two successive codes is prevented.

self organizing—Having the capability of classification or internal rearrangement, depending on the environment in accordance with given instructions or a set of rules.

self organizing machine—A class of machines which may be characterized loosely as containing a variable network in which the elements are organized by the machine itself, without external intervention, to meet criteria of successful operation.

semantic matrix—A graphical device for plotting in a standard conventional form whatever precise elements of meaning have been ascertained from the semantic analysis of a concept.

semiconductor—A solid with an electrical conductivity that lies between the high conductivity of metals and the low conductivity of insulators. Semiconductor circuit elements include crystal diodes and transistors.

sense—(1) To examine, particularly relative to a criterion; (2) to determine the present arrangement of some element of hardware, especially a manually set switch; (3) to read punched holes or other manually se⁺ switch; (4) to read punched holes or other marks.

sensitivity—The degree of response of an instrument or control unit to a change in the incoming signal.

sentinel—*Same as* flag (3).

septenary number—A number, usually of more than one figure representing a sum, in which the quantity represented by each figure is based on a radix of seven. The figures used are 0, 1, 2, 3, 4, 5, and 6.

sequence—(1) To put a set of symbols into an arbitrarily defined order; i.e., to select A if A is greater than B. (2) An arbitrarily defined order of a set of symbols; i.e., an orderly progression of items of information or of operations in accordance with some rule.

sequence check—A data processing operation designed to check the sequence of the items in a file assumed to be already in sequence.

sequence checking routine—A routine which checks every instruction executed, and prints out certain data; e.g., to print out the coded instructions with addresses, and the contents of each of several registers, or it may be designed to print out only selected data, such as transfer instructions and the quantity actually transferred.

sequencer—*Same as* sorter.

sequential access storage—A storage technique in which the items of information stored become available only in a one after the other sequence, whether or not all the information or only some of it is desired; e.g., magnetic tape storage.

sequential control—A mode of computer operation in which instructions are executed in consecutive order by ascending or descending addresses of storage locations, unless otherwise specified by a jump.

sequential operation—The performance of actions one after the other in time. The actions referred to are of a large scale as opposed to the smaller scale operations referred to by the term serial operation. For an example of sequential operation consider $A \times (B \times C)$. The two multiplications indicated follow each other sequentially. However, the processing of the individual digits in each multiplication may be either parallel or serial.

serial—(1) The handling of one after the other in a single facility, such as transfer or store in a digit-by-digit time sequence, or to process a sequence of instructions one at a time; i.e., sequentially. (2) The time sequence transmission of, storage of, or logical operations on the parts of a word, with the same facilities for successive parts.

serial access—Pertaining to the process of obtaining information from or placing information into storage where the time required for such access is dependent on the necessity for waiting while nondesired storage locations are processed turn.

serial computer—A computer in which digits or data lines are handled sequentially by separate units of the computer. Mixed serial and parallel machines are frequently called serial or parallel according to the way arithmetic processes are performed. An example of a serial computer is one which handles decimal digits serially although it might handle the bits which comprise a digit either serially or in parallel.

serial operation—The flow of information through a computer in time sequence using only one digit, word, line or channel at a time.

serial-parallel—(1) A combination of serial and parallel; e.g., serial by character, parallel by bits comprising the character. (2) Descriptive of a device which converts a serial input into a parallel output.

serial programming—The programming of a computer by which only one arithmetical or logical operation can be executed at one time; e.g., a sequential operation.

serial storage—A storage technique in which time is one of the factors used to locate any given bit, character, word, or groups of words appearing one after the other in time sequence, and in which access time includes a variable latency or waiting time of from zero to many word times. A storage is said to be serial by word when the individual bits comprising a word appear serially in time; or a storage is serial by character when the characters representing coded decimal or other non binary numbers appear serially in time; e.g., magnetic drums are usually serial by word but may be serial by bit, or parallel by bit, or serial by character and parallel by bit. *Related to* storage, sequential access.

serial transfer—A method of data transfer in which the characters of an element are transferred in sequence over a signal path in consecutive time positions.

serial transmission—To move data in sequence, one character at a time as contrasted with parallel transmission.

series, time—*See* time series.

service routine—A broad class of routines which are standardized at a particular installation for the purpose of assisting in maintenance and operation of the computer as well as the preparation of programs as opposed to routines for the actual solution of production problems. This class includes monitoring or supervisory routines, assemblers, compilers, diagnostics for computer malfunctions, simulation of peripheral equipment, general diagnostics and input data. The distinguishing quality of service routines is that they are generally standardized so as to meet the servicing needs at a particular installation, independent of any specific production type routine requiring such services.

servicing time—*Same as* engineering time.

servomechanism—A device to monitor an operation as it proceeds, and make necessary adjustments to keep the operation under control. A furnace thermostat is an example of a servomechanism.

set—(1) To place a storage device in a prescribed state. (2) To place a binary cell in the one state. (3) A collection of elements having some feature in common or which bear a certain relation to one another; e.g., all even numbers, geometrical figures, terms in a series, a group of irrational numbers, all positive even integers less than 100 may be a set or a sub-set.

set up time—The portion of the elapsed time between machine operations which is devoted to such tasks as changing reels of tape, and moving cards, tapes, and supplies to and from the equipment.

sexadecimal number—A number, usually of more than one figure, representing a sum in which the quantity represented by each figure is based on a radix of sixteen. Also called Hexadecimal.

shift—To move the characters of a unit of information columnwise right to left. For a number, this is equivalent to multiplying or dividing by a power of the base of notation.

shift, circular—*Same as* cyclic shift.

shift, end around—*Same as* cyclic shift.

shift, logical—*Same as* cyclic shift.

shift, non arithmetic—*Same as* cyclic shift.

shift register—A register in which the characters may be shifted one or more positions to the right or left. In a right shift, the rightmost character(s) are lost. In a left shift, the leftmost character(s) are lost.

shift, ring—*Same as* cyclic shift.

short word—The fixed word of lesser length in computers capable of handling words of two different lengths. In many computers this is referred to as a half word because the length is exactly the half-length of the full word.

sign—(1) In arithmetic, a symbol which distinguishes negative quantities from positive ones. (2) An indication of whether a quantity is greater than zero, or less than zero. The signs often are the marks = and −, respectively; but other arbitrarily selected symbols may be used; such as a 0 and 1, or 0 and 9, then used as codes at a predetermined location, can be interpreted by a person or machine.

sign bit—A binary digit used as a sign draft.

sign check indicator—An error checking device, indicating no sign or improper signing of a field used for arithmetic processes. The machine can, upon interrogation be made to stop or enter into a correction routine.

sign digit—A character, frequently a single bit, used to designate the algebraic sign of the quantity.

signal—The event, phenomenon or electrical quantity which conveys information from one point to another.

signal attenuation—The reduction in the strength of electrical signals.

signal conditioning—To process the form or mode of a signal so as to make it intelligible to or compatible with a given device, including such manipulation as pulse shaping, pulse clipping, digitizing, and linearizing.

signal to noise ratio—The ratio of the amount of signals conveying information to the amount of signals not conveying information.

signalling rate—The rate at which signals are transmitted.

signed field—A field which has a plus or minus character coding over the units position to designate the algebraic sign of the entire number.

significant digits—A set of digits, usually from consecutive columns beginning with the most significant digit different from zero and ending with the least significant digit whose value is known and assumed relevant, e.g., 2300.0 has five significant digits, whereas 2300 probably has two significant digits; however, 2301 has four significant digits and 0.0023 has two significant digits.

simulation—(1) The representation of physical systems and phenomena by computers, models or other equipment; e.g., an imitative type of data processing in which an automatic computer is used as a model of some entity; e.g., a chemical process. Information enters the computer to represent the factors entering the real process, the computer produces information that represents the results of the process, and the processing done by the computer programming, the technique of setting up a routine for one computer to make it operate as nearly as possible like some other computer.

simulator—(1) A computer or model which represents a system or phenomenon and which mirrors or maps the effects of various changes in the original, enabling the original to be studied, analyzed, and understood by means of the behaviour of the model; (2) a program or routine corresponding to a mathematical model or representing a physical model; (3) a routine which is executed by one computer but which imitates the operations of another computer.

simultaneous access—*Same as* parallel access.

single address—*Same as* one address (2).

single step operation—A method of operating an automatic computer manually in which a single instruction or part of an instruction is performed in response to a single operation of a manual control. This method is generally used for detecting mistakes.

skeletal code—The framework of a routine which is completed by a generalized routine using input parameters.

skip—*Same as* skip instruction.

skip instruction—An instruction having no effect other than directing the processor to proceed to another instruction designated in the storage portion.

skip, tape—*See* tape skip.

snapshot dump—A dynamic partial print out during computing, at breakpoints and checkpoints, or selected items in storage.

software—The totality of programs and routines used to extend the capabilities of computers, such as compilers, assemblers, narrators, routines, and subroutines.

solid state—The electronic components that convey or control electrons within solid materials; e.g., transistors, germanium diodes, and magnetic cores. Thus, vacuum and gas tubes are not included.

solid state computer—A computer built primarily from solid state electronic circuit elements.

sonic delay line—*Same as* acoustic delay line.

sophisticated vocabulary—An advanced and elaborate set of instructions. Some computers can perform only the more common mathematical calculations such as addition, multiplication, and subtraction. A computer with a sophisticated vocabulary can go beyond this and perform operations such as linearize, extract square root, and select highest number.

sort—To arrange items of information according to rules dependent upon a key or field contained in the items or records; e.g., to digital sort is to sort first the keys on the least significant digit, and to resort on each higher order digit until the items are sorted on the most significant digit.

sort, four-tape—To four-tape sort is to merge sort in which input data are supplied on two tapes, and are sorted into incomplete sequences alternately on two output tapes, the output tapes are used for input on the succeeding pass, resulting in longer and longer sequences after each pass until the data are all in one sequence on one output tape.

sort, merge—To produce a single sequence of items, ordered according to some rule, from two or more previously unordered sequences, without changing the items in size, structure, or total number, although more than one pass may be required for a complete sort, items are selected during each pass on the basis of the entire key.

sorter—A machine which puts items of information into a particular order; e.g., it will determine whether A is greater than, equal to or less than B and sort or order accordingly.

source data automation—The many methods of recording information in coded forms on paper tapes, punched cards, or tags that can be used over and over again to produce many other records without rewriting.

source document—A document from which basic data is extracted.

source language—The original form in which a program is prepared prior to processing by the machine.

source program—A computer program written in a language designed for ease of expression of a class of problems or procedures, by humans; e.g., symbolic or algebraic. A generator, assembler translator or compiler routines is used to perform the mechanics of translating the source program into an object program in machine language.

space—*Same as* blank (1).

space, dead—*Same as* dead band.

space, working—*Same as* working storage.

special purpose computer—A computer designed to solve a specific class or narrow range of problems.

specific address—*Same as* absolute address.

specific code—*Same as* absolute code.

specific program—A program for solving a specific problem only.

specific routine—A routine to solve a particular mathematical, logical, or data handling problem in which each address refers to explicitly stated registers and locations.

speed, transmission—*See* transmission speed.

spot punch—A hand operated device resembling a pair of pliers, for selectively punching holes in punch cards.

sprocket pulse—(1) A pulse generated by a magnetized spot which accompanies every character recorded on magnetic tape. This pulse is used during read operations to regulate the timing of the read circuits and also to provide a count on the number of characters read from tape. (2) A pulse generated by the sprocket or driving hole in paper tape which serves as the timing pulse for reading or punching the paper tape.

stacker, input—*Same as* input magazine.

stacker, output—*Same as* output magazine.

standard subroutine—A subroutine which is applicable to a class of problems.

standing-on-nines carry—A carry out of a digit position generated by a carry into the digit position and the normal adding circuit is bypassed.

standby application—An application in which two or more computers are tied together as a part of a single over-all system and which, as in the case of an inquiry application, stand ready for immediate activation and appropriate action.

underpunch—A punch in one of the lower rows, 1-9, of an 80 column 12 row punch card.

ultrasonics—The field of science devoted to frequencies of sound above the human audio range; i.e., above 20 kilocycles per second.

unconditional branch—*Same as* unconditional transfer.

unconditional jump—*Same as* unconditional transfer.

unconditional transfer—An instruction which switches the sequence of control to some specified location.

unconditional transfer of control—*Same as* transfer, unconditional.

underflow—(1) The condition which arises when a machine computation yields a result which is smaller than the smallest possible quantity which the machine is capable of storing, (2) a condition in which the exponent plus the excess becomes negative in a floating point arithmetic operation.

unit—A portion or subassembly of a computer which constitutes the means of accomplishing some inclusive operation or function.

unit, card punch—*Same as* card punch.

unit, card reader—*Same as* card reader (2).

unit, central processing—*Same as* main frame (1).

unit, paper tape—The mechanism which handles punched paper tape and usually consists of a paper tape transport, sensing and recording or perforating heads and associated electrical and electronic equipments.

unit record—(1) A separate record that is similar in form and content to other records, e.g., a summary of a particular employee's earnings to date. (2) Sometimes refers to a piece of non-tape auxiliary equipment; e.g., card reader, printer or console typewriter.

unit, tape—*See* tape unit.

uniterm—A word, symbol, or number used as a descriptor for retrieval of information from a collection; especially such a descriptor used in a coordinate indexing system.

uniterm indexing—A system of coordinate indexing which utilizes single terms, called Uniterms, to define a document uniquely.

uniterm system—An information retrieval system which uses uniterm cards. Cards representing words of interest in a search are selected and compared visually. If identical numbers are found to appear on the uniterm card undergoing comparison these numbers represent documents to be examined in connection with the search.

uniterming—The selection of words, considered to be important and descriptive of the contents of a paper for later retrieval of the articles, reports, or other documents. The selected words are then included in a uniterm index.

universal turing machine—A turing machine that can simulate any other turing machine.

unpack—To separate various sections of a tape record or computer word, and store them in separate locations. The sections usually correspond to format fields within the record or word.

unwind—To code explicitly, at length and in full all the operations of a cycle thus eliminating all redtape operations in the final problem coding. Unwinding may be performed automatically by the computer during assembly, generation, or compilation of a program.

update—(1) To put into a master file changes required by current information or transactions, (2) to modify an instruction so that the address numbers it contains are increased by a stated amount each time the instruction is performed.

up time—The time during which equipment is either producing work or is available for productive work.

utility program—*Same as* utility routine.

utility routine—A standard routine used to assist in the operation of the computer; e.g., a conversion routine, a sorting routine, a printout routine, or a tracing routine.

validity—The correctness; especially the degree of the closeness by which iterated results approach the correct result.

validity check—A check based upon known limits or upon given information or computer results; e.g., a calendar month will not be numbered greater than 12, and a week does not have more than 168 hours.

variable—(1) A quantity which can assume any of the numbers of some set of numbers, (2) a condition, transaction or event which changes or may be changed as a result of processing additional data thru the system.

variable connector—(1) A flow chart symbol representing a sequence connection which is not fixed, but which can be varied by the flow-charted procedure itself. (2) The device which inserts instructions in a program corresponding to selection of paths appearing in a flow chart. (3) The computer instructions which cause a logical chain to take one of several alternative paths.

variable cycle operation—A computer action in which any cycle of action or operation may be of a different time length. Such action is characteristic of an asynchronous computer.

variable, two state—*Same as* two valued variable.

variable, two valued—*See* two valued variable.

variable word length—Having the property that a machine word may have a variable number of characters. It may be applied either to a single entry whose information content may be changed from time to time, or to a group of functionally similar entries whose corresponding components are of different lengths.

vector—A quantity having magnitude and direction, as contrasted with a scaler which has quantity only.

Venn diagram—A diagram in which each point represents an individual. Sets are represented by closed regions including all members of the set and excluding all nonmembers. The diagram is used to facilitate determination whether several sets include or exclude the same individuals.

verifier—A device on which a record can be compared or tested for identity character-by-character with a retranscription or copy as it is being prepared.

verify—To check a transcribing operation, by a compare operation. It usually applies to transcriptions which can be read mechanically or electrically.

vocabulary—A list of operating codes or instructions available to the programmer for writing the program for a given problem for a specific computer.

volatile storage—A storage medium in which information cannot be retained without continuous power dissipation.

volume test—The processing of a volume of actual data to check for program malfunctions.

Williams tube—A cathode ray tube used as an electrostatic storage device and of the type designed by F.C. Williams, University of Manchester, England.

wire printer—A high speed printer that prints character-like configurations of dots through the proper selection of wire ends from a matrix of wire ends, rather than conventional characters through the selection of type faces.

wired program computer—A computer in which the instructions that specify the operations to be performed are specified by the placement and interconnection of wires. The wires are usually held by a removable control panel, allowing flexibility of operation, but the term is also applied to permanently wired machines which are then called fixed program computers.

word—An ordered set of characters which occupies one storage location and is treated by the computer circuits as a unit and transferred as such. Ordinarily a word is treated by the control unit as an instruction, and by the arithmetic unit as a quantity. Word lengths may be fixed or variable depending on the particular computer.

word length—The number of characters in a machine word. In a given computer, the number may be constant or variable.

word mark—An indicator to signal the beginning or end of a word.

word time—(1) The amount of time required to move one word past a given point. The term is used especially in reference to words stored serially. (2) The time required to transport one word from one storage device to another.

working storage—A portion of the internal storage reserved for the data upon which operations are being performed.

write—(1) To transfer information, usually from main storage, to an output device; (2) to record data in a register, location, or other storage device or medium.

x punch—(1) A punch in the X or 11 row of an 80 column card. (2) A punch in position 11 of a column. The X punch is often used to control or select, or to indicate a negative number as if it were a minus sign.

xerographic printer—A device for printing an optical image on paper in which dark and light areas of the original are represented by electrostatically charged and uncharged areas on the paper. The paper is dusted with particles of finely powdered dry ink and the particles adhere only to the electrically charged areas. The paper with ink particles is then heated, causing the ink to melt and become permanently fixed to paper.

xerography—A dry copying process involving the photo electric discharge of an electrostatically charged plate. The copy is made by tumbling a resinous powder over the plate, the remaining electrostatic charge discharged and the resin transferred to paper or an offset printing master.

xy plotter—A device used in conjunction with a computer to plot coordinate points in the form of a graph.

y punch—(1) A punch in the Y or 12 row of an 80 column card; i.e., the top row of the card. (2) A punch in position 12 of a column. It is often used for additional control or selection, or to indicate a positive number as if it were a plus sign.

zero—A numeral normally denoting lack of magnitude. In many computers there are distinct representations for plus and minus zero.

zero access storage—The storage for which the latency (waiting time) is small. Though once widely used, this term is becoming less acceptable, since it constitutes a misnomer.

zero address instruction—An instruction consisting of an operation which does not require the designation of an address in the usual sense; e.g., the instruction, "shift left 0003", has in its normal address position the amount of the shift desired.

zero level address—*Same as* immediate address.

zero suppression—The elimination of nonsignificant zeros to the left of significant digits usually before printing.

zone—(1) A portion of internal storage allocated for a particular function or purpose. (2) The three top positions of 12, 11 and 0 on certain punch cards. In these positions, a second punch can be inserted so that with punches in the remaining positions 1 to 9, alphabetic characters may be represented.

zone bit—(1) One of the two left most bits in a commonly used system in which six bits are used for each character. (2) Any bit in a group of bit positions that are used to indicate a specific class of items; e.g., numbers, letters, special signs, and commands.

zone punch—*Same as* overpunch.

Appendix A

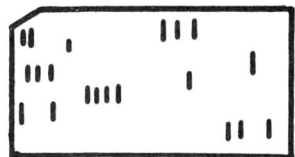

Operation of Computers

The modern computer can be compared to an automobile with its engine running. Until the auto is put into gear, the transportation possibility is still a potential. The computer may also be compared somewhat to an electric circuit with a voltage potential present (say, 240 volts) but with no load connected to the circuit no current will flow. Similarly, until a computer is provided with a program, its capabilities remain a mere potential. A computer program is a set of binary patterns that directs the computer, step by step, in the solution of a given problem.

In general, there are two basic types of computers; digital, and analog. Digital computers represent everything in terms of binary digits. Even letters of the alphabet and punctuation are represented as digits. There are some hybrid computers that connect digital computers to analog computers, but most of today's computers are digital.

An analog computer uses one quantity, such as an electrical voltage, as an analog of some numeric value to be represented. For example, 3.145 volts in an electrical circuit might represent a velocity of 3,145 fps in a ballistics simulation program for an analog computer. Analog computers are fast for certain kinds of problems, such as solution of mathematical systems of partial differential equations, but they are generally too imprecise for most applications.

The name computer was applied to these devices early in the history of their use because arithmetic computation was the only significant application to which they had been put. The first computers were built to replace armies of mathematicians operating desk calculators in the computation of ballistic trajectories. Today's variety of applications have made "general purpose information processing machine" a more appropriate name, but "computer" has stuck.

One way to better understand the essential elements of a digital computer is to create a well known analogy. Imagine a faithful, loyal, dedicated employee, such as a secretary, who follows every instruction to the letter. This secretary, given a manual of procedures and some documents to work with, can refer to history files and produce required reports. He or she needs only a calculator (to perform computations) and a sheet of instructions. If she unerringly follows those instructions, she will produce a stack of papers in her OUT basket that represents a transformed version of the information contained on papers in the IN basket. If the secretary transforms legitimate inputs into correct outputs by following the instruction sheet, those instructions can be considered as a correct and valid program.

In the above example, the secretary performs five distinct functions:

1. Reading source information (both the documents in the IN basket, and the list of instructions).

2. Storing intermediate results (remembers information for a short time, either in her head or on a scratch pad).

3. Computing, using a desk top calculator (to create totals, or to arrange data into proper order).

4. Writing transformed information (the required results in the OUT basket, or records in files for future use).

5. Controlling these activities (sequencing of these four activities to achieve the required result).

Figure A-1 shows that a computer can perform these five functions, but all of the data and instructions must be supplied in a special computer readable form. In other words, the *program* is a computer's equivalent of a manual of procedures. Under the guidance of the steps in that program, the computer may read input data, store intermediate results, perform arithmetic using numbers from inputs and from previous computations, and write outputs in many forms. The control element of the computer selects which of the other four elements are to be used at any given time. The computer, then, performs five functions similar to those performed by a secretary:

SECRETARY	COMPUTER
Read	Input
Store	Storage
Compute	Arithmetic
Write	Output
Control	Control

As human beings, we perform input functions through our senses; taste, smell, touch, sight, and hearing. Most computers sense inputs by sight (optical character readers, for example) or feel (wire contacts through holes in punched paper tape). Some inputs are simple electrical on-off signals from remote sources. Sound also plays an important part in allowing computers to read.

Humans store information for short term retention in their memory, relying on a variety of filing systems for more permanent storage. Computers also have memory. Their capacity to store information may vary from machine to machine, depending on the number of external devices such as tapes, disks, and drums, that are used. The storage capacity of computers using several of these devices is almost infinite.

Both man and his machines can perform arithmetic. The arithmetic capability of digital computers ranges from elementary to complex. Computers perform all arithmetic operations using binary numbers. The computer can also perform other logical functions, such as determining whether one number is greater than another.

We create output by our actions. The computer produces output in the form of rewritten magnetic tapes, disks and drums, printed reports, and even motor on-off controls. Since the computer operates electronically, it can also control electronic circuitry, such as the circuitry necessary to automatically open or close a flow valve in a water supply system.

We can control both ourselves and our machines. Machines can control only what they are instructed and permitted to control. When the secretary does some work, she is responsible for controlling the order in which various steps of the procedure are performed. She can, under the guidance of the detailed instruction list, read some information, perform some computations, and produce some output in the order specified in the program.

Computers are controlled by turning them on and off, and by supplying a computer program. The program is a description of a detailed procedure that is to be followed. Just as a theater program outlines the events that are to

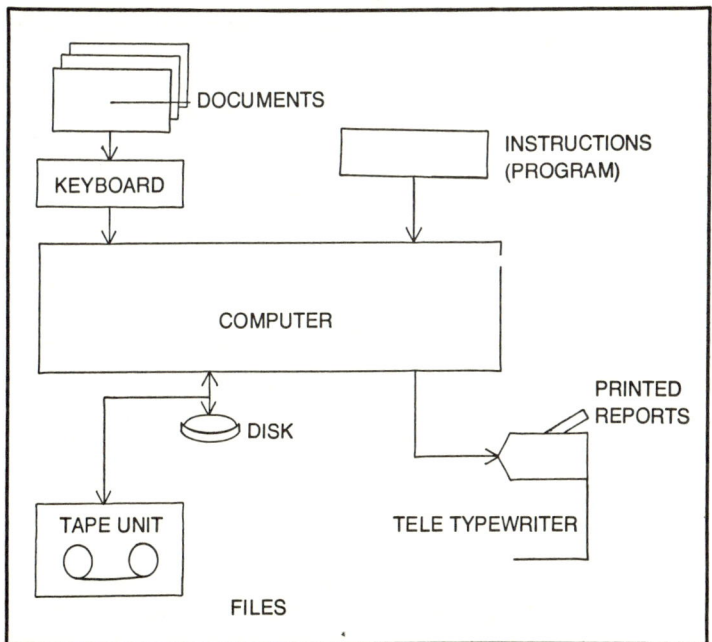

Fig. A-1. A computer performs functions that are similar to those performed by a clerk.

follow, a computer program outlines the steps to be followed to arrive at a solution to the problem presented. The program is interpreted by the computer to turn various circuits on and off in the necessary sequence to produce a solution.

COMPUTER STRUCTURE

The diagram in Fig. A-2 shows the five basic elements of a digital computer. Every digital computer, no matter how large or small, has these five elements plus the set of instructions that tells the computer what to do. A computer then must be able to accept input data, process it through arithmetic or logical operations, store some intermediate results, and eventually produce output data, all under the guidance of a central control element. The control element is guided in its operations by the instructions supplied by a programmer. The five basic elements comprise the hardware of the computer. Hardware can be touched, squeezed, observed; that it is tangible. The instructions, on the other hand, represent the software of a computer. Software is an intangible arrangement of bits. We may be able to observe, touch, or squeeze a storage medium, but the specific bit patterns held within are not physical, they are information.

Nearly all computers require inputs from one or more external sources. A computer that has no input signals can only repeat the same sequence of instructions over and over again. Some small computers are used in precisely this way, but most computers have inputs that can be brought into the computer for subsequent processing.

To compute a payroll check, for example, the computer must have the ability to fetch an employee record from a file, and to read in the number of hours worked in the week. These both require an input path to the computer. In some simple applications where small computers are used to replace older electromechanical logic, inputs may not be required. A programmable controller of a numerically controlled milling machine may not require inputs. The program contains the sequence of instructions to cause the machine to repeatedly mill the same part. External inputs are of no value in this case.

Inputs to the computer may take the form of punched cards, magnetic tapes or disks, or simple switch closures. When a keyboard is operated by a human, each key depression results in a switch closure. The computer can accept this switch closure as a binary signal and convert the key depression into a binary pattern. That binary pattern, in turn, can then be used to print a selected character on a printer, or display it on a video crt.

A computer must produce outputs to be useful. A computer's output may be in the form of printed results on paper, graphic plots drawn with special plotting equipment, or simply an electrical signal that can turn a lamp on and off. The range of possible outputs from a computer is virtually unlimited. The output element of a computer is selected when the control unit executes an instruction that transfers data from the ALU, storage, or an input to the output element. Most often, the data comes from storage, and

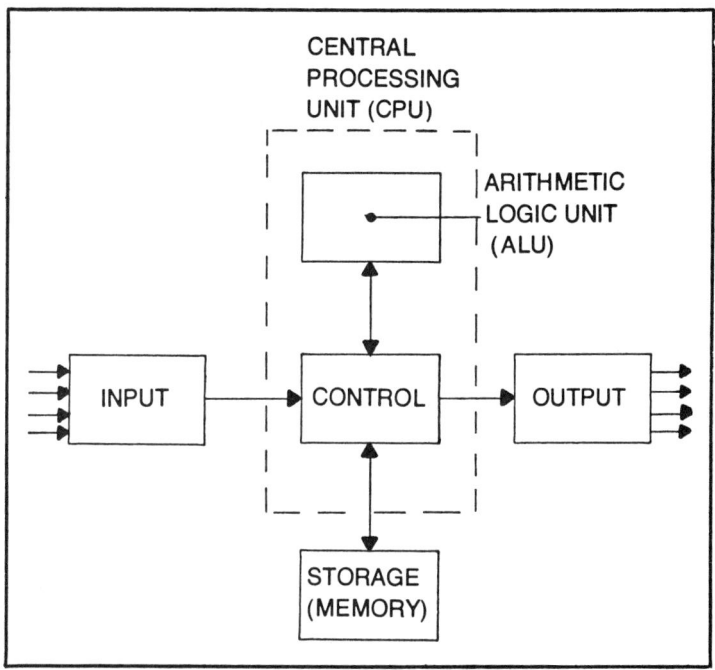

Fig. A-2. All digital computers have these five elements.

was created as a complex combination of inputs that were modified by the ALU.

The input and output devices are points at which humans interact with the computer. Much care must be taken to make computers easy for people to use, rather than making people adapt to poorly designed or poorly programmed computers.

In most computer applications, data must be stored before it is processed completely or used to produce outputs. The electrical digital signals that represent the data values are placed in the storage element, or memory. Instructions can also be read into storage and held for future use.

A computer processes information, and that processing is performed by the ALU which accepts data from input and storage elements and produces computed results for storage or output. To add a pair of numbers, the ALU is directed to fetch the values from storage, and to place the sum back into storage. The ALU may include capacities for addition, subtraction, comparison, logical operations, and even multiplication and division.

All elements of a computer operate under the direction of the control element which opens and closes the various pathways for data: from input to storage, from storage to the ALU, and from the ALU to output. The control element operates as directed by the instructions provided in storage. By writing the proper sequence of instructions, the computer programmer can completely control the detailed transfers of data within the computer to produce varied results. Thus, with different programs, the computer can be made to perform different functions, even though the underlying electronic circuitry remains unchanged.

SOFTWARE

The software consists of a collection of instructions that can be followed by the control element of the computer. These instructions must be detailed step-by-step instructions. Unlike humans, who can inject common sense into the completion of a task, a computer is not capable of logical reasoning. A computer must be ordered to do even the simplest part of a task. There are four major classes of computer instructions:

1. Input/output instructions cause data to be accepted from inputs to the computer, or to be produced on outputs.
2. Arithmetic - Logic instructions cause data to be transformed through simple operations in the ALU, including addition, subtraction, shifting, and logical operations (AND, OR, ETC.)
3. Storage instructions move data between storage and other elements.
4. Control instructions specify changes in the normal sequence of instruction execution.

The set of instructions for the computer is the best set of working drawings of that computer's architecture. The number and type of instructions are an indication of the ease with which the computer can perform operations. Some computers, for example, have a multiply instruction. Given two numbers, this instruction will produce the product. Most microcomputers, on the other hand, do not have a multiply instruction. Multiplication can be done on these computers, but only through the execution of many more instructions. Since most microcomputers are used in applications that do not require multiplication, the lack of a multiply instruction is seldom a restraining influence on successful applications. However, it is important to note that those facilities that are not provided in the instruction set can be created through the execution of the right sequence of simpler instructions.

INTERCONNECTION OF THE ELEMENTS

Each element of a computer can be treated as a sub-system. Each element has certain inputs and outputs, and certain actions take place internally to transform those inputs into outputs. A revised view of the five block model of the computer is shown in Fig. A-3. Here, all of the inputs and outputs to each element of the computer are identified. Note that except for the interfaces between the computer and the outside world, one element's output is some other element's input. By analyzing how these paths between elements operate, we can discover how a computer functions in detail.

Most of the pathways for data are bidirectional. However, issuing data to an input source, or attempting to acquire data from an output destination, is meaningless. These data pathways can be easily limited to a single direction. On the other hand, data must move in both directions between control and storage and between control and the ALU. Since data may flow both ways, these paths are called bidirectional.

Notice that all of the control signals originate in the control element, and that all data passes through control. Control may be thought of as a gigantic switchboard that operates at microsecond rates to switch data from one source to another destination. In fact, this is precisely how contemporary computers work.

At any one time, control may be directing one of the other four elements to perform some operation. In very complex computers, more than one element may be commanded at a time. The input element of the computer has many possible data sources, but only one of them is to be selected at a time. When reading from input data sources, the control element must first specify which input source is to be selected. Control places some bit pattern on the wires that comprise the input selection lines. The selected data is then placed on the input data lines. Once input data has been acquired, the control element must store that data somewhere for future use. The data might be shipped off to the ALU, or to storage, or even to one of the output destinations.

If the input data is to be saved in storage, the control element must specify where in storage the data is to be placed. Since many numbers can be stored, each one must be stored in a unique place so each can be selectively retrieved. The data is placed on the data lines, and the storage module is commanded to write the data. The command is issued by the control element through the Read/Write selection line. The specific register into which the data is to be stored is specified as a pattern of bits on the register selection lines.

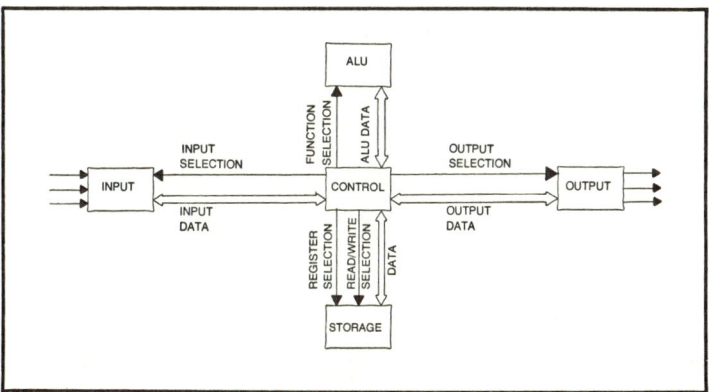

Fig. A-3. The interconnections between elements consist of both data and control signals.

The specification of which input lines to read, and into which register to place the data in storage, is carried in an instruction. That instruction contains three essential items of information:

1. The operation to be performed (read data from an input and store it away).
2. The source of the data (the specific input source to select).
3. The destination of the data (the specific register into which the data is to be placed).

One way to visualize this operation is to examine a small sequence of instructions that might be found in a large program. This brief instruction sequence (program segment) acquires two input numbers and produces a sum on an output. This program can be summarized as the following sequence of instructions.

1. Accept a number from input source 5, and save that number in storage at register 83.
2. Accept a number from input source 2, and save that number in storage at register 43.
3. Read the first number (from register 83) and pass it to the ALU, commanding the ALU to save that number.
4. Read the other number (from register 43) and pass it to the ALU, commanding the ALU to add it to the previously saved number.
5. Accept the sum from the ALU and pass it to output destination 7.

Each of these instructions can be described in more detail by referring to the signals that appear on the wires between the various computer elements. For example, the first step above (accept a number and place it in storage) can be described in more detail like this:

1. Control issues the number of the required input source (5) on the input selection lines. The input element accepts that number and selects that data source.
2. The data source presents some data (say, the number 113) on the input data lines to control. Control accepts that number and holds it temporarily.
3. Control issues the storage register number (83) to storage by placing that number on the register selection lines. Control also commands the writing action on the Read/Write selection line. Storage accepts the register number and gains access to that register.
4. Control places the temporarily held data (113) on the data lines. Storage writes that number into the selected register.

Obviously, such detailed English explanations could be difficult to follow for any reasonably complex set of instructions. Therefore a shorthand method is sometimes used to describe those sequences. The narrative description for reading and storing a number could be written in a briefer form like this:

1. Input selection←control (5);
    Input←input selection (5)

2. Input data←input (113, from source 5);
   Temporary←input data (113)
3. Register selection←control (83);
   Read/Write selection←control (Write);
   Storage←register selection (83)
4. Data←temporary (113);
   Storage (at register 83)←data

Each of the items named in this brief example is a register of the computer. One of the control registers (which happens, in this example, to contain the number 5) supplies its contents to the input selection register. The left-pointing arrow implies the transfer of some information from one register to another.

Now, reconsider the application posed earlier-the production of the sum of two numbers. In the following example, each of the original instructions has been broken down into a number of detailed steps. These steps are represented in the shorthand form. You should fill in the descriptive shorthand for the last instruction yourself to be certain that you understand exactly how the computer works:

1. Input selection←control (5);
   Input←input selection
   Input data←input (113);
   Temporary←input data
   Register selection←control (83);
   Read/Write selection←control (Write);
   Storage←register selection
   Data←temporary;
   Storage register 83←data (113)
2. Input selection←control (2);
   Input←input selection
   Input data←input (102);
   Temporary←input data
   Register selection←control (43);
   Read/Write selection←control (Write);
   Storage←register selection
   Data←temporary;
   Storage register 43←data (102)
3. Register selection←control (83);
   Read/Write selection←control (Read);
   Storage←register selection
   Data←storage (113);
   Temporary←data
   Function selection←control (Save);
   ALU data←temporary (113)
4. Register selection←control (43);
   Read/Write selection←control (Read);
   Storage←register selection

```
    Data ← storage (102);
      Temporary ← data
    Function selection ← control (Add);
    ALU data ← temporary (102)
 5. Function selection ← ____ (Fetch);
    Temporary ← _____
    Output selection ← _____ ( );
    _____ ← output selection
    _____ ← _____ ;
    Output ← _____ (215)
```

SCALING OF COMPUTERS

It might appear that the size of numbers is limited by the widths (number of data lines) of the data paths that exist between elements. Actually, in the example, data path widths of eight bits would be sufficient, since the numbers never got larger than 215 (an 8-bit register can hold numbers up to decimal 255). However, even larger numbers can be handled by breaking them up into pieces. Then, each part of the number has to be handled independently, and that would require more instructions.

Large computers have wide data paths; smaller computers have narrower paths. Some of the largest computers have paths as wide as 64 bits for numbers Programmers seldom have to resort to the slow technique of breaking a number up into pieces and processing each piece separately. On the other hand, a small microprocessor may have paths as narrow as four bits. Processing a 64 bit number would take *at least* 16 times as long on the 4 bit machine as it would on the 64 bit machine.

There are special electronic techniques that can be used with large computers to make them operate much, much faster. However, because these techniques are only economical with very large computers, they are seldom used with microprocessors. Some of the largest computers can execute instructions 400 times faster than a typical microprocessor. That speed advantage, multiplied by the speed advantage of wide data paths, marks the difference between large, medium, and small scale computers.

Large scale computers, or supercomputers, have thousands of ICs and require huge rooms for installation. Purchasing one hour of computer time may cost more than $3000. The only way these fast, powerful computers can be economical is to have a large number of users. Each user occupies only a small percentage of the computer resources, and for only a short period of time. By using only 1/10 of the computer for two minutes, a scientist can perform thousands of necessary computations at a cost of about $10.

These large computers have large input/output systems with millions (or even trillions) of bits of storage on magnetic tapes and disks. The main storage module of the computer may have over one million registers, and the ALU control element may be designed to permit hundreds of simultaneous users on the computer. Most of these users use supercomputers to solve mathematical and engineering problems. These kinds of computers are seldom used for commercial data processing.

Commercial data processing is most often done on a computer scaled to the size of the business. For example, large insurance firms use complex medium scale computers. Accessing information about policies and billing data requires the support of large input/output media (disks and tapes), but the processing is relatively small. However, a medium scale computer might be required in this kind of application to support hundreds of computer terminals in agents' offices throughout the country.

A typical medium scale computer might have disk and tape storage that rivals that used with a supercomputer for capacity. However, the CPU will seldom be as large or complex, and storage may be limited to 250,000 registers or so. An hour of computer time in such a system might cost $800. By using ¼ of the computer for three minutes, a business executive can process a complete list at a cost of about $10.

Small scale computers are usually called minicomputers. Some minicomputers are used in small to medium sized organizations for business data processing. However, more of them are used to perform communication chores for a larger computer. The minicomputer may service hundreds of telephone lines on the front end of the computer, passing data to the central medium sized computer over a high speed set of wires. Other minicomputers are used to effect on line control of production processes.

A typical minicomputer might have 65,000 registers of main storage, and a relatively simple ALU control element. Some applications might demand disk or tape storage, but many do not. The operating cost of a minicomputer might be as low as $40.00 an hour. By occupying the entire computer for 15 minutes, an engineer may be able to quantify some equations at a cost of about $10.

The least expensive computers are microcomputers. Some of these are used in small businesses as data processing tools, others are used for personal entertainment, and still others are installed inside other equipment for internal control. These computers are so inexpensive that dedicating one to an application is feasible. A small retail establishment might use a microcomputer with disk storage, 16,000 registers of main storage, and a simple ALU control element. The cost of operating such a microcomputer system might be as low as $10 a day. By occupying the entire computer at all times, the retailer may be able to better control store operations at a cost of about $10 per day.

Technologically, all of these computer alternatives are alike except for their underlying power. But, that power can be traded for time. The lower power computers cost less, but take longer to perform their tasks. Finding an account balance for a customer in a bank might require 1/10,000 of a second on a large supercomputer, and two seconds on a microcomputer. Will the customer notice? Is the faster speed necessary, especially in view of the fact that the teller's terminal may require 20 seconds to print out the account information? In other words, in many applications, time is not a critical issue, and a less expensive computer can be used.

MICROPROCESSORS

When the CPU (combined ALU & control element) of a computer is implemented in a single integrated circuit, we call that central processor a microprocessor. The term is a contraction of microelectronics and central processor, and indicates the technology used in the heart of the computer.

A microprocessor is not an entire computer. It is only the ALU & control portion of a computer. When the microprocessor is combined with storage, input, and output, however, the result may be properly called a microcomputer. A microcomputer is any computer based on a microprocessor.

At this point, it is important to distinquish between two different kinds of microcomputers. One kind is based solely on microelectronics with the integration of all computer elements in one IC or a very small number of ICs. A one chip microcomputer cannot be distinguished from its microprocessor counterpart by simple inspection. However, one chip microcomputers are small, powerful computers that are useful for a wide range of special applications. They are found in consumer goods, electronic games, and electronic interfaces between larger computers and peripheral devices like cassette tape drives.

One chip microcomputers are inexpensive, but limited. They are useful in certain low cost applications that demand little in the way of computing power or storage capacity, however, the pins of the IC are devoted to input and output lines limiting expansion capability.

The more popular kind of microcomputer is made up of separate ICs for the CPU, storage, input, and output that are all interconnected by wiring etched on a printed circuit board. When a microcomputer is created out of many individual elements, as are many of the popular single board computers, more power is available to the user. If the application demands more memory, more memory boards can be added to the configuration. If special I/O capabilities are required, they can be installed as special boards. Although more expensive than the one chip microcomputers, microcomputers in printed circuit board form are capable of vastly more complex configurations, and an almost limitless variety of storage and I/O capabilities.

Many of the general purpose single board computers use many one chip microcomputers to act as I/O interfaces. A single computer complex might, in fact, have dozens of one chip microcomputers performing peripheral interface chores under internal software control, all supporting a single fast microprocessor with a large amount of storage on other boards. More and more interface systems are being implemented as one chip microcomputers that have been suitably programmed. Most of these can be treated, however, as dedicated ICs. Internally, they've been programmed to perform some specific task. However, since the user or maintenance technician cannot change any of that software, the programmed one chip microcomputer is effectively a special purpose IC developed for the intended interface application. The trend is away from huge centralized computer systems to distributed systems of computers, in which the computing power is distributed among many small one chip microcomputers.

COMPUTER BUS SYSTEMS

One of the best ways to achieve high speed operation in a computer is to keep all of the pathways between various computer elements separated. In addition to the pathways to and from control as shown in Fig. 14-3, very fast computers include special pathways between other elements. A special circuit path called direct memory access (DMA) may exist between input and storage elements so that data can be rapidly transferred into storage while other operations are performed. The more complex the computer, the more likely it is to have some special inter-element paths. However, most microcomputers are designed with only simple pathways. Efficiency is sacrificed for the simplicity of a more organized structure.

MASTER BUS CONTROL

The bus system can be used to transfer information between a master and a slave element of the computer. The design of the master element defines the order, arrangement, and timing of the various electrical signals that affect information transfer. All slave elements must be compatible with the rules laid down by the master element.

Data is always transferred between one of the slaves and the master in control of the bus system. Since there is only one address on the address bus at a time, only a source or destination register can be specified. One of the bits of the control bus specifies whether the master is the source (and, hence, the slave is the destination) or the destination (in which case data is being read from the slave.) Of course, with two separate address buses, data could be transferred directly between two slaves under master element control. However, the improvements in information transfer rates that can be obtained by having more than one address bus are generally not worth the effort on small computers. Such multi-bus systems are found on large computer systems where speed is paramount.

THE CONTROL BUS

The key to understanding a computer is to examine its control bus. The address and data buses of a computer may be wider, but the control bus is always the most complex of the three. The address bus is always used to select one particular register to be involved in a transfer to or from the microprocessor. The data bus is always used to transfer data. But the control bus is composed of many different kinds of signals, all of which have complex interpretations over time.

WRITING TO STORAGE

Writing takes place in a fashion analogous to reading, except that data is supplied on the data bus by the CPU. As shown in Fig. A-4, the address bus

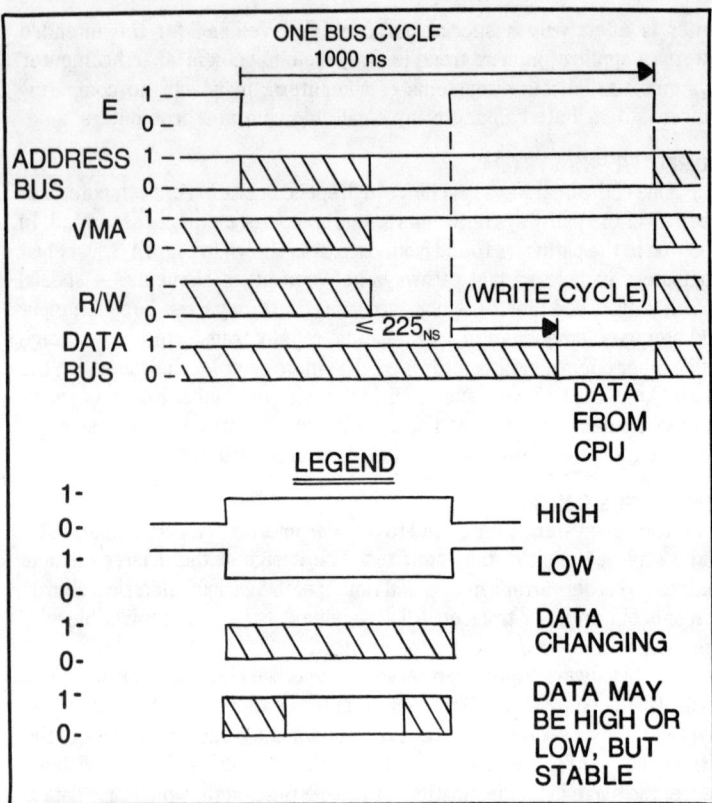

Fig. A-4. The 6800/6802 timing diagram for a write to storage.

VMA, and −W signals are produced just like the equivalent signals used during reading. However, the storage element cannot take the data from the data bus until the specific register has been addressed. Just like reading, it takes time to gain access to the required register. This is called the access time. In most computers with a sequence of this kind, the storage element would cause writing to occur at the instant the E signal made the end-of-cycle, high-to-low transition.

Transferring data from one storage register to another simply requires two successive read and write storage cycles. Some instructions in the computer cause successive cycles like this to happen automatically. Invariably, however, the process ends with another storage read operation which will retrieve another instruction for execution.

MASTER CLOCKS

To create the enable signal for controlling the bus cycle, some central clock is required for the microprocessor, or a part of the microprocessor IC. In either event, an external frequency determining component is necessary.

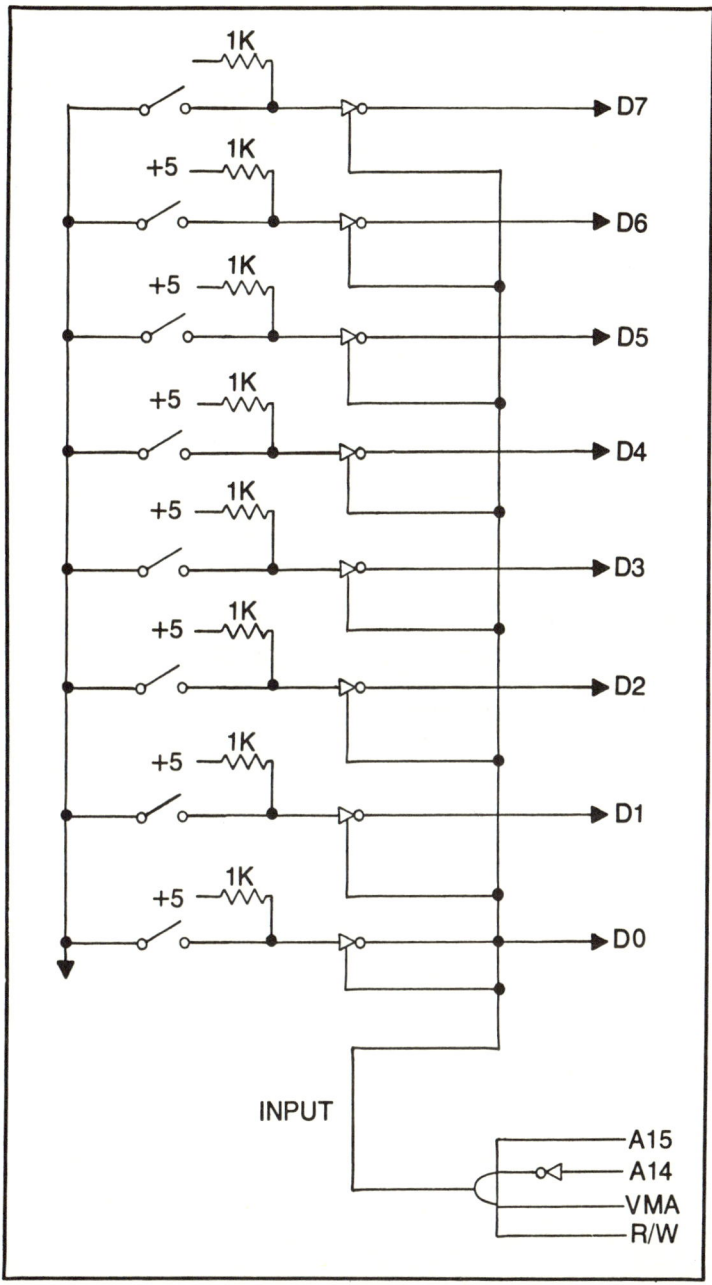

Fig. A-5. A simple input port places the input data on the data bus only when addressed for reading with a valid memory address.

STORAGE AND THE BUSES

The signals on the address and control buses, and on the data bus during writing, are all produced directly by the microprocessor. Sometimes there may be digital logic required external to the microprocessor itself to create all of these signals, but these support ICs are considered part of the microprocessor complex. How these signals are used, however, determines the complexity of the input, output, and storage elements of the microcomputer.

Storage in a microcomputer is usually made up of read only memory (ROM) ICs for operating system storage, and random access memory (RAM) ICs for data and program storage. The ROMs are written once, before installation in the microcomputer, and contain the operating system. Since these storage elements are not written into by the microprocessor, they can be permanently encoded with an operating program, and that program will be ready to execute whenever power is turned on. The data storage, on the other hand, is in semiconductor storage ICs that can be both read and written. When power is first applied, their initial data conditions are random. Data cannot be stored in semiconductor RAMs while power is turned off.

BUS CONTROL OF I/O

Input signals can be connected to the data bus during those instructions that call for reading of input data by using a simplified version of the techniques used for storage shown in Fig. A-5. The address bus, and parts of the control bus, are combined together to create an INPUT signal. When that signal is high, the input data from the switches is enabled onto the data bus lines.

Appendix B

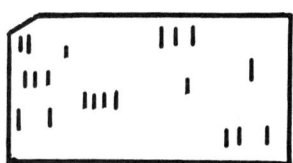

Assignment Codes

IBM SYSTEM/360 AND SYSTEM/370

SOURCE COMPUTER. computer-name.
OBJECT COMPUTER. computer-name.

System/360		System/370 Model 165		System/370 Model 155	
Code Letter	Capacity	Code Letter	Capacity	Code Letter	Capacity
C	8K	I	512K	H	256K
D	16K	J	1024K	HG	348K
E	32K	JI	1536K	I	512K
F	65K	K	2048K	IH	768K
G	131K	KJ	3072K	J	1024K
H	262K			JI	1536K
I	524K			K	2048K
J	1048K				

```
SELECT file-name ASSIGN TO system-name

    DOS
    SYSnnn-class-device-organization [-name]

    OS
    Class [-device]-organization-name
```

GE SERIES 6000/600

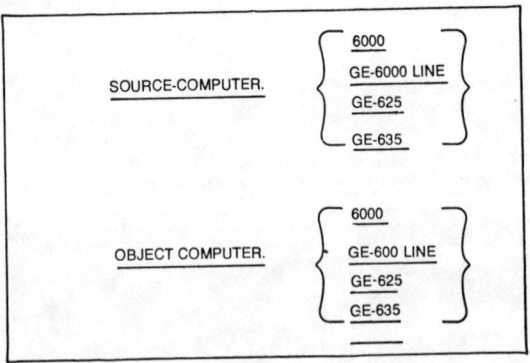

```
ASSIGN TO file-code-1 [FOR { CARDS / LISTING } ]
```

BURROUGHS B2500 AND B3500

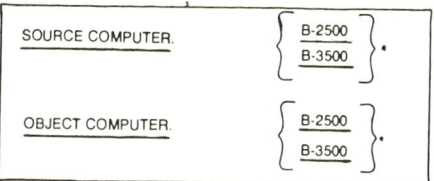

```
          ASSIGN TO hardware-name-1

  Some of the allowable hardware-names are:

     PRINTER    TAPE      (7 or 9 channel tape)
     PUNCH      TAPE-7    (7 channel tape)
     READER     TAPE-9    (9 channel tape)
```

CDC 3170, 3300, AND 3500

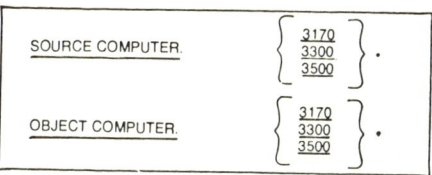

```
       ASSIGN TO hardware-name-1 dis-1

    Allowable hardware-names are:

     READER      DISK
     PUNCH       SYSTEM-INPUT
     PRINTER     SYSTEM-OUTPUT
     TAPE        SYSTEM-PUNCH
```

UNIVAC 1100 SERIES

```
    SOURCE-COMPUTER. UNIVAC-1108.
    OBJECT-COMPUTER. UNIVAC-1108.
```

```
   ASSIGN TO implementer-name [ system-file-name]

  The implementer-name may be one of the following:

       CARD-READER
       CARD-PUNCH        UNISERVO
       PRINTER           MASS-STORAGE
       FORM-PRINTER
```

IBM 1130

<u>SELECT</u> file-name <u>ASSIGN</u> TO system-name

System Names for Card and Printer Devices on 1130

RD-1442	for a 1442 Model 6 or 7 used for reading only.
PU-1442	for a 1442 Model 6 or 7 used for punching only.
RP-1442	for a 1442 Model 6 or 7 used for reading and punching.
PO-1442	for a 1442 Model 5 (punching only).
RD-2501	for 2501 card reader.
PR-1132	for the 1132 printer when no carriage control is used.
PR-1132-C	for the 1132 printer when carriage control is used.
PR-1403	for the 1403 printer when no carriage control is used.
PR-1403-C	for the 1403 printer when carriage control is used.

Index

Index

A
Address bus	279
ALU	270, 271, 273, 274, 276
American Standards Associations	5
Analog computers	267
Arithmatic hierarchy	51
Assembler	11, 76

B
Business Equipment Manufacturer's Association	5

C
Character set	23
COBOL-Edition 1965	4
1960	3
1961	3
CODASYL	vii, 3
Collating	52
Compiler	7, 8, 10, 12, 16, 20, 23, 26, 30, 31, 32, 33, 44, 54, 56, 73, 75, 76, 87, 95, 100
Computer speed	276
time costs	276
Constants	25, 26
Contributing Organizations	3, 4
Control lines	273
CPU	278, 279
Crt	270

D
Data checking	54
paths	273, 276
Development Committee	4
Differential equations	267
Dimensions	108
Disks	269, 270
DMA	279
Documentation	28, 29, 75, 92, 94
Drum storage	269

E
Editing	34, 37, 39, 41, 61, 66, 68
Elementary item	12, 13, 14, 30, 32
Evaluation subcommittee	4
Executive Committee	2, 3, 4

F
Federal Government	vii

G
Graphic plots	270

H
Human discourse	1, 6
interaction	271
Hybrid computers	267

IC chips	278	**R**	
Improved readability	1	RAM	282
Interface	272	Random access	134
Intermediate Range Committee	2, 4	Registers	275, 279
Internal representation		Reprogramming costs	6
of data	33, 41, 127, 136	ROM	282
program	100		
Interpreters	10	**S**	
Inventory	16, 49, 84	Semiconductor	282
		Short Range Committee	2, 3
L		Source program	11, 76, 85, 95, 103, 105
Language Structure Group	4	Spacing	58
Language subcommittee	4	Special Task Group	3
Long Range Committee	2, 4	Sperry Rand Corp.	vii
		Status switch	53, 86
M		Subroutines	8, 72
Magnetic tape	13, 57, 87, 90, 125, 134, 269, 270	Superintendent of Documents	vii
		Systems Group	4
Maintenance Committee	3, 4		
Memory	268, 284	**T**	
Memory dump	88	Time card	12
Milling machine	270	Timing diagram	280
Modular structure	8	Transaction	16, 66
Multi-bus systems	279		
		U	
O		U.S. Government Printing Office	vii, 3
Optical reader	268	USA SI	vii, 4, 5
P			
Paper tape	268	**V**	
Payroll	270	Variables	25, 26, 107
Pentagon	2		
Ports	281	**X**	
Programmer training	6	X3 Committee	5
Publication subcommittee	4	X3. 4 Committee	5
Punch card	13, 17, 57, 90, 95, 270	X3. 4.4 Committee	5